READING
WOMEN

READING
WOMEN

How the great books of feminism changed my life

STEPHANIE
STAAL

PUBLICAFFAIRS
New York

Book Design by Pauline Brown
Text set in 10-point Caslon 224

Library of Congress Cataloging-in-Publication Data
Staal, Stephanie.
    Reading women : how the great books of feminism changed my life /
Stephanie Staal.
        p. cm.
    Includes index.
    ISBN 978-1-58648-872-7 (alk. paper)
    ISBN 978-1-58648-876-5 (E-book)
    1. Feminism. 2. Motherhood. 3. Marriage. 4. Interpersonal relations.
I. Title.
    HQ1155.S83 2011
    306.874'30973—dc22

                                                    2010037606

First Edition
10 9 8 7 6 5 4 3 2 1

For Sylvia

．．．．．．．．．．．．．

When a subject is highly controversial—and any question about sex is that—one cannot hope to tell the truth. One can only show how one came to hold whatever opinion one does hold. One can only give one's audience the chance of drawing their own conclusions, as they observe the limitations, the prejudices, the idiosyncrasies of the speaker.

—VIRGINIA WOOLF, *A Room of One's Own*

．．．．．．．．．．．．．

CONTENTS

Preface   ix

PART I: Discovery   I

Understanding Backwards   3

Revisiting Feminism   8

Day One   15

Adam, Eve, and the Serpent   19

Natural Woman, Unnatural World   27

You Can Run, but You Can't Hide   41

PART II: Destiny   47

Perpetua   49

Rewriting Motherhood   54

A Vindication of the Rights of Woman   62

Marital Destiny   76

The Awakening   83

Coming Home   99

PART III: Divisions   105

A Room of One's Own   107

The Second Sex   113

The Feminine Mystique   136

Daughter of the Revolution   141

Who Has Time for "Happy"? 151

The Dialectic of Sex 157

How Does a Feminist Do Laundry? 166

I Want a Wife 178

Sexual Politics 184

Object Lesson 194

PART IV: Desire **203**

Fear of Flying 205

Dora 217

In a Different Voice 224

The Morning After 233

Gender Trouble 240

Riverbend Girl Blog 252

Living Forwards 256

Author's Note *261*

Acknowledgments *263*

Reading Lists *265*

Reading Group Guide *269*

PREFACE

I graduated from Barnard, an all women's college in New York City, in the early 1990s. As a woman born in the '70s, who came of age in the '80s, I entered adulthood with a certain set of expectations. The ideals of feminism were not so much a crescendo that crashed through my life but rather the steady beat to which I grew up. Anything boys could do, girls could do—better. To me, feminism was evolution, not revolution. Many of the achievements that women only a generation ago might have viewed as groundbreaking, I took for granted. Of course, women could be doctors and lawyers, run governments and corporations. In college, these assumptions accepted during my youth were emphasized, underlined, spoken aloud; indeed, attending a single-sex college, in which our gender was treated as a glory, the opening up of opportunities for women appeared not so much as options but mandates. We were, all of us on that graduation day almost two decades ago, poised to take over the world.

Life, however, is not lived by directive, and there has been much talk in recent years of the false promises of feminism, the disillusionment and disappointments, the lash and backlash, especially for those of us who married, who became mothers—or perhaps it has always been thus? Each generation, I suppose, forges new paths over the same old terrain. The role of feminist has never been easily reconciled with that of wife and mother, particularly in the public eye, but neither, it's true, has it rested easily in the privacy of our own homes. Parental love and professional ambition make for uneasy allies. And for my generation—women empowered by feminism as our due course—the contradictions can strike at the heart of who we are, or at least the way we see ourselves. The same women who grew up believing we could have it all now understand the toll of the transformations into wife and mother, the ambiguities and compromises they raise, the pledges broken both to ourselves and to others, the stark realization that perhaps we are not the heroines we once thought we were.

It was only after I got married and became a mother that I fully grasped the common refrain that the older you get, the less you know. Motherhood introduced a new range of emotions, from crazy love to mad frustration, emotions I could never have imagined that changed the tenor of my existence. As a mother, linked to my child in a million ways, I could not ignore the difficulties of applying my feminist ideals to my life's realities, yet I could not turn my back on feminism, either; I could not throw out the baby with the bathwater, so to speak. I longed to fashion my own incarnations, the personal with the political. In those early years, I thought a lot about the young woman captured in the graduation photo on my wall, brimming with hopes about the future, always sensing the framed glass that separated us. But to say I started this book in search of her, and ended up finding myself, is only part of my story.

PART I
DISCOVERY

Curiously enough, one cannot read a book; one can only reread it. A good reader, a major reader, an active and creative reader is a rereader.

—Vladimir Nabokov, *Lectures on Literature*

Understanding Backwards

....

2:47 A.M.

My daughter's thin wail slices through the silence, waking me from an already fitful slumber. I roll over and squint at the clock beside my bed, then close my eyes and lie very still, hoping her cries will subside. Already, though, it is too late. My heart is beating faster, humming through my body, an engine of awareness. Her cries grow louder, more insistent. Finally, she calls out my name. Mama. *Maaa-Maaa*. My feet touch the wood floor, hard and cold, navigating the path from my bedroom, down the hallway, to my daughter's bedroom. From her window, I can see the moon, round like an owl's eye.

She is lying in her crib, favorite blanket wrapped and knotted around her small body. Sweat plasters her hair to her head like a golden cap, and her cheeks are flushed, blooming bright pink. Instantly, my chest floods with love and concern. Her eyes swerve back and forth beneath closed lids and crinkled little brow. She has had a nightmare. I scoop her up in my arms and carry her back to my bedroom, first laying her gently in the middle of the bed and then crawling in next to her. My husband, John, raises his head and glances over at us through sleep-encrusted eyes, then groans and flops over onto his stomach, pulling the blanket around his ears. My daughter's forehead is damp against my chest, and her arms and legs cling to me with surprising strength, her grip desperate, as if she were trying to press her way inside of me, make us one. Our skin sticks together, damp from the warmth. I rock her, singing softly under my breath. She smells of milk and lotion, sweet and sweaty. My touch soothes her, I can tell; her lips are slightly parted now, her eyes at rest, and her fists uncurl from tight buds on my chest to flowers, the fingers loose and curled slightly upward.

It's a weird power, this effect of mother on child. I am still getting used to it. Soon she is asleep, her breathing shallow and rhythmic. Fearful of waking her, I silence the twitch in my muscles, allowing my arms and legs to go numb. Inside, though, the thoughts swirl. I am a mother, a wife, and—for a moment, my imagination fails me. As dawn breaks, sunlight creeping up the bedroom walls, I am still awake, wondering how I got here, to this place.

• • •

How familiar the plot: *And then I got married, had a baby, and everything changed*. Part of me understood perfectly how I arrived in that bed, a child entwined around me as if another limb, while I myself felt adrift. Even before I became a wife and mother myself, I had heard how this particular story unfolded. Like many women who came of age between the second and third waves of feminism, I had been taught that throughout the ages, the transitions into marriage and motherhood were the vulnerable points at which we might lose our voices, might cease to be the narrators of our own lives.

But, lucky for us, feminism—with its emphasis on equality and empowerment—offered women a different plot, with a different ending. I happily subscribed. I worked like a dog in college, winning honors, awards, and coveted internships, then landed a fairly glamorous job upon graduation as a literary scout for foreign publishers and Hollywood producers. A few years later, I enrolled in a master's program in journalism and then worked as a newspaper reporter, my stories regularly appearing on the front page of the features section. At nights I worked on a book proposal, and when a major New York publisher made me an offer, I took leave of my job to finish it. During this time, I married a progressive and supportive man, the kind of man who, when I informed him I would not be changing my last name to his after the wedding, responded with genuine surprise, "Why would you?" Yet not so long after John and I married and Sylvia was born, I found myself in the midst of an identity crisis much like our feminist foremothers had described, feeling especially disquieted given that I, perhaps naively, had not quite expected it would happen to *me*.

I suppose my entry into marriage and motherhood was not exactly smooth. John and I had been living together for five years and were engaged when I unexpectedly got pregnant. We were thrilled at the news and decided to hasten the timetable of our wedding. So in the span of only one year, I published my first book, got married, gave birth to my daughter, and exchanged a one-bedroom apartment in Manhattan's bustling West Village for a three-story Victorian house in Annapolis, Maryland. The changes came so fast, I hardly had time to absorb them all. And then I turned thirty, with all the attendant cultural baggage *that* entails.

The age of thirty, as nineteenth-century French novelist Honoré de Balzac once noted, is one of the most dangerous periods for a woman, and indeed, it was at this particular juncture in my own life, the turning from one decade to the next, that I—somewhat predictably, somewhat ashamedly—started to unravel. Around that time, I started to feel as if I no longer recognized myself. In the years following college graduation, my days had been filled with work and social engagements—late nights at the office or out to dinner with friends—and the constant activity gave me the feeling of being propelled forward and up toward the familiar and definable goals of promotion and achievement. Pregnancy had swerved my career path by bringing new considerations to the fore, and after my daughter was born, I chose to work as a freelance writer rather than return to a full-time job as a newspaper reporter. The decision was the complicated product of emotion and economics. After weighing the costs of hiring child care against the potential salary and hectic schedule of a journalist, it was not so much a choice as, really, the only course that seemed practical. Still, the night of my thirtieth birthday, as John and I hurriedly wolfed down our linguine at a local Italian restaurant, too exhausted to have a conversation and anxiously trying to finish dinner before our daughter's nightly nursing, I couldn't help but wonder whether I was making the best choices for myself.

The doubts started to creep in after that, toward the end of my daughter's first year, as the immediacy of her infancy started to transform into toddlerhood. I waited for the melancholy to subside, chalking it up to postnuptial, postpartum blues spiked with a healthy dose of turn-of-the-millennium angst. Surely, I told myself, these feelings of alienation were perfectly normal. I chastised myself for being self-indulgent: I had a beautiful and healthy baby, a roof over my head, and the flexibility to work from home; I knew how fortunate I was. In my best inner-drill-sergeant voice, I ordered myself to get over it. But as the weeks, then months, dragged by, it got worse. I felt as if I were following some tired traditional script, yet somehow I couldn't stop myself. I made vows to carve out more time to write, squeezing in an hour here and there during my daughter's nap time, but my mind was always elsewhere, listening for the sounds of her waking. Too often, I ended up staring at the solitary cursor animating an otherwise blank computer screen.

The days passed, veiled in a lulling sameness, until eventually I found myself unable to picture my own future, to see beyond the seemingly endless cycle of domestic rituals that nailed down my life, even to discern what appeared to be the vanishing contours of character. By the time Sylvia started preschool at the age of two, I found myself living the life I had always been warned against. Professionally, I had lost an astonishing amount of ground by stepping off the pre-scribed job track; personally, John and I had grown apart, worn out and grouchy from the daily demands and pressures of family life. Our relationship was becoming so strained that words like *marriage counseling* and *separation* had started to invade our arguments.

In the midst of all this turmoil, my mother came to visit for the holidays. We were in the kitchen, talking. As she perched on a bar stool, elbows propped on the granite countertop, I circled around her, a dervish in perpetual motion, alternating between helping Sylvia eat strawberry yogurt as she sat in her booster seat and basting the beef tenderloin in the oven for Christmas Eve dinner. My mother looked on, slightly amazed.

"Wow. I never thought my daughter would be so *domestic*." She laughed.

My mother is a research scientist and retired university professor, renowned in her field. And while career success and domestic prowess are not necessarily mutually exclusive, they are for my mother. She can make exactly one dish—roasted red peppers—and other than that, my sister and I try to keep her as far away from the kitchen as possible. So when she made a point to comment on my June Cleaver–ness, I laughed, too, because she was making a joke at least partially at her own expense; nonetheless, her words stung, be-cause I knew she meant them, and because *I'd* never thought I would be so domestic, either.

With that, my identity crisis swung into full gear. What the hell was happening to me? I had been steeped in feminism and even had a mother who was the ideal role model for the Strong Career Woman, but I felt quite unable to articulate the woman I wanted to be. Anxiety constantly shimmered underneath my skin. When I tried to discuss my fears with John, he shrugged his shoulders, bewildered and not a little annoyed, and suggested I take a break, maybe go see a movie at the local mall. My closest friends listened and sighed in understanding, their voices filled with join-the-club empathy, but there was little they could do to help. The "neighborhood mommies," on the other hand, stared at me as if I had grown a second head and it was purple. Sometimes, alone in the bathroom, I would drop my head into my hands in frustration, certain that there must be some way out of this limbo, if only I knew what it was. Everyone had advice. But I didn't listen to any of it.

Instead, I turned to books.

Revisiting Feminism

On a rainy afternoon, after picking up Sylvia from her morning at preschool, I let her loose in the aisles of the local Barnes and Noble, while I settled myself into a secluded corner and sat cross-legged on the floor, encircled by every book on womanhood I could find, each one a potential crystal ball offering me insight into what I should do, how I should act, what to expect. Some of the books came from the self-help section, others from the family and parenting section, a few from the fiction aisles. Each claimed to address the myths, the masks, the madness of womanhood.

I coaxed Sylvia over to me with a few picture books, and once she had plopped down at my side, I started to read—well, as much as one can read with a frolicsome three year old nearby. I flipped through political manifestos blaming feminism for women's evident unhappiness and books reproaching women for wanting too much, or for asking too little. The more I read, the louder the din of discordant opinions. Regarding marriage, I was urged to either surrender or rebel, give in or give up. As for motherhood, I was informed that, after the arrival of a baby, even the most egalitarian marriages tend to break down along traditional gender lines, that I had a 20 percent chance of getting postpartum depression, that I might forever pee a little when I laugh. The rather lame rejoinders to these books were wrapped in pastel covers and expressed in Hallmark verse; I skipped those altogether. All of these voices of dissatisfaction were buzzing through my head—the detailed accounts of apathetic husbands, perfectionist mothers, unsympathetic bosses—and momentarily overwhelmed, I pulled my knees up to my chest.

Sylvia was giggling over one of her favorite books, a clever twist on *The Three Little Pigs*. In this version, the three little pigs literally escape from their own story, haphazardly dropping into other popular fairy tales, before finally returning home with an entourage of new friends to defeat the big bad wolf and live together in communal bliss. I looked at my daughter and smiled, then hoisted myself up again. I walked over to the women's studies section—not a section, really, more a couple of shelves—my searching finger dragging along the various spines before stopping at Betty Friedan's *Feminine Mystique*.

I have been a fanatical reader since childhood, when my father and I used to spend every Saturday morning happily perusing the stacks at the Bethesda public library. I would walk between the library shelves as if in a trance, my fingers trailing across row after row of colorful spines, and leave hours later with a stack of books delicately balanced between my flattened arms and my chin. At home, I would lay the books out on the floor one by one, examining their flaps and covers, before deciding which one to read first.

I devoured everything I could get my hands on, from obscure biographies to the trashiest of best-sellers. I went from *Jane Eyre* to Jackie Collins without so much as a blink. My parents would scold me for reading at the dinner table, even though I always thought I was being so crafty by hiding the book on my lap, glancing down only between bites. But eventually they gave up, realizing there were worse vices, and my addiction was brought out into the open, where it has remained ever since.

I read constantly—in cars, walking the dog, lying in bed with my legs resting up against the wall, yoga-style. At any given time, I am in the middle of several books at once, my place marked by whatever scrap of paper happens to be close by, whether it's my latest credit card bill or one of my daughter's crayon drawings. My bookshelves are three books deep, and piles of books spread and teeter on every open surface of my home. If reading has always been a journey of imagination, a means of escape, it has also been, perhaps at least as importantly, a way of absorbing the intricate complexities of life and experience. To me, books are like magic: They inform the mind and transform the spirit. I have finished a book and felt so bereft at taking leave of its characters that I have immediately turned it over to begin again from page 1. In a special section, old favorites, their pages by now soft as worn cotton, lure me again and again, sometimes just to savor a passage or two for a moment's inspiration.

The act of rereading, as I have learned over the years, is an especially revealing one; in its capacity to conjure up our previous selves, rereading contains, I think, a hint of voodoo. I cannot read Emily Brontë's *Wuthering Heights* without remembering myself at fifteen, sprawled on my twin bed, deep in the throes of first love, and therefore secretly enthralled by the tragic proportions of Heathcliff and Cathy's passion; but there, too, is my twenty-five-year-old self who had by then been through heartbreak more than once—for her, the primacy of their passion recedes into the background, as instead the damaging repercussions of this passion come into relief. In coming back to the same book like this, again, over time, I not only see how my notions of love have changed but gain insight into *why*; I have uncovered clues to myself. Books may appear as so many words on a page, static, when actually they are ever changing—shifting, a palimpsest onto which the narrative of the reader's life is continually taking form.

Perhaps this explains what happened that day at the bookstore. When I pulled *The Feminine Mystique* off the shelf and read through its pages, I experienced something transcendent, revelatory.

I first read Friedan as an undergraduate at Barnard. To a college student in the early 1990s, *The Feminine Mystique* was a mildly interesting relic from another era—a time when girls wore poodle skirts, angled for an engagement ring before graduation, and defined success as two kids and a house in the suburbs. These things were about as far from my reality as I could imagine. Back then, I was on the brink of independence, and unlike the women Friedan described, opportunity seemed to spread out before me like a pair of wings, delicate, but strong and broad enough, I hoped, to carry me into the future. Long cocooned in the classroom, bred on heady ideas, radicalized and politicized, I was impatient to swoop into what I saw as the real world. No dream was too big. I fantasized about becoming a foreign correspondent, writing the Great American Novel, basically nothing short of changing the world; any thoughts of marriage and motherhood trailed distantly behind.

I'm not sure what I expected exactly on that rainy afternoon, but looking through *The Feminine Mystique* a second time, one eye on the page and the other on my daughter, I was startled. As I read Friedan's descriptions of women compressing their hopes and dreams to fit into "occupation: housewife," with some educators going so far as to suggest, in all seriousness, that women no longer be admitted to four-year colleges and universities, my college self began to emerge, indignant, an apparition given voice and form in my memory. This cultural collusion against women was *wrong*. Suddenly, I was reminded of my old passions, my earlier convictions, and past and present collided. I sat up a little straighter.

At the same time, the women's stories sounded so familiar, *too* familiar for comfort. I encountered the desperation of a mother of four who had left college at nineteen to get married, a woman who would have been an utter foreigner to me when I first read the book as a nineteen year old myself. Now I could inhabit her words. "I begin to feel I have no personality: I'm a server of food and a putter-on of pants and a bedmaker, somebody who can be called on when you want something," she tells Friedan. "But who am I?"

That night, after the dinner dishes had been loaded into the dishwasher and Sylvia had been bathed and tucked into bed, I shook off my fatigue and climbed up the two flights of stairs to the attic, where I kept the enormous cedar chest holding the mementos of my youth. After wading through old love letters, silly notes from junior high, and class photos yellowing with age, I uncovered what I was looking for: a black-marbled composition notebook from college with the title "Feminist Texts" penned neatly across the front.

Ah, yes, Fem Texts. I sat back on my heels, notebook in my hands. Above me, the bare lightbulb dangled from the ceiling. Randomly turning to a page, I stared at my cursive handwriting, the doodles in the margins. I had signed up for this course as a junior at Barnard, and the books I read had a profound effect on my early conception of womanhood. While the specifics of what they said had been mostly forgotten, I could still recall the emotional impressions the books left behind, the way they stimulated and challenged and provoked. It was well after midnight when I finally started to put all the scattered papers, notebooks, and photographs back into the chest, and rising to my feet in the attic, I had the brief sensation that I was packing up for a journey.

• • •

In some sense, I was. Over the next few months, a plan slowly began to take shape: Why not return to my alma mater to take Fem Texts? Was that a nutty idea? Was it even possible? I wondered if by retracing my steps down a clear and carefully charted route through the female experience I might more easily find my way forward. I ran the idea by John over breakfast one morning.

"Uh-hum," he murmured, barely looking up from the paper, his hand groping for his cup of coffee.

I tried again, tapping the newspaper to get his attention, but all I got was a slightly annoyed look. Plainly, he did not get either the point or the appeal of such a project, though perhaps it was not really his fault: He's an MIT-educated computer engineer who probably doesn't know Betty Friedan from Betty White. Still. In a spasm of frustration, I pushed my stool back from the kitchen counter, a little too abruptly, and went to call my friend Nina.

Nina also graduated from Barnard, a couple years before I did, and gave me my first job out of college. She had started her own literary scouting company—at the age of twenty-three—and was about six months pregnant when she interviewed me at a café in Chelsea. She was beautiful, confident, and fitted exactly my image of what a Barnard grad would be doing with her life after graduation; I clicked with her at once. We spent the next few years working together, first out of her Soho loft and then, as the company grew, from a rented office space on Broadway. We often worked late into the night, driven by an acidlike ambition to succeed—reading manuscripts, going to publishing events, dealing with clients—and soon we had more clients than the two of us could handle, and several more employees came on board. During those years, Nina was my mentor and role model. She was a tough and demanding boss, but at the same time always generous and fair. When I left publishing to go to journalism school, we remained close, our friendship forged by the excitement and challenge of those earlier years.

"I love the idea! You have to do it!" she said when I told her of my plan, and I could hear real enthusiasm in her voice. Other friends, dealing with the constant juggling of career, family, and self, were no less supportive. As I discussed the idea with them, I realized I was eager not only to find out how such writers as Mary Wollstonecraft, Simone de Beauvoir, and Betty Friedan would stand up to my rereading and what new inspiration they might provide but also to discover

how feminism was evolving under the scrutiny of a younger generation of women. Buoyed by the encouragement of my friends, I began
to map out a proposal.

An introductory survey of the major works of feminism, Feminist
Texts is a yearlong course broken down into two semesters: Feminist Texts I, which covers pre–second wave feminist texts, and
Feminist Texts II, which looks at more contemporary authors. Both
sections are offered each semester through either Barnard or its sibling school, Columbia College—although classes are filled mostly
with Barnard students in either case. That fall, the class, I learned,
was scheduled to meet for two hours once a week, in the afternoon.
As a logistical matter, if I took an early-morning train from Annapolis,
I would arrive in New York City in time for class and could still catch
the late-afternoon train home the same day. With a little careful
planning, Fem Texts would not cause any dramatic disruptions of
the family schedule. I could do it. All I needed was permission from
the professor. Since the class is a discussion-based seminar, enrollment is capped at around twenty students. I wasn't sure it would be
possible to talk my way into such an intimate classroom setting, especially as an alumna and not a registered student.

The beginning of the semester fast approaching, I finally took the
plunge. Sitting at the kitchen counter with my laptop, I shot an e-
mail to the professor asking if I could audit the course. Then I held
my breath, obsessively clicking "check mail" every other minute,
waiting for her reply. Luckily, I didn't have to wait too long. That
very same day, she sent back a response, welcoming me into her
class. I sat, blinking at the screen, letting the news sink in. Giddy
now, I pushed myself off the stool, grabbed my purse, and hurried
down to the drugstore on Main Street, boosted by the realization that
it was actually happening. I was going back to school. When I came
home, I was carrying a brand-new black-marbled composition book,
its clean, white pages ready to be filled.

Day One

··

A few weeks later, I was in New York City, heading to my first class at Barnard; like any homecoming, this one was bittersweet. As I walked, time bent, and I was briefly transported back to another stage of my life, a distant chapter of dorm rooms, final exams, and late-night bagels. Outside, the air still carried the summer's humidity, and I wove through the crowds of scantily dressed people ambling along Broadway in their tank tops and flip-flops, almost believing that I had been shuttled back to the early 1990s—that is, until the cell phone vibrated in my pocket.

"Hey." John's voice sounded in my ear. "Where are the Band-Aids? I can't find them."

Right. The setting may have been familiar, but I was no typical bright-eyed college student. It had been a long time since I walked this same path toward the campus gates: Before I became a wife. Before I became a mother. Before the passage of time had inscribed itself onto my face, my body, my memory. As I continued down the sidewalk, feeling suddenly conspicuous among the other students with their carefree gaits and brilliant smiles, I told myself that bridging the gap between my present self and that younger one—or, at the very least, understanding the breach that now seemed to separate us—was precisely the point.

The first time I saw the Barnard campus, I was nineteen years old and hungering to live in New York City after spending two years at a university tucked away in the redwood forests of northern California. My father had driven me up to the city from Maryland, and I remember coming around a curve on the New Jersey Turnpike to behold the entire Manhattan skyline stretched out across the river, a vision of promise and possibility to my teenage eyes. After we paid the toll, our white Acura plunged into the darkness of the Holland Tunnel, and then, only a few minutes later, we were greeted by blue skies and crowded streets, honking horns, and the warm scent of exhaust and perfume so peculiar to the city, the throng of people on the move. I rolled down the window so as not to miss a single detail. We spent the next two hours crawling through traffic, and by the time we approached the Barnard gates on 116th Street and Broadway, I was so jittery with anticipation that my door was open, my foot dangling toward pavement, before the car had even stopped. I stood on the sidewalk, mesmerized, taking in the bustle of Broadway as far as the eye could see until a peppy red-haired young woman came up to direct me to the registration table. Following her lead, baggage in tow, I entered the cast iron gates. Just as I was now doing so many years later.

I stopped in front of Barnard Hall, the Greek-columned brick and limestone building directly in front of the main gates, to get my bearings. On the surface the Barnard campus looked about the same. The campus still spanned the same four city blocks, somewhat dwarfed by the more imposing campus of Columbia University across the street. I made my way down the winding redbrick walkway, taking note of the familiar signposts. The statue of Athena, Greek goddess of wisdom, a gift from the class of 1905 to commemorate the establishment of the Barnard Greek Games, still stood frozen in flight; posters announcing various club meetings still fluttered from bulletin boards and lampposts; the more modern library and the grassy lawn had not changed.

Barnard College received its inaugural class of fourteen women in 1889. The college was named after Columbia College's tenth president, Frederick A. P. Barnard, a vocal champion of extending university education to women. First located in a rented brownstone on Madison Avenue, Barnard eventually moved to its current location on Broadway, where it was able to increase enrollment to more than two thousand students. From this quiet oasis, the college has fiercely remained an independent women's college, despite the ever-looming shadow of Columbia. The pressure has been intense for Barnard to give up its single-sex status. Columbia and Barnard spent almost a decade in negotiations to merge the two schools, along the lines of Radcliffe's union with Harvard, back in the 1970s and '80s. Those discussions ultimately broke down, with Columbia going coed in 1983 and Barnard remaining an all-women's college. In a rather unique and, some would argue, dysfunctional relationship, the two schools continue to retain a high level of integration, sharing instruction and facilities but keeping admissions and administration separate.

For whatever reason—whether it's the David-and-Goliath positioning with Columbia, or simply the type of student Barnard attracts— an almost palpable air of proud defiance hangs over the small, grassy campus. More than a hundred years ago, Barnard's students were pioneers, fighting against societal norms for the right to an education despite their sex; today, the women who attend Barnard are usually pioneers of a different sort, selecting a single-sex institution in an era when women's work for equality is supposedly done. That afternoon I saw the hints of rebellion in their faces, the confident posture of their bodies; I heard it in the rise and lilt of their voices as I caught snippets of their conversations floating through the air about classes, summer vacations, that night's dinner plans. Falling into step beside them, my step quickened and grew more assured as I walked down again this well-trodden path.

• • •

"Call me T." With those three words, our professor breezed into the room and took a seat at the large discussion table, officially kicking off our first day of Fem Texts. Until then, the students had been exchanging sidelong looks, furtively assessing one another. Now T. was the focus of our undivided attention. The first thing I noticed was how tall she was; even without the high-heeled black boots she was wearing, she must have been six feet. Next I was taken aback by how young she was—around my age—though she probably didn't appear quite so young to most of the students in the class, who, according to a quick calculation in my head, must have barely been in elementary school when I was an undergraduate. My head started to spin in a litany of age-related angst: *I was backpacking around Europe before some of these kids were born! When I took this class the first time, they were younger than my daughter is now! I was walking down the aisle at my Barnard graduation when many of them were learning how to walk, period!* I forced myself to turn my attention back to the class.

T. smiled broadly and ran her fingers through her spiky auburn hair. In her black lace shirt and dangly silver earrings, she looked more like she should be on her way to a bar in the East Village, not some cramped college classroom. Her blue eyes peered at us from behind cat-eye tortoiseshell glasses, gliding over each of the twenty faces staring back at her. "I'm not into titles or hierarchy," she said, and several students nodded approvingly. I liked her immediately and felt a ripple of relief. I had forgotten how critical a professor is to the chemistry of a class. Before my eyes, the nervous anticipation of the students was dissolving, settling, transforming. Responding to T.'s own energetic and easygoing manner, we were starting to relax. The collective body language of the class shifted shape, elbows propping forward on the table, heads tilting toward T.

"I am not going to expose you to my brand of feminism, if I even have one," she said. "This class is about exploring the texts. If we don't agree with something, that's great. We're here to rip these books apart. If we *do* agree with them, that's good, too." She paused and gave us a devilish grin. "But certainly not as interesting."

A doctor of theology, T. had selected as our first reading Elaine Pagels's *Adam, Eve, and the Serpent*, an intellectual history of the first two chapters of Genesis that traces traditional patterns of gender and sexuality back to ideas formed during the first four centuries of Christianity. I was a bit surprised when I saw the title as our first assignment, not having discussed religion in my Fem Texts class as an undergrad. But I later learned that the Women's Studies Department had since decided to give professors some discretion in crafting the syllabus for this course in an effort to "decanonize" feminist texts, allowing a more diverse set of voices, experiences, and perspectives into the conversation. In practice, this approach meant that, depending on who was teaching the class, the readings could vary widely; one professor might start with Sappho, another with Christine de Pizan. Since theology was T.'s specialty, naturally she wanted to talk about Eve and the way her story laid the foundation for Western notions of women throughout history.

"After all," as she told the class, "why not start at the beginning?"

Adam, Eve, and the Serpent

Eve was an interesting starting point for me. I'm not religious, or rather, I come from a quilt work of religious backgrounds, and somehow all the religions present in my family have effectively neutralized each other. Between my nonpracticing Jewish grandfather and my baptized Catholic, yet essentially neo-pagan, grandmother on my father's side, and my Buddhist and Taoist grandparents on my mother's—not to mention my parents, both devout scientists—I had emerged with a vague agnosticism of my own design.

Any early education in biblical lore came from watching Cecil B. DeMille's Hollywood epic *The Ten Commandments*, starring a young and improbably tan Charlton Heston as Moses. I don't think I had come into contact with an actual Bible, other than perhaps as a fixture in hotel rooms, until it appeared on the syllabus of my eighth grade Western Civilization class. In a windowless junior high classroom, as we each took turns reading passages from Genesis over the static purr of fluorescent lights, I was first introduced to Eve and suddenly made aware of the immense burdens placed on women, simply because of their—*my*—sex. Right there, laid bare on the pages before me, unfolded the tale of how a single woman's transgression cast all mankind from paradise. For, Eve, beguiled by the serpent, plucks an apple from the forbidden tree, takes a bite, and then cunningly feeds the fruit to her husband, Adam, implicating him in her sin. As punishment for their disobedience, God banishes the once blissful couple from the Garden of Eden and into a world of suffering. Adam is sentenced to a lifetime of hardship and toil for heeding his rebellious wife. As for Eve, God declares, "I will greatly multiply your pain in childbearing; in pain you shall bring forth children, yet your desire shall be for your husband, and he shall rule over you."

Spoken aloud in a classroom full of adolescents running mostly on hormones, the story appeared to be a ringing endorsement for the propositions that men should never listen to women and women must always obey men, enduring any suffering as their due. Some of the boys snickered at this, pleased to have more ammunition for teasing the girls after class. My friend Barbara, who sat at the desk in front of me, turned around and made a face. I nodded and rolled my eyes.

Mr. Corbin, a weathered veteran of the Montgomery County public school system, spotted the trouble brewing at once. "Shut your traps!" he barked, his eyes scanning the room, seeking a reason to issue a detention or pass out one of his infamous pop quizzes on biblical genealogy. Instantly, we went blank-faced and silent.

But the damage had already been done. Eve was the malcontent who dared defy the rule of God, creator of the world; she was the temptress who deliberately persuaded her husband to partake in sin, her feminine wiles more potent, apparently, than the Almighty's wrath; she was the first libertine, the original desperate housewife, the ultimate bad girl. And despite my discomfort at having all women besmirched by Eve's original sin, I was also secretly fascinated. At fourteen years old, I was very much a good girl, a rule-following, bespectacled honor-roll student. The *idea* of Eve and her power had a magnetic appeal.

As an adolescent girl, I was in the midst of my own personal metamorphosis. Not only was my body changing, lengthening and rounding, but I was becoming increasingly influenced and shaped by others' perceptions of me. Always outspoken in class, I began to bite my tongue, nervous about saying the wrong thing. Embarrassment blushed across my face at the slightest awkwardness, real or imagined. Like Eve, whose eyes were opened after the Fall, I suppose I tried to fashion fig leaves that might hide my vulnerability. Every night, I fretted over what to wear to school the next day, or how best to tame the frizz in my hair, or whether to camouflage the latest blemish that had burst onto my face, uninvited. Hair, skin, nails, face, legs, breasts (or lack thereof), butt, belly—I had never been so acutely aware of every single part of my body. My reflection had become such a distraction that at one point my father threatened to remove all the mirrors from the house. He could not understand that my preoccupation had nothing to do with vanity and everything to do with trying to claim my body as my own. Unknowingly, I had been exposed to one of the first principles of sexism, that a woman's biology dictates her destiny, and I was struggling to overcome the disconnect between my body and my *self*.

I spent the rest of my teenage years teetering on this seesaw of shame and desire, courage and fear, obedience and rebellion, although Eve herself had pretty much vanished from my consciousness as quickly as she had appeared, replaced by Madonna and the other idols of my teen world. I had hardly thought about Eve since then, believing I knew all I needed to know about her.

Reading Pagels's book, however, I discovered that I actually knew very little about Eve. I never knew, for instance, that her origins were a good deal more complex and contested than generally acknowledged. In our junior high dictation of Genesis, I'd missed this subtlety: Genesis tells not one, but two, versions of the creation story, a fact that has confounded scholars and theologians for centuries.

Genesis 1 and 2 were originally separate stories, probably the work of several authors from different schools of thought, only later grafted together into its current biblical form. Therefore, some obvious inconsistencies arise. Genesis 1, the more recent version, reflects a transcendent God who exists outside time and space. This God creates from above, bringing into existence both heaven and earth, light and dark, land and water, flora and fauna; most important for our purposes, though, God creates man: "In the image of God he created them; male and female he created them." Genesis 2, on the other hand, reveals quite another God, or, as T. put it, "Here, God gets his hands a little dirty." He walks, he talks, he gets personal. This God is in the details.

In Genesis 2, the creation of man and woman does not happen simultaneously as it does in Genesis 1 but, rather, occurs in sequence. Man, whom God names Adam, is formed from the dust of the earth and granted dominion over the Garden of Eden. But Adam is lonely, and so God decides to make a "helper fit for him." While Adam sleeps, God steals one of his ribs, from which he creates Eve. He presents the new creature to Adam, who says, "This at last is bone of my bones and flesh of my flesh; she shall be called Woman, because she was taken out of Man." With this declaration, T. pointed out, Adam justifies the hierarchy of men over women. Adam was created in the image of God, yet Eve was created in the image of man, so she is only a secondary image, a vestige.

For centuries, writes Pagels, the battle of interpretations between these twin tales of Genesis raged within the Christian community, partly because Christianity itself was in flux. During its first four hundred years, when the religion was still regarded as a "dangerous superstition," the majority of Christians viewed original sin as a parable of moral freedom and responsibility. Regularly persecuted and killed for their beliefs, the followers of Christianity embraced the theme of disobedience presented in Genesis, considering the story a call to fight against the political forces of the state. Then, in 313 CE, the pagan emperor Constantine decided to tolerate Christianity within his empire, and, by permitting Christians to openly practice their religion, set off a quiet revolution in sexual attitudes and practices; within a couple of centuries, Christianity was the official state religion. Christianity's martyrs—translated from the ancient Greek as "witnesses"—slowly faded from memory. And as the religion gained respect and power in this vastly altered landscape of acceptance, Genesis 1 and 2 mutated from an illustration of free will into a paragon of its opposite—human bondage and corruption.

Which brings us to Augustine, whose interpretation of Genesis provides the cornerstone of *Adam, Eve, and the Serpent*. By his own lengthy account, Augustine did not start out as a model Christian, if by model Christian we mean sober and celibate. As Augustine vividly describes in his *Confessions*, his was a dissolute youth that preceded his eventual embrace of Christianity. He recalls how "in the sixteenth year of the age of my flesh . . . the madness of raging lust exercised its supreme dominion over me." This raging lust led to a string of sexual escapades and the birth of an illegitimate child. As Pagels explains, such racy anecdotes from Augustine's life are more than idle gossip, but reveal how Augustine's views on Genesis developed. With Eve cast as the predatory woman, Augustine came to see himself as representing her vulnerable male victim. He then took his struggle with his sexual impulses—his own personal voyage from sin to salvation—and expanded it into a paradigm for all of humanity.

At its core, Augustine's *Confessions* is a conversion tale. Drawing on his personal experiences, Augustine reasoned that individual free will is merely an illusion, and attempts to master one's bodily functions— let alone one's destiny—are fruitless. To his way of thinking, if we accept the notion that human nature is a fundamentally unreliable guide, how can we possibly be trusted to know our true wants and needs? Take sexual attraction as a prime example. Augustine believed that sex is shameful and dangerous, chaining men to unhealthy desires and dividing their spirit, and men's sexual urges are therefore little more than evil temptation. Women bear the brunt of the blame for causing men's displays of lust. They consciously inflame men's desire, Augustine claimed, leading more susceptible brutes to utter ruin with but a beckoning finger and a swish of the hips. In order to gain salvation, Augustine instructed men to attain a state of "free slavery" by submitting to the rule of government, even if that means bowing to tyranny. According to Augustine's "natural" order of things, the state controls man, man controls woman, and God controls all. And so, with a slash of his pen, Augustine rewrote three centuries of thought that had promoted Christianity as a celebration of freedom.

The message encoded by the Augustinian view of Genesis is this: We have entered into bondage as a result of Adam and Eve's original sin, which caused the sexual corruption and the loss of our moral freedom. We went from paradise to purgatory. Lust, pain, death— these are the proof, for such miseries would not exist unless all of us are, in fact, living in a state of dystopia. No human being is exempt from God's punishment, because, in Augustine's mind, every infant born is infected from the very moment of conception through the man's semen, and thus "shackled by the bond of death."

Not everyone agreed with this relatively grim view of humanity. Augustine's most ardent opponent, Julian, bishop of Eclanum, argued that the natural world, as God's creation, was essentially a good place, not the miserable limbo Augustine envisioned. For twelve years, Julian and Augustine openly debated their clashing interpretations of

Genesis. Julian reckoned that Genesis provided a simple cautionary tale about the power of choice and that God's punishment was limited to Adam and Eve alone, not all of humankind. Seen in this light, the lesson Julian drew from Genesis was that our individual perceptions are what make and unmake the world around us. Those who consistently choose to sin will see the world in oppressive shades of gray, while those who make virtuous choices will build a world colored by hope and love. In other words, the world may contain illness, death, and suffering, but our choices can transform our experiences within that world.

Augustine, meanwhile, insisted that the only path to eventual salvation in heaven is obedience and repentance—a message all too friendly to authority. After Augustine died, the church officially accepted his view. Julian was branded a heretic. Augustine became a saint.

• • •

"Any thoughts?" T. asked the class.

We had been relatively quiet so far, listening to T.'s introduction of Pagels's book. In the wake of her question, we looked at each other uneasily, trying to guess which of us would be the first to speak. A tall, athletic woman named Deanne finally stretched her arm up in the air.

"I don't understand why anyone would subscribe to Augustine's view," she said. "It just seems so . . . *dark*."

"Well, Pagels has an interesting theory about that," T. answered. "She points out the obvious answer: that Augustine's views won out because they supported the power and hierarchy of the church and state; they were politically expedient. But there was probably another, more psychological, reason as well—people would rather feel guilty than helpless. Our guilt reassures us that our suffering is rooted in moral ground, and therefore has both cause and meaning."

T. looked around and got a few nods, as well as a few blank stares. She took a deep breath and tried again. "When something tragic happens to us, we will usually say, 'Why me?' It's a question often asked in the face of tragedy. Well, Augustine would answer it's not *you*, but the steep price we must pay for the sins of Adam and Eve. According to Augustine's view, we can, at least theoretically, banish the specter of pain. Julian, on the other hand, would respond that pain is a normal, an unavoidable, part of daily life, and the power lies solely in how you confront it. Think about it." T. paused. "People want to feel that bad things happen for a *reason*. Which is the more comfortable view: 'We're living in a fallen world' or 'That's just the way the world is'? Isn't it better to believe we're all striving toward heaven?"

The class, unsure how to react, remained silent.

"Isn't it comforting to have a 'devil made me do it' excuse?" T. prodded.

"I don't think it's better to feel guilty than helpless," Deanne said, pulling on an ash-blond ponytail, "because, in the end, aren't you still helpless?"

T. shrugged and smiled. "What about Augustine's views on women?" she asked. "He succeeded in typifying women as temptresses held in check only by submission and childbearing, which, unfortunately, is a theme we will see again and again throughout the semester."

Maria, a petite woman with curly, dark hair, tentatively raised her hand. "I've always wondered—why are women so defined by their bodies?" she asked. "I mean, you always hear how women are, like, *earthier* and closer to nature, but where did that come from?"

For a moment, T. appeared nonplussed. "That's a complicated one to answer. Well, to start, we didn't always understand childbirth and menstruation," she explained carefully. "Back then they were mysterious, sometimes even frightening, events. The problem is that these biological processes became acculturated and ultimately mandates for men's domination over women. Biology and destiny effectively merged."

I sat back in my chair. *Now* we were entering territory I remembered well from my college days. Feminist ire has always burned bright at this intersection of biology and destiny and with good reason. For centuries, a woman's body has been used against her as a tool to ignore, overlook, denigrate, control, and, sometimes, terrorize her. Women throughout the ages have been told to submit to the will of their husbands and God, no matter if they must dull their minds and suppress their spirits to do so. For, if they do not follow their divine duty to practice selfless obedience and devotion to husband, child, and home—terrible things will happen. Just look at our feisty, rebellious Eve. Consigned to a life of painful childbirth after the Fall—suitably chastened, if not chaste—Eve is hardly heard from again. Eve gets another shot at grace only through Mary, the perpetual virgin who gives birth to a savior. In a rather telling linguistic play on words, when the angel Gabriel announces his presence to the Virgin Mary in the Vulgate version of the Bible, he calls out "Ave," which, when read backward, is the Latin *Eva*, as if what had been wrong might finally be put right.

But "what if women can't, or don't want to, become mothers? Should they still be considered women?" T. asked the class.

"Yes! Of *course!*" called out a couple of students, in amused indignation, amid general nods.

And I agreed with them—of course I did. But then, in a flash, I was thinking something else. The words rearranged themselves in my mind to ask, "What if a woman *does* want to become a mother? Can she still be considered a feminist?"

Natural Woman, Unnatural World

This question continued to pester me as I sat on the train heading home to Annapolis, my mind split between thoughts about Eve and the curses laid upon the female body and Augustine's conversion tale, which pitted man's higher calling against a woman's wiles. Women could achieve salvation, too, but whereas Augustine's conversion marks the beginning of his path to sainthood and glory, the parallel transformation of Eve to Mary, from girl into wife and mother, is itself where most women's stories end: "Reader, I married him."

With eyes opened by the class discussion, I found myself spotting the many faces of Eve everywhere. Turning the pages of a magazine somewhere outside of Philadelphia, I noticed how many modern images of women played on the story of Genesis. A jewelry ad featured a model with moist, ruby lips holding forth an apple, icy diamonds dripping from her wrist, a python slithering around her neck. A full-page spread announcing a new season of television's *Desperate Housewives* showed the actresses lolling, Eve-like, on a blanket of apples, with the slogan "Tempting, isn't it?" Article after article described the wild party girl—or her older twin, the brittle career woman—who settled down after she had a baby because she now understood the error of her ways. She had conquered selfishness, ambition, curiosity—all those characteristics that drew Eve to the apple and impelled her to sink her teeth into its flesh—in favor of compliance and complacency. Or at least that is how the popular myth goes.

As a suburban girl growing up in the 1970s era of *Free to Be You and Me*, I developed a healthy skepticism of such gender-specific fairy tales. Yet even I have to admit I found myself beguiled by conversion stories once I became a mother. Like Maria, and the other students in class, I always believed that women's lives should be defined neither by their bodies nor by their sex. I had little clue, as a college coed, about the realities of pregnancy and motherhood. A dark curtain had been dropped around these particular experiences.

And so, in line with many women of my generation—the first generation, really, to be raised, on the whole, with the full expectation of success or professional fulfillment—I spent my early twenties focusing on my career and dodging the issue of motherhood entirely. If pressed, I said I wanted children, but only if and when I was *ready*. I am not sure what I meant precisely by "ready," but I must have assumed it was one of those inexplicable feelings akin to knowing when you had met "The One." In the meantime, the idea of motherhood remained rather like an abstract painting on a distant wall that I peered at occasionally but couldn't really fathom.

Whenever I did try to contemplate motherhood, I ended up relying with some apprehension on the popular stories of women retreating from public lives to private homes after they had babies; of doctors, bankers, lawyers who were suddenly interested only in the minutiae of playground politics, not current events. From the outside, marriage and motherhood seemed to work some deep alchemical magic on women, some incontrovertible proof that you can run but cannot hide from destiny.

When I found out I was pregnant, at the age of twenty-eight, my initial reaction was shock. I was not a young mother by many people's standards, I know, but in my narrow slice of the world—Gen X, urban professional, chronically angst ridden and excruciatingly self-analytical—most of my friends were still debating whether they could take on the responsibilities of a puppy, let alone a baby. Among my peers, I was the equivalent of a teenage mom. Probably if I had been a few years older, with babies on the brain, I wouldn't have felt as if that little plastic wand had emitted some sort of stun ray. At the sight of it, I leaned against the bathroom sink so I could gaze closely at myself in the mirror. Shouldn't I look different? Shouldn't I feel different? Shouldn't I have *known*? I pressed my hands against my stomach, gently, my body suddenly beyond my comprehension and control. I closed my eyes and tried to detect a shift, a change in my being, but felt nothing except perhaps mild panic.

There was a soft knock at the door. Distracted by the news, I had forgotten all about John waiting in the other room. "Everything okay in there?" he called in, a little nervously.

I took a deep breath and opened the door. Without a word, I handed him the pregnancy test, with the thin blue line facing up. He looked down at the wand, up at me, and blinked. He blinked again. "Does this mean? . . ." His voice cracked slightly.

I nodded.

Holding the pregnancy wand in his hands, he sat down on the edge of the bed. I sat down next to him, the outside of our thighs lightly touching. Together, we stared at the piece of plastic that was about to change the course of our lives. He rested his hand on my arm. I pressed my leg into his. Minutes passed in silence.

Finally, he turned to me. "What are you thinking?" he asked. "You know I'll support you in whatever decision you make."

I nodded. We looked at each other. Then I smiled, and his face lit up. I nodded again. We were going to have a baby.

• • •

The week after I found out I was pregnant, I went out to dinner with my friends Tasha and Jenny at our favorite West Village standby, the Grange Hall. The three of us had taken jobs in book publishing straight out of college and soon became close friends. Although we had all left the industry to follow other paths—Jenny to become a marketing executive, Tasha to pursue a master's in creative writing, and I to attend journalism school—we still got together regularly at the Grange. We were there so often that I used to call it an extension of the closet-size galley kitchen in my apartment, which was right around the corner.

The bartender nodded and waved at us as we came in through the side door. The place was crowded, as usual, but we managed to snag a good booth in the corner and quickly stripped off our heavy winter coats and scarves. Candlelight burnished the walls of the cozy dining room, and voices rose and fell around us. As we scanned the menus,

I wondered just how I would make it through the evening with my two closest confidantes without divulging the news. Since it was very early in my pregnancy, John and I had decided to wait a few more weeks before telling our family and friends. But I wasn't sure I would be able to hold out. Already my face was starting to feel stiff from the strain.

A waiter came to take our drink order. Tasha ordered a glass of red wine, Jenny ordered a strawberry margarita, and, with forced casualness, I said that I was fine with tap water.

"What's up?" Tasha asked, motioning to my water glass.

"What do you mean?" I continued to study the menu intently.

"No Aviation cocktail tonight?"

"Oh . . . I'm still on antibiotics for that cold I had last week," I lied. "No drinking allowed."

Tasha arched her eyebrow but said nothing. One dubious look from her, and my resolve started to crumble. I sighed, knowing I was sunk. Damn, I had always been an awful liar.

"I'm pregnant," I blurted out. Tasha and Jenny stared back at me, speechless. Within minutes, I had spilled every detail about our recent visit to the obstetrician, how John and I had seen the baby's heart via ultrasound, how we had watched, enthralled by the minuscule pulse on the screen.

"I *knew* something was up!" Tasha crowed. "Antibiotics. *Please*."

After a round of congratulations, though, the sheer gravity of my news started to sink in. For a moment, the noise of other people's conversations surged around us. Our drinks arrived.

"You're not going to completely change after the baby, are you?" Tasha asked.

"No, of course not," I said with more bravado than I felt. "I'll still be the same old me, just with a baby."

"I feel like it's the end of an era," Jenny said, raising her margarita in a toast. We clinked glasses.

After we had finished dinner and said our good-byes, I walked back to my apartment and plunked down on the couch. The place was a mess—papers and books strewn everywhere, and a couple of old pizza boxes piled in the corner for good measure. The worry that had been nagging at me for days underneath all the excitement now rang clearly in my mind: Really, how could I become a mother? Pulling a pair of John's socks out from under my thigh and tossing them in the corner, I stared up at a hairline crack in the ceiling. Weren't mothers supposed to be older, wiser? Weren't they supposed to have all of life's answers fanned out at their fingertips like a deck of cards? They did not live in messy one-bedroom apartments, eating take-out meals cross-legged on the floor for lack of a dining room table. Babies belonged in a less precarious world of extended families, of regular dinner hours, and parents in the bloom of full-fledged adulthood; they were for people who had their identities grounded in place, not for someone like me, still basking in the waning light of adolescence, still searching for the best version of herself. I was terrified that I would not be up to the task. Yet I knew I wanted to have this baby. There was even serenity in this surrender to my body, a sweet relief.

As the months passed, surrender to my body I did. I remember how strangely anchored I felt in my pregnant body, with its growing belly, the skin rolling every time the baby kicked, the breasts heavy and exotic; actually, everything seemed exotic to me during those months. The world curved and closed, as I plodded ever slower through the streets of Manhattan, often wrinkling my nose at some foul odor. My pregnancy had endowed me with a nearly superhuman sense of smell, not exactly an asset during a New York City summer; I swear, I once sniffed out a fire thirty blocks away. I was attuned to my body's every change, but my body was not entirely my own. Every now and then, I would catch my wavering reflection in a store window and, disoriented, stop to ask myself, who *is* that woman?

It was during my last trimester, as my body had swelled to gigantic proportions and the trash piled up on the city sidewalks, steaming in the summer heat, that John and I rather impulsively decided that we should leave New York. At the time, the move, like so many of our other choices back then, made sense. Since I had adopted the more flexible schedule of a freelance writer and John had recently left his corporate job for consulting, we didn't have any daily obligations in the city, and when we looked around our tiny apartment— ever aware of our cantankerous downstairs neighbor who, from his many complaints about my "stomping around," seemed to object to my weight gain as much as I did—we found it hard to justify staying. We had some money saved up for a down payment, and for a mortgage payment smaller than what we were paying in rent for our one-bedroom apartment, we could get an entire house in Annapolis, a city close to where my father lived. A *house*. Not only would a move give the baby her own room, but I could finally claim a room of my own within which to write. Besides, we reasoned, Annapolis was more a family town, friendly and quaint, with its cobblestone streets, fluttering white sails on the water, and pristine flower baskets bursting into rainbow-colored blooms all summer long.

"But wait, I don't understand. How can you leave?" Tasha asked me when I told her we would be moving shortly after the baby was born. "You *love* the city—plus all your friends are here. Your life is here."

"I know, I know," I said. "But it seems like the right thing to do." We were going to be parents, after all.

• • •

But first, childbirth. For all the changes pregnancy had wrought on my body, the full biological implications of being a woman didn't hit me until I was lying in a hospital room, my body wracked with continuous contractions, conveniently illustrated by the jagged red peaks playing out on a nearby monitor. My body had taken charge, and there was no reasoning with it—not that I was in any state to reason. We later discovered that, in his fluster, John had forgotten to turn off the video camera when I went into labor, thus leaving us with a little keepsake—the harrowing soundtrack of my daughter's delivery. I sounded like a cross between a groaning ox and a banshee. When my daughter finally arrived, screaming, into my arms, I was overjoyed, but also overwhelmed, and both sore and worn out. Nurses were crowding around me, pulling, stitching, wiping. Within minutes, I was being escorted into the bathroom and told to urinate under the nurse's watchful eye. I grimaced and did as I was told.

Somehow I had believed that giving birth would be the toughest part, and afterward my baby would fall asleep in my arms, bathed in a dewy glow, as maternal instinct kicked in. I was not prepared when, for the first twenty-four hours of her life, my daughter wailed nonstop, choking and red-faced, as I fumblingly tried to nurse her. Nothing about it felt natural to me. John tried his best to help, hovering by the bed, reading out instructive passages from *The Womanly Art of Breastfeeding*, but there really was not much he could do, other than maybe sprout a pair of lactating breasts himself. In no time, our egalitarian relationship had gone topsy-turvy. All eyes were looking to me to nourish and comfort this obviously very unhappy baby. Meanwhile, I was leaking in all the wrong places, my hard, round stomach having dissolved into a disturbingly pliable pouch of skin, and everything below the waist hurt like hell. That first night John finally dozed off in a chair, and I could hear his snores under the baby's cries, loud and rhythmic. At midnight, after being awake for almost forty hours, I finally broke down and rang the night nurse, begging her to take my daughter to the nursery so I could rest.

"No one does that," she said reproachfully. "The nursery's empty."

After I explained I was having trouble nursing, she spent the next hour tugging on my breasts, while my daughter continued to scream.

Sitting hunched in bed, my tender breasts being roughly handled by some strange woman, I remember thinking, "I should be horrified at this, but I am just so beyond the point of caring. I would happily parade naked down Broadway if this baby would just stop crying."

I barely slept that night, and the next day was not much better. The baby continued to scream, before falling into an agitated sleep for a time, only to wake up and start screaming again. She screamed with an anger I could never have imagined; she screamed with the anger of the gods. I tried to nurse, but to no avail. My body was raw. I could barely sit up.

I rang the nurse, and someone I had never met before came in. "Do you have a donut pillow or something?" I asked.

"Sorry, no donut pillows," she replied. "When did you have your last Motrin?"

I shook my head. "I don't think I've had *any* Motrin," I mumbled. She left and returned with a small paper cup and two pills. I swallowed them greedily, then lay back and closed my eyes.

"Try to get some sleep," John said. The baby had passed out on his shoulder, and he was rocking her as if he'd been doing it his whole life.

I started to cry. "I don't think I can do this," I said.

That afternoon, the pediatrician came by. As he examined the baby, he asked about her feeding, and we told him that she hadn't nursed yet. "We can't release you until she has a bowel movement," he said.

Release? I thought. You mean you're actually going to let us take this adorable, helpless baby home with us? Can't you see we have no idea what we're doing?

The pediatrician stood up, all business. "She's also looking a bit jaundiced," he said. "Don't worry. We'll just put her under an ultraviolet light. That should take care of the problem." He swaddled her up and carried her out of the room, while John and I stared after him. We were alone in the hospital room, and the sudden silence was almost eerie.

I felt on the verge of hysteria. "I don't want to leave," I said to John, clutching his hand.

But the next morning, September 8, we were duly discharged from St. Vincent's Hospital. I hobbled out the sliding glass doors, blinking in the blast of outdoor air. I pushed the baby stroller toward Seventh Avenue as John ran ahead to get the car, a hatchback Honda Accord that could barely accommodate a car seat. Waiting for him on the sidewalk, I was consumed by the jitters. A jackhammer was roaring in front of the hospital, kicking up clouds of dust, yet now the baby slept, oblivious. I covered her with a blanket as best I could, telling myself everything would be all right.

• • •

We spent the first couple of days back home in a state of panic. Because the baby had arrived almost two weeks late, my parents had already come and gone back to work, leaving John and me alone in our apartment with a squalling newborn. Four days after birth, and she still had not nursed properly. Realizing that we were in desperate need of help, I hired a doula. She came barging into the apartment and, during the span of her brief visit, reprimanded me for getting an epidural, ordered me not to give my daughter a drop of formula, and insisted we all pile into a taxi and go to Greenpoint, Brooklyn, where a Hasidic rabbi could easily clip my daughter's frenulum (the fleshy tissue underneath the tongue) and thereby solve all of our breast-feeding woes. When we ventured that we might want a second opinion before we started clipping anything on our daughter's body, she accused us of being elitist. John promptly fired her, while I broke down and, against the advice of the hospital nurses and the doula, tried to feed the baby a bottle of formula; she only screamed louder. Both John and I were barely holding on. He started sobbing while walking the dog. I sobbed on the phone to friends, who, without children of their own, could do little more than offer nervous clucks of sympathy.

I was at my wit's end when Kathy, a lactation specialist who had taught our childbirth education class, answered my distressed call. Arriving at my door a few hours later, Kathy quickly assessed my tear-stained face and peered over my shoulder at the shrieking baby floundering in her car seat in the middle of the living room. She gave me a hug and then pulled her blond corkscrew curls back into a ponytail. "Don't worry," she said soothingly. "This is *normal*. Everything will be okay."

The reassurance sounded so much better coming from her. Two hours later, calmed by a few spoonfuls of formula, Sylvia had latched on to a painfully swollen breast and was nursing. I thought I might collapse from relief. After the fears and fatigue of the past few days, I caught at last a glimpse or two of the enchanted existence of a new mother. As she nursed, I played with her fingers and toes, marveling at their miniature size. I beamed when she fell into the blissful drunken stupor, lips slightly apart, dark eyelashes curling from closed lids; that night, for the first time in days, I was finally able to shut my eyes for a few hours, too, and I slept heavily, peacefully, with my baby snuggled up against my chest.

The next morning, I woke up in a stream of buttery sunlight pouring through the window. It was a crisp autumn day, the kind of day that makes people fall in love with New York City. I lay there, thinking it was the perfect day for a stroll with Sylvia around the neighborhood. She was still asleep, one tiny fist resting on my chest, and I cautiously turned onto my side to get into a more comfortable position—perhaps I might be able to steal an hour or two more of sleep. But as I moved, Sylvia began to stir in the bed beside me, her little arms and legs moving in unison, working up to a slow flail. And then her face scrunched up in preparation for that thundering cry of hunger. A few moments later, the dog was also up and thumping her tail on the floor. Taking his cue, John rolled out of bed to walk the dog, giving voice to the groan I had stifled, and I picked up the baby and held my breath as I guided her to my right breast, which, mirabile dictu, worked as well this morning as it had the night before.

Feeling pretty confident now, I cradled the baby against me with one hand and clicked on the twelve-inch television by the bed with the other, expecting to find some light talk-show fare. A blazing building filled the screen. From the newscaster's frantic reporting, I gathered that a plane had only minutes before slammed into one of the World Trade Center's towers, not twenty blocks from our apartment. At first I wasn't too worried, assuming it must have been an accident, some amateur piloted Cessna gone horribly off course. I burped Sylvia, switched her to the other side of my lap, and sat up to get a better look. The camera zoomed in on a burning section of the tower, which looked like a wide, livid scar, and that's when it dawned on me that no single-engine flyer could do that kind of damage.

Then, without warning, another plane hit the other tower. I couldn't even process what I'd just seen. The newscasters live on the scene talked over each other in confusion. A few moments later, I heard the front door to our apartment slam shut and Emma's paws clacking across the wood floor. John appeared in the doorway of the bedroom, and the dog ran up to me, her tail wagging.

"Have you heard?" he asked.

I pointed to the television screen, nodding.

"I saw it happen," he said as he crossed the room. "I saw the second plane crash." His voice was shaking.

The news reports soon confirmed our worst fears, that the plane crashes were suspected acts of terrorism. My mind snagged on the word *terrorism*, and I could not pull it away. I stared down at Sylvia resting so peacefully in my arms—her chest rising with each breath, her fists rounded now in soft Os—and hugged her close, as if to shield her from the images on the screen.

I don't think I had ever really known the meaning of terror until that moment. In the hours that followed, John and I huddled together on the bed, our baby nestled between us, as we watched the wave of disaster unfold before us. I sat with my arms wrapped around my body—utterly motionless, save for the beating in my chest, fast as hummingbird wings, so fast that it felt like my heart no longer belonged to me. Over and over again, I kept counting my daughter's impossibly tiny toes, one through ten, willing my racing pulse to calm. But there was more to come. As we watched, the Twin Towers suddenly heaved, shuddered, and, in swift succession, crumbled to the ground.

It was over before I knew what had happened. The crash-and-burn images on the screen had started to seem surreal, and John and I decided to see for ourselves what was happening on our doorstep. I carefully swaddled Sylvia up in a green blanket dotted with cartoon characters, placed her in the stroller, and popped up the hood to protect her from whatever we might find once we left our apartment building.

Outside, everything was almost the same, but not quite. The guys at the local deli were scrambling eggs on the grill, but they were uncharacteristically somber. The resident transvestite was walking his quivering Chihuahua around the block as usual, but his face was strikingly bare of rouge, lipstick, and mascara. A young couple embraced in the middle of the street, her brown hair falling on his shoulder as she wept. Most noticeably, the swift pace of the city had staggered into slow motion. Police had restricted traffic from entering our neighborhood, and the usually crowded streets were now empty of cars. People drifted crooked paths across empty thoroughfares, dazed and confused, with no clear destination. Strangers congregated on street corners, in front of cafés, and on apartment building stoops, as if they were old friends. Save for the steady alarm of police and fire truck sirens passing down the West Side Highway, the air was so very still and quiet, the sky so blue except for the smoke.

Looking north from Seventh Avenue, I could make out St. Vincent's Hospital in the distance, where, only a few days before, I had given birth. The driveway was mobbed with ambulances carrying victims to the hospital for emergency care. To the south, the Twin Towers that used to scrape the sky had been replaced by a thick wall of rubble and dust. My chest ached, from sadness, from smoke, and I had trouble swallowing. John and I looked at each other and headed back to the apartment.

All day and all night, the remains burned. Eventually, the wind shifted direction, carrying those particles of destruction into the air we were breathing. Our eyes watered, and our throats stung, and although I pressed wet towels around our windows and put a fan next to the baby bassinet, it was no use; there was no blocking out the acrid odor.

The decision to go stay with John's parents on Long Island was an easy one. I packed quickly, with the urgency of a civilian fleeing a war zone. We were waved through the police barricade that surrounded our neighborhood, and as we made our way out of the city, I gazed though the closed window at the hundreds of people holding silent candlelight vigils, their lit faces floating ghostlike along the sidewalk. John and I did not speak for the entire car ride.

We stayed on Long Island for two weeks, sleeping on the pullout couch in his parents' den. Everything around me had been reduced to extremes: love and loss, life and death, talk of diapers and of terrorism. While I tended to Sylvia, feeding and rocking and changing her, the images of destruction aired over and over on the television, creating an otherworldly, flickering glow in the darkened living room. I could not turn them off. When we returned to our West Village apartment, it was only to pack up all of our belongings, load them into a truck, and move to Annapolis, leaving behind the city we loved, the place we had called home.

You Can Run, but You Can't Hide

Although we had already been planning to move to Annapolis before Sylvia was born, the tragedy of 9/11, of course, lent an unexpected solemnity to our departure. Looking back, I see now that with the dual shock of new parenthood and the attack on the World Trade Center, John and I dove for cover under what we fancied was the ultimate domestic fantasy. We had traded big-city for small-city life, a tiny postwar apartment for a sprawling Victorian home. The house we moved into in Annapolis was, in a word, gorgeous, with mahogany window frames and pocket doors. Its wavy leaded-glass windows offered peeks of the South River, and, at serendipitous moments in the afternoon, refracted the sunlight just so, splitting it into sprays of gold. I had not lived in a house in more than a decade, not since before college, and the sheer amount of space took some getting used to. For weeks, John and I holed up in one of the smaller bedrooms on the second floor, where we had transferred all the furniture from our old apartment living room. This hideaway was our dirty little secret, until one day my father dropped by unannounced and appeared in the doorway of our "New York" room. I let out a yelp of surprise, as he stood there, surveying the scene.

"You have got to be kidding," he said dryly.

"What?" I retorted. "We're *nesting*."

"It's like you never left your apartment," he said. He walked across the room and squeezed onto our already crowded Jennifer convertible sofa, the dog shifting position to lean against his leg.

We spent those first few months in Annapolis in a dreamlike haze, my memories from that period coming forward only as montage, as if I were playing a role cobbled together from every sentimental movie I had seen on family life: Strolling by the bay at sunset with Sylvia asleep in the sling. Planning meticulously home-cooked meals to serve at our new dining room table. Posing on our front steps, all four of us, including the dog, wearing Santa hats, for our first family Christmas card. I threw myself into the role, but once the novelty wore off, a sense of unease set in. I felt isolated and alone. Often I would come home from my weekly trip to the grocery store and, pulling up in front of our gray-shingled house, feel the muscles at the back of my neck constrict; sometimes I had to fight the urge to keep driving. But to where—and from *what* exactly?

I decided to focus on work, hoping a new project would reconnect me to the outside world. John had staked out the first floor, near the kitchen, as his workspace, and I claimed the attic as my sanctuary. It was a bit of an odd room, small and lined entirely with garish Victorian-style wallpaper made up of brightly plumed birds and tropical flowers. The room's A-line ceiling, which, even at its highest point, I could graze with my fingertips, gave the space a cavelike feel that was simultaneously comforting and claustrophobic. From a small round window, I could make out the water's edge, and against that wall I set up my desk, a telephone, and my laptop.

Every day after I had put Sylvia down for her morning nap, I would dutifully walk up the two flights of stairs and sit down to write. And sit, and sit, and sit. Then I would stand, pacing. As soon as I heard Sylvia stirring in her crib, I would hurtle down the stairs to scoop her up, gaining a brief reprieve before the cycle started all over again. The less I found myself able to concentrate on my writing, the more antsy I became. I sent my agent rambling pitches for magazine articles.

"Don't worry so much about work," she chided me over the phone, clearly exhausted by my barrage of e-mails. "Relax and enjoy being a mom for a while."

I could not relax.

Motherhood itself was not the problem. In the hushed parenthesis of dawn, I would sit in a rocking chair by the window and lull Sylvia to sleep in my arms, watching her skin turn golden with the rising sun; whenever she smiled at me, my heart grew wings. All this, yet

I saw in myself the same prematernal me, even if, to the rest of the world, it was like I had emerged from the nine-month pod of pregnancy as some *new* person. What had been my livelihood was suddenly referred to as something "fun and creative" to pass the time when I was not doing my primary job of being a mom. Now that I had a baby on my hip, many people assumed I wanted only to discuss how long she had napped that afternoon or the benefits of grinding my own baby food, even though, frankly, these conversations bored me to no end. When Adrienne Rich writes of feeling alienated by the "institution—not the fact—of motherhood," I know exactly what she means. It goes without saying that I loved my baby—intensely—but the institution of motherhood rests not so much on love as on the conversion tale: the belief that a mother need no longer feel any ambition, any curiosity, any desire of her own.

Not that I didn't try to convert. For the first year after I arrived in Annapolis, I went out of my way to sign up for music classes or go to the park with Sylvia, eager for these occasional escapes from the house. Stay-at-home moms dominated the neighborhood during the day when the city emptied out of almost everyone else but government employees, students, and retirees. Nowhere in evidence was the electrifying diversity and cool anonymity of New York. Designed for eighteenth-century living, downtown Annapolis, where we lived, is mostly made up of narrow streets crammed with brightly painted row houses. Given these close quarters, I soon got to know many of the other mothers in town. Mornings I would see the same women at the local coffee shop, toting Vera Bradley bags filled with Ziploc containers of Cheerios and Yo baby yogurts and gathering in small groups, absentmindedly jiggling the strollers next to them as they chatted. I tried my best to fit in, if only out of a sense of survival, but they quickly sniffed out that I wasn't really one of them.

Marion was one of the first moms I met after moving to Annapolis. Her son was about the same age as Sylvia, and she very graciously invited me to the morning coffee klatch she had put together with some of the other mothers in the neighborhood. I thought we might have a lot in common. She had lived for a couple of years in New York before moving to Washington, D.C., to work as an attorney, but by the time I met her she had quit her job and taken to the job of mother with an impressive officiousness. Pretty early on, we realized that we were not going to become fast friends.

"So what's the theme of Sylvia's room?" Marion asked me at one of these coffee klatches I attended, where five of us moms sat, packed in together, around a square table for two at the front of the café. Everyone looked at me.

I put my coffee cup down, resisting the urge to wipe my sleeve across my upper lip. "Theme?" I said, tugging on a loose thread hanging from the hem of my shirt.

"Yes, *theme*," Marion continued. "Your nursery theme. Christopher's theme is baseball. I got the most *adorable* baseball lamp last week—special order."

The other moms cooed approvingly, but Marion turned her gaze back to me. I was not off the hook yet.

"Oh, Sylvia's theme is 'storage room,'" I joked lamely, although it wasn't so far from the truth. We still had not finished unpacking the boxes from our move eight months earlier, and they remained stacked from floor to ceiling against one wall of her room. No one laughed. I took a sip of coffee. "But I'm thinking I'll do her room in a mythical-creatures theme," I added, quickly improvising. "You know—unicorns and leprechauns, maybe a wood nymph or two."

Marion nodded approvingly, but soon after that, whenever I saw these moms congregated inside, I would wave hello from afar and then keep pushing Sylvia's stroller past the coffee-shop window, around the corner and out of sight.

• • •

John, for his part, seemed immune to any of the sociopolitical nuances of parenthood. When he took Sylvia to Kindermusik classes, the mothers all fussed over him and invited him out to lunch. When he pushed Sylvia in her sun hat and stroller through the streets of downtown Annapolis, he would positively beam as passersby smiled at our baby. Never one for small talk before he became a dad, John was now striking up casual conversations with every stranger who commented on her cuteness. Neighbors would pull me aside and tell me I was *so lucky* to have such a great husband who was *so involved* in raising our child. And it was true. We had moved to Annapolis in large part so we could afford to both work at home and share childrearing responsibilities. We worked out a schedule in which I took Sylvia in the mornings; John took care of her in the afternoons. Our shared parenting time appeared astonishingly equal to outsiders— maybe *too* equal. It didn't take long to discover that they viewed my time as a duty, whereas John's was a gift—he was saint to my sinner.

From my perspective, however, this split was not quite as equitable as I had hoped. True, we divided the actual hours of child care, but I had also assumed responsibility for a host of other household matters: food shopping, finding a pediatrician, making appointments, looking for kid-friendly activities, buying baby clothes, researching preschools, and so on. On top of that, I continued to nurse Sylvia for her entire first year, which meant I could never wander too far, for too long. Whenever we tried to give her a bottle of pumped milk, she would turn her head and wail, and pushing her to take the bottle didn't seem worth the hassle. While John single-mindedly worked through the morning, during his afternoons with Sylvia as she napped, and again after dinner, I could never achieve his level of concentration. At night, I would nurse Sylvia, put her to bed, and then stay upstairs, often watching television alone in the dark.

We may both have been involved in our daughter's care, but I soon realized that John and I were not experiencing parenthood on the same psychological plane. I was the "Mother," and I both relished and resented the responsibility. No matter how unfair my feelings, I was infuriated that John seemed able to compartmentalize his life so neatly into work and family, while I was struggling to make the pieces fit together. Without being fully aware of what was happening, by the time Sylvia was walking and talking, John and I had drifted into two separate orbits: upstairs and downstairs; his and hers. Once I calculated months—*months*—had gone by since we had exchanged a real conversation that didn't include a rundown of our domestic to-do list. Perhaps if we still had been living in New York City or had not suffered through the trauma of 9/11, or if I had been born under Venus instead of Mercury, things would have been different. All I know is that by the time I walked into that college classroom at Barnard, I felt like a starving woman who had stumbled onto a feast.

PART II
DESTINY

The beginning is always today.

—MARY WOLLSTONECRAFT

Perpetua

....

To say I was an avid student would be an understatement. Liberated from the stress of papers, exams, and grades, I had the luxury to reflect on what I was reading and go beyond the assigned pages. With our first class discussion of Eve and the story of Genesis, T. had exposed the great weight of cultural expectation that had been pressing women into submission since ancient times. But for me, she had also inadvertently offered insight into my own susceptibility to the conversion myth of motherhood. Although the rest of the semester would be spent studying the feminists who challenged the prevailing notions of a woman's destiny, who themselves lived their lives against the grain, already I wanted more. I wanted the female response to Augustine's male perspective, for perhaps if I understood how women lived under such severe limitations as existed back then, I would be able to test the boundaries of my own destiny in the present.

Locating such a woman's story called for some digging. History transmits the voices of few women from antiquity. Barred from education, women usually remained illiterate, and, thus, their lives, as told in their own words, are all but absent from the pages of the past. We are mostly left to guess at their inner fears and hopes, their thoughts and reflections. In *Adam, Eve, and the Serpent*, however,

Pagels had briefly described a chronicle belonging to Vibia Perpetua, an aristocratic woman who lived in North Africa at the end of the second century AD. As a young woman, Perpetua had devoted herself to Christianity, still a religion far from the mainstream at that time, and shortly after giving birth to her first child, a son, she was arrested as a heretic for refusing to perform a pagan act of worship to the emperor, Septimus Severus. Her slave Felicity, also a Christian and pregnant with her own child, was arrested and thrown in jail with her mistress. Perpetua, who was fluent in both Greek and Latin, managed to keep a diary of her imprisonment up until the day of her execution, offering us a rare inside look into a woman's life during that period.

How could I resist this invitation? With the help of the Internet, I tracked down a book called *Perpetua's Passion: The Death and Memory of a Young Roman Woman*, which included extensive excerpts from Perpetua's diary. The book, a battered, deaccessioned library copy ordered from a used bookstore in Boston, landed on my porch in Annapolis two days later. The next morning, after dropping off Sylvia for the morning at preschool, I tucked the book into my purse and headed for my favorite tiny café off Main Street.

Walking toward downtown, I ran into Marion corralling her toddler and infant into her station wagon. I might have tried to slither down a different street if she hadn't spotted me first. Now it was too late. She waved, motioning for me to come over. Even after I stopped going to the coffee klatches, Marion was always exceedingly polite when we bumped into each other, although I nevertheless picked up on an undercurrent of awkwardness, probably emanating from me and not her. As she strapped her youngest into the car seat, I made funny faces at her toddler to make him laugh. She gave me a look, winked, and asked when I was going to have "another one."

"Ah, who knows," I said evasively. "I feel like I have my hands full with one."

"I'm sure Sylvia would love a little brother or sister," she said. "Besides, you want to strike while the iron's hot, if you know what I mean." She looked at me pointedly, and a beat of silence ensued.

I changed the subject. "Where are you off to?" I asked.

"Gymnastics class, then Whole Foods. How about you?"

"Going to do some reading." I regretted the words as soon as I said them.

"Good for you," she singsonged. "What are you reading?"

Oh, what did I have to lose? I pulled *Perpetua's Passion* out of my bag and showed it to her.

Her eyes widened as she read the back flap, and she gave an exaggerated shudder. "Sounds pretty gruesome," she said, handing the book back to me.

Her daughter squirmed in the backseat, and Marion pulled down her sunglasses from the top of her head. "Stephanie, you're so . . . *eccentric*," she said. "Better run or we'll be late, but it was *so* great to see you." She air-kissed me on the cheek, and I continued walking on with a sigh of relief.

• • •

I made it to the café without too many more encounters, taking a seat on the old futon by the window where I often liked to covertly people-watch as I read. But before too long I was completely engrossed by Perpetua's diary excerpts, too sucked into her world to notice what was happening in mine. Her prison descriptions are vivid, the pages filled with a bristling fear over her infant son's welfare. "I was terrified," Perpetua writes, "as I had never before been in such a dark hole. What a difficult time it was! With the crowd the heat was stifling; then there was the extortion of the soldiers; and to crown all, I was tortured with worry for my baby there." She writes about her father's many visits to the prison and how he begs her to recant

Christianity—if not for her own sake, then for the sake of her child—but Perpetua remains steadfast.

During her incarceration, Perpetua has four vivid dreams, which she records in her journal. In her last vision, the night before her execution, Perpetua dreams she has entered the arena where she is to die and discovers that she has turned into a man. She is pitted against an Egyptian "of vicious appearance" and emerges from their combat victorious. "The crowd began to shout and my assistants started to sing psalms. Then I walked up to the trainer and took the branch. He kissed me and said to me: 'Peace be with you, my daughter!' I began to walk in triumph towards the Gate of Life. Then I awoke," she writes.

On the actual day of her execution, Perpetua, with her former slave Felicity, is thrown naked into the arena in front of some thirty thousand spectators. The sight of Perpetua's slight, shivering body and Felicity's breasts, still dripping with milk from her recent childbirth, sobers even this bloodthirsty crowd, and the two women are quickly retrieved and clothed in tunics. Their female bodies suitably covered, they are led back into the arena to await their fate. Paired with a mad heifer, Perpetua and Felicity are tossed, bruised, and smothered—wounded, yet still alive. Although the crowd is incredulous at their strength, their survival is no salvation. Perpetua must die, if not under the hooves of a beast, then by the sword. The last martyr to climb the scaffold that day, Perpetua bravely exposes her neck, but her execution is neither swift nor kind. The gladiator dealing death lowers his sword and misses, hitting her collarbone instead and causing the young woman to scream out in pain. But this does not stop Perpetua from taking the gladiator's trembling hand and guiding it to her throat. She was twenty-two years old.

Even after I closed the book, I could not erase from my mind the image of that pale hand, that sharp blade, that tender throat. Although the city of Carthage celebrated the anniversary of Perpetua's martyrdom with an annual festival in her honor, the Catholic Church over the years began—literally—to rewrite her role. By the fourth century, accounts of Perpetua's trial and death had been severely edited. A nonexistent husband, for one, was written into the plot. Perpetua's inner anguish about leaving her child was utterly deleted. Despite Perpetua's own words to the contrary, a misleading version of Perpetua's martyrdom materialized in which she rejected her infant son and family without any remorse, physically pushing them away, calling them evil. Augustine, too, tarnished Perpetua's reputation by constantly comparing her to Eve, emphasizing that, for all her virtue, she remained a member of the frailer sex.

Although the truth of what happened remains preserved in Perpetua's diary, the need to revise the circumstances of Perpetua's death shows how history tends to obscure the bravery of mothers: bravery wielded in a broader social context by women determined not to go silently into the private oblivion of Eve but to risk their lives to stand up publicly for their beliefs. Through her story, told across the millennia, Perpetua tugged on the thin thread of doubt that had wound itself around my thoughts ever since I became a mother: that, by becoming a mother, I no longer controlled my own destiny; indeed, that despite all I had learned to the contrary, biology *is* destiny.

"Think again," I could almost hear Perpetua whispering in my ear. The feminist story, she reminded me, is a counternarrative, a narrative of disobedience, a chronicle of battle, not of surrender. Women who do not fit the mold are too often maneuvered, manipulated, and mangled into some culturally safe archetype. The makers of history transformed Perpetua into a cold, unfeeling mother—a villain of sorts. But who is to say that becoming a mother didn't also push Perpetua to *become* a martyr, didn't cause her to passionately uphold her religious ideals because she wanted to offer her son the greatest gift she could—an ideal? Maybe, in the end, Perpetua's maternal instincts

were precisely what gave her the strength to confront the burliest
Roman gladiator and then to lie down with dignity before death.

Rewriting Motherhood

One morning, a couple of weeks into the semester, John groggily hit
the snooze button on the alarm clock and promptly went back to
sleep; I woke up about a half hour later, looked at the clock in dismay,
and then ran down the hall to rouse Sylvia out of bed. She moaned
in protest, and soon I was teetering down the stairs, my daughter's
arms and legs wrapped around me like a monkey's, her head buried
in my neck. As we walked into the kitchen, I unpeeled her body from
mine and then deposited her onto a stool.

"I want scrambled eggs with cheese," she said sleepily.

"How about a bowl of cereal?"

"NO! Scrambled eggs with cheese."

"How do you ask?"

"*Pleeeaaaaasssssssse*," she intoned.

One eye on the clock, I went into a well-choreographed and highly
synchronized routine like some character out of the *Matrix*: I pulled
the eggs, milk, and butter out of the refrigerator; put the pan on the
stove with a dab of butter; poured Sylvia a glass of milk; cracked
the eggs and whipped them with a fork; let the dog (whimpering at
the back door right on schedule) into the yard; returned to find the
butter sizzling and poured the eggs into the pan; grabbed a paper
towel to wipe up the spilled milk on the countertop; stirred the eggs;
let the dog (who was now scratching at the back door) back into the
house; put the milk, eggs, and butter back into the refrigerator and

got the cheese out; sprinkled cheese on the eggs; and then swirled the eggs once more, spooned them onto a plate, and put the plate in front of Sylvia.

Breakfast, check.

I took a breath, ready to move on to making her lunch for school.

Sylvia ate two bites of her scrambled eggs and announced she was full.

"What?" I screeched two octaves above my normal voice. "You hardly ate anything!"

But I didn't have time for a proper confrontation. I gathered the makings for a turkey and cheese sandwich. *Damn*, no more juice boxes.

"Ten more bites," I said.

"Five," she bargained. "And I want my sandwich cut in triangles."

"Fine. Seven."

We went for a few more rounds as I finished making her lunch. At last, she took three small, tortured bites before clutching her stomach dramatically. "Mommy," she declared, "I have a tummy ache."

A moment's hesitation as I decided whether to argue further or save myself for the inevitable battle we were about to have upstairs when I tried to get her dressed. I chose the latter, pouring the rest of the scrambled eggs into the dog's food bowl in defeat; both the dog and Sylvia were delighted.

Upstairs, ten minutes and three outfits later, I snapped.

"Mommy, I want to wear something pretty!" Sylvia screamed. "I want to wear something *pink*!"

"I already *told* you, all of your pink clothes are dirty!" I yelled back, wrestling my clawing, writhing four year old into a T-shirt and jeans, feeling every bit as mean as I sounded. Her face crumpled, and she started to howl.

John popped his head into her room. "What's going on?" he asked, bleary-eyed, scratching his head. "Anything I can do to help?"

I shot him a wilting look, and he wisely disappeared.

I spent another fifteen minutes trying to calm Sylvia down so that I could get her into her car seat, and finally we were off. I glanced at the clock. We might just make it, I thought. I stepped on the gas, but luck had flown my side, and I hit every red light between our house and her preschool. We arrived five minutes after drop-off had officially ended, which meant we had to make the walk of shame to the school office. My daughter was somber, her face blotchy, her hair barely combed. I was not looking much better and with some horror realized that I was wearing the same outfit I had been wearing when I signed Sylvia in late two days earlier. Sheepishly, I entered the office.

"Another tardy," Marge, the school secretary, tut-tutted, as I filled out the pink slip and signed my name. "You know," she said, "it's up to the parents to teach children the importance of punctuality." I nodded and smiled, gritting my teeth. Then I fled.

Back at home, I sat down at the kitchen counter, poured myself another cup of coffee, and slipped the *New York Times* out of its blue plastic wrapper. My eye was caught at once by this front-page headline: "Many Women at Elite Colleges Set Career Path to Motherhood." Instead of unwinding with the crossword puzzle as was my custom, I started to read. The trend of Ivy League–educated mothers "opting out" of the workforce had been a subject of heated debate only a year or two earlier, but now, according to the article, the Ivy League's female students were *pre*opting out, that is, they were already planning to drop out of their careers to be stay-at-home mothers while still single and childless coeds, taking classes like Cellular Biology and Renaissance Literature.

The article, based on informal surveys and interviews with a handful of students at Yale, proclaimed this latest trend with some alarm. What did it mean that Ivy League women, presumably the future leaders of our country, were already planning to suspend their careers or abandon them entirely in order to make motherhood their only priority? Take Yale sophomore Cynthia Liu—1,510 SAT score, 4.0 GPA, pianist, runner, and hospital volunteer. Although she planned to attend law school for her J.D. after graduating from college, she expected to practice law for no more than a few years before quitting, trading in the money and the prestige for an MRS and MOM. "My mother always told me you can't be the best career woman *and* the best mother at the same time," Liu was quoted as saying. "You always have to choose one over the other."

Here the experts weighed in. Women are finally "turning realistic," said Cynthia E. Russert, Yale professor of American history. Laura Wexler, Yale professor of American studies and women's and gender studies, attributed women's retrograde attitudes to the failure to build a social infrastructure that supports working mothers. "I really believed 25 years ago that this would be solved by now," she added. Among the students interviewed for the article, the gender divide was apparent. The female students were extremely aware of the problems caused by trying to balance work and family, while male students, in general, approved of a woman's decision to stay at home. One woman described a guy in her class who went so far as to say, "I think that's sexy." (Ha, *that* guy's in for a rude awakening, I thought, staring down at my food-stained, five-day-old outfit of T-shirt and sweat pants.)

My coffee cup was barely empty when my phone rang.

"I'm really starting to think feminism *is* dead," Jenny declared.

My other line beeped.

"I'm sorry, but those girls have no clue what the everyday reality of motherhood is like," said Tasha, who recently had her first baby and had not gotten more than three continuous hours of sleep in more than six months.

We all agreed that the article was depressing, not so much because these young women wanted to be stay-at-home mothers, but for their seeming readiness, at nineteen years old, to resort to traditional gender roles without a peep. As Yale student Angie Ku summed up toward the end of the article, "I accept how things are. I don't mind the status quo. I don't see why I have to go against it."

I mulled over this last quote, thinking back to when I was Ku's age, back to all those late nights in college, conversing with friends as we draped ourselves over the couch in the dorm's common lounge, hopped up on ambition and caffeine. Not one of us ever raised the subject of marriage or motherhood. *Status quo?* No way. We were too busy picking apart the beauty myth and taking back the night. We nursed our plans of becoming doctors or lawyers, artists or writers, dreaming big and promising ourselves we would worry about the details later. As far as we were concerned, the path was linear and went only one way: up.

Sure, many of us had revised our plans since then. A few of us had chosen to stay at home or to work part-time after husbands and children arrived on the scene; some of us had soared professionally over the years, while others had suffered career disappointments or scaled back our expectations. Even so, I would never give up those heady days of youth.

Or would I? Was my own reaction just as knee-jerk as any conservative notion of "proper" womanhood? I folded up the newspaper and set it down on the counter. The previous week I had gone to a panel discussion at Barnard called "Rewriting Motherhood," aimed at moving beyond the common tropes we encounter when we talk about motherhood: Are women who return to work after having children turning their backs on their social and biological destiny? Are stay-at-home moms betraying the advances of feminism? The panel, which included *New York Times* columnist Lisa Belkin, who acted as moderator, and Judith Warner, author of the recent best-seller *Perfect Madness: Motherhood in the Age of Anxiety*, drew an enormous crowd. Every foldout chair was filled, and still more people— mostly women, but some men, too—lined up against the wall or sat cross-legged on the linoleum floor.

Together, and individually, the panelists eloquently identified the tensions created by motherhood, both within their own lives and within the culture as a whole. But toward the end of the hour, when Belkin moved the conversation toward how best to handle the dilemmas of modern motherhood, a disagreement broke out. Recounting an episode in which a woman stood up at a charity dinner and insisted we tell our daughters to tone down their ambitions so they will be prepared for motherhood, Warner remarked, "Every time I think back on this, I pretty much have tears in my eyes, because I think that is the *worst* possible thing that we could do. We can't cut our daughters off at the knees. We all need to be working to make things change."

Cecelie Berry, editor of the anthology *Rise Up Singing: Black Women Writers on Motherhood*, cut in. A Harvard Law School graduate who left corporate litigation to stay home with her two sons, Berry had throughout the evening injected a note of realism—sometimes a harsh realism—into the conversation. She had opened up the presentation by reading an essay she had written about motherhood titled "Nobody Can Tell You." The audience sat riveted as she described the "erosion of self" that comes with motherhood and depression as the "bastard of an extramarital liaison, me and Domesticity," but also the incredible love she has for her children and, more mysterious, she said, the love they have for her. As a black woman, Berry felt the added social obligation to remain in the professional world, to become *someone*, and was torn between staying at home and working. Of all the panelists, Berry seemed most deeply entrenched in the contradictory feelings of love and anger, guilt and frustration.

"Well, I don't know if we should tell our daughters they have *limitless* possibilities," said Berry. "If you want to include a meaningful experience with motherhood in your lives, I don't know if that's possible."

Warner's mouth dropped open at Berry's comment, but she quickly recovered. "I guess a lot of this breaks down according to what *kind* of career you're going to have," she said, glancing at Berry, "what kind of *life* you want to have. But I think if we can just give girls the ability to remain true to themselves, then that sort of takes care of part of the problem."

"Yeah, it does break down to what kind of career you want to have," agreed Berry, "but that's exactly why I don't want to tell girls, 'You have limitless options.' I don't know if it's possible to really be a mother who experiences motherhood and at the same time have a dynamic, high-profile career."

Murmurs erupted from the audience, hands shot in the air. Unfortunately, Belkin cut in to conclude the event, which had already run over by a half hour, leaving the attendees to choke back their questions for the panelists. We broke out in a frustrated smattering of applause, while student volunteers quickly descended, herding members of the audience out the glass doors. As I filed out of the auditorium into the breezy night, walking across the very campus where I had groomed a self who was intended for the larger world, the impossibility of the predicament pressed upon me. That part of me was useless in the making of sandwiches, dressing of writhing bodies, wiping of noses and spills. In the cool autumn air, I felt the simmer of my own unpursued ambitions rising up against my desire to fully experience motherhood. I did not know how to reconcile them.

At the time, I had wondered if Berry was right: Maybe girls should be carefully apprised of the limits imposed by family. But reading the *New York Times* article that morning convinced me otherwise. I pictured my daughter growing up believing that she had to choose either a career or motherhood, and I shook my head with the gut conviction that no, she deserved more. If anything, the books we had been reading in Fem Texts had reminded me that we could always push further the limits of the impossible, if we only dared to do so.

• • •

Interested to hear what my classmates thought of the *New York Times* piece, I arrived early in order to stake out my usual seat on the coffee-splattered couch in the back of the classroom, near the window, the better to listen to the discussion and observe the students without intruding. Sitting around the table as I had on the first day, I felt too conspicuous, bent over my black-marbled composition book, scribbling notes, while all the other students typed away on their laptops. I might as well have been wearing a sign advertising that I went to college before the invention of e-mail, and besides, those chairs were designed for nimbler bodies. As the rest of the students trickled into the classroom, I gathered from their conversations that the article had already been widely disseminated and discussed in other classes.

T. swept into the room, arms weighed down by a folder crammed with papers. "So what did you think?" she asked. No one needed to ask about what.

"It made me really mad," said Janine. "The reporter took, what, a small handful of women at Yale and turned their beliefs into a trend. I mean, it creates a false impression that all college women think that way."

"I heard the reporter just graduated from Yale," added Maria. "Probably just interviewed a bunch of her friends."

"Not that there's anything *wrong* with wanting to be a stay-at-home mom, but just the way it was presented in the article . . ."

"*I know*—just wasn't helpful at all . . ."

"Personally, I don't know anyone like the women she interviewed in the article . . ."

"No, there *are*! Maybe not here at Barnard, but I have a friend at Georgetown who says there's, like, an MRS club on campus—and girls all talk about getting their MRS degree all the time . . ."

"No—*really*?"

"Seriously!"

"That's just so depressing . . ."

"I've heard that, too . . . Scary . . ."

T. intervened, trying to rein in the conversation, as it grew more agitated and free-range. "Something to keep in mind," she told the class, "is that an article like this comes out every year or two—I don't know how many times I have seen this 'trend' of women flocking back to the home." She sighed. "I'm always hoping that someday my job as a gender-studies professor will become obsolete, but looks like I'm going to have this job for a *looonnngg* time." The class chuckled.

T. leaned forward in her chair. "Now, let's rewind back to two centuries ago when women could barely get *any* kind of education," said T., "and let me introduce you to the woman who has been called the mother of feminism: Mary Wollstonecraft."

A Vindication of the Rights of Woman

Almost everyone who knows anything about feminism has heard of Mary Wollstonecraft. Her *Vindication of the Rights of Woman* is perhaps the most famous case ever made for educating women. Published in 1792, in the wake of both the American and the French revolutions, Wollstonecraft's treatise maintained that, rather than being groomed to act like docile, frivolous creatures, women should be given the same opportunities to exercise their bodies and develop their intellectual capacities as men. Her argument is deceptively simple. "If she [woman] be not prepared by education to become the companion of man," she writes, "she will stop the progress of knowledge and virtue, for truth must be common to all, or it will be inefficacious with respect to its influence on general practice."

When I read *A Vindication of the Rights of Woman* as an undergraduate, my reaction was basically something along the lines of— *duh*! Wollstonecraft's contention that women were capable of rational thought appeared superfluous, if not insulting; I mean, I was in college, wasn't I? And she was reasoning that the most important goal of educating women was to produce better wives and mothers?

What a difference the intervening years made. After rereading *A Vindication of the Rights of Woman*, Mary Wollstonecraft was my new hero. Her polemic is a textual tornado, written over a span of just six weeks, and her passion comes through on every page. This is who Mary Wollstonecraft was—impetuous, opinionated, and wickedly clever. Plainly addressing a male audience as well as a female one, Wollstonecraft sets out to prove that if women are educated, men—nay, humanity—will be better off. She chooses her words carefully, conducting them with such precision that one never knows for sure whether she is speaking earnestly or with tongue firmly in cheek to make abundantly clear the absurdity of women's position in society; I vote for shrewd wit. "Make women rational creatures and free citizens," she writes, "and they will quickly become good wives and mothers, that is if men are good husbands and fathers." I smile at her use of *make*, taking it as a little jab to the men who have "made" us otherwise.

My newfound respect for Wollstonecraft, however, was not shared by my classmates. As the discussion got under way, it became clear that they viewed the text as a musty screed, no longer relevant and too focused on educating women simply to enhance their roles as wife and mother, just as I had so many years back.

Certainly, Wollstonecraft put great stock in the profession of motherhood and even held many progressive ideas about parenting. At a time when the majority of mothers hired wet nurses to care for their infants, Wollstonecraft urged mothers to breast-feed their babies themselves. Likewise, she believed that a child needed to be continually held and touched, not hung by the rafters—sometimes until they were nearly sick with fatigue and hunger—which was not uncommon to do back then. For these notions, many women derisively called her a "raven mother"; today we might call her an advocate of "attachment parenting."

Believing that mothers, too, were responsible for developing their children's moral character, Wollstonecraft argued that the level of a woman's education and her ability to mother were closely allied. "To be a good mother—a woman must have sense, and that independence of mind which few women possess who are taught to depend entirely on their husbands," she writes. "Meek wives are, in general, foolish mothers; wanting their children to love them best, and take their part, in secret, against the father, who is held up as a scarecrow."

Such sentiments were fine. What many of the students in the class faulted Wollstonecraft for was not being radical *enough*—she does not propose to upturn traditional gender roles entirely, but rather suggests only to perform a bit of nip and tuck. Wollstonecraft even says as much herself:

> Let it not be concluded that I wish to invert the order of things; I have already granted, that, from the constitution of their bodies, men seem to be designed by Providence to attain a greater degree of virtue. I speak collectively of the whole sex; but I see not the shadow of a reason to conclude that their virtue should differ in respect to their nature. In fact, how can they, if virtue has only one eternal standard? I must therefore, if I reason consequentially, as strenuously maintain that they have the same simple direction, as that there is a God.

Seems pretty innocuous, doesn't it? Perhaps. But I like to think that I saw beyond the words to Wollstonecraft's meaning and intent, which were, it seemed to me at least, far more extensive and, indeed, more subversive than simply educating women to be noble companions, mothers, and wives, following in the shadows of their men on the climb to virtue. Lest we forget, Wollstonecraft was battling the belief that knowledge had no place in a woman's life, for woman neither needed nor wanted an education to fulfill her destiny as wife and mother; knowledge would just confuse her, upset her, or make her dangerous. In *A Vindication of the Rights of Woman*, then, Wollstonecraft makes a case for the opposite. By striving for the shared goal of virtue, or excellence, she proposes that women would better contribute to the benefit of all of society.

A Vindication of the Rights of Woman was very much a product of the Enlightenment rationalism that took hold during the French and American revolutions. Like her fellow rationalists, Wollstonecraft hoped to create a perfect society by developing reason, virtue, and knowledge—but among both men *and* women. Freedom of thought followed the path of truth, while ignorance would lead to a breakdown of family structure, sexual debasement, and moral loss.

I suspect Wollstonecraft was to some extent sugarcoating her radical case for women's education in talk of marriage and motherhood in order to appeal to both sexes. On closer inspection, her words, I think, reveal her true aim. "It is plain from the history of all nations," she writes, "that women cannot be confined to merely domestic pursuits, for they will not fulfil family duties, unless their minds take a wider range, and whilst they are kept in ignorance they become in the same proportion the slaves of pleasure as they are the slaves of man." She was determined, then, to break women free from the "fetters" of imposed obedience and utter domesticity, which, no matter how silken, were fetters nonetheless.

"Remember when this was written," T. kindly admonished the class in response to their growing criticism. "We have to see these as beginning steps."

Taking in the room of young women, so comfortably disposed—legs stretched out, elbows on the table, most of them in tank tops and cargo pants—I considered what it was like in Mary Wollstonecraft's day, when women were restricted not just intellectually but physically as well. Today we may have Botox and Wonderbras. Back in the eighteenth century, women plastered their faces with a face powder containing a lethal white lead to mask any natural flush or expression, while their bodies were confined within cumbersome corsets, layers, and hoops. "It was indecent for any woman to appear without encasing her flesh in a whalebone cage that lifted the breasts and held the frame upright from shoulder to thigh," writes Lyndall Gordon in her biography of Mary Wollstonecraft, *Vindication*. "Stays limited a woman's movement: when she read, she could not recline but must hold the book upright; when she curtsied, she sank from the knees with a rigid back. The head, rising from the cage on the pliant column of the neck, could turn from side to side, the lowered lids or widened eyes transmitting the coded signals of their class."

This was Mary's world. Women were not only imprisoned by their dress and their class but also considered the property of their husbands, effectively deprived of any legal rights of their own. The Hardwicke Act of 1753 ruled that a wife, her money, her earnings, and her children all belonged to her husband. Without fear of reprisal, a man could beat, rape, and commit his wife to a lunatic asylum at his own discretion, and, according to Gordon, this fear of being sent to a madhouse hung over every wife in eighteenth-century England; in short, a married woman did not exist in the eyes of the law.

Wollstonecraft knew the precariousness of a woman's position intimately—she had witnessed up close the anguish of women in her own family. The daughter of a temperamental, alcoholic father, who squandered his inheritance in one failed scheme after another, Mary had grown up attentive to her mother's vulnerability. Whenever her father descended into one of his violent moods and began to beat his wife, the young Mary would throw her own small body in front of her mother's to shield her from the falling blows; sometimes she slept on the landing of her parents' bedroom, ready to rush in and protect her mother, should she cry out in the night. Later, when her younger sister Bess became desperately unhappy in her marriage, Mary interceded—"to snatch Bess from extreme wretchedness," as she wrote to their other sister, Everina—and helped her to leave her husband. From all she had seen, the young Mary vowed never to marry.

But what was an eighteenth-century woman to do, if not marry? It was a question that Mary had to face when she came of age. Barely educated, and coming from a family that over the years had declined in wealth and status, Mary had to scramble to find alternatives. Unless she inherited her family's wealth, an unmarried woman had few prospects—that is, a *respectable* unmarried woman—aside from becoming a teacher, a paid companion, or a governess; Mary took a crack at all three, proving she was not like most women of her time. For most women, confronted with such limited options, even an undesirable marriage would have been regarded as their best chance at a decent life. Winning a husband was therefore considered a woman's paramount achievement, and from a young age, girls were encouraged to cultivate what Wollstonecraft called their "illegitimate power" over men—to allure and seduce, holding men in their sway through beauty, feigned helplessness, and coquetry; remarkably, Wollstonecraft herself evaded those social pressures, escaping what would have seemed her fate through a lively intelligence and bluntedged charm.

Wollstonecraft's chosen path of resistance wasn't an easy one, but the ingenuity it entailed brought her into contact with like-minded people. Desperate to leave home, Mary found a job as a lady's companion to an aging widow, and during that time she met a family called the Bloods, becoming close with the daughter, Fanny. With dreams of creating a strong female community, Mary, Fanny, and

Mary's sisters founded a progressive school that enjoyed some moderate success. Then Fanny, who had always had a weak constitution, married and fell gravely ill while pregnant, causing Mary to abandon the school so she could nurse Fanny back to health. Fanny never recovered, and after her death, a heartbroken Mary fled to Ireland to work as a governess. It wasn't long after that Mary decided to devote herself entirely to her writing career. A woman supporting herself as a writer was practically unheard of, but Mary was determined to become the "first of a new genus." After many years spent barely eking out enough money to survive, she won the backing of an anonymous angel investor.

Before she wrote *A Vindication of the Rights of Woman*, Wollstonecraft had already published several books, including *Thoughts on the Education of Daughters*, a semiautobiographical novel titled *Mary*, and *A Vindication of the Rights of Man*, a pamphlet in support of the French Revolution of 1789. But it was her *Vindication of the Rights of Woman* that would win Wollstonecraft widest acclaim— and censure. At last she could unleash her mounting fury at society's treatment of women as little more than decorative objects, a position that deeply offended her. "I have a heart that scorns disguise," she once wrote to a friend, "and a countenance which will not dissemble." In her bald style, Mary thus set herself forth as of the spokeswoman for promoting women and men as equal companions and, in this crusade of hers, ended up crossing words with some formidable adversaries.

For one, there was Jean-Jacques Rousseau, the controversial, yet influential, author of *The Social Contract*, among other major works, including *Emile*, his classic treatise on education. Wollstonecraft generally admired Rousseau and his theories about the goodness of "natural man," whose inherent virtue is distorted only by the corrupting forces of society, but she raised her pen in challenge to his opinions of a woman's place. In *Emile*, Rousseau describes a woman's fundamental role as "to please, to be useful to us, to make us love and esteem them, to educate us when young, and take care of us when grown up, to advise, to console us, to render our lives easy and agreeable, these are the duties of women at all times, and what they should be taught in their infancy." Rousseau creates his ideal woman in the form of Sophia, Emilius's future wife, whom he trains to be the perfect coquette: Emilius may be her master, but she, by orchestrating their relationship correctly, may direct his heart. "You will long maintain the authority in love," instructs Rousseau, "if you know, but how to render your favours rare and valuable. It is thus you may employ even the arts of coquetry in the service of virtue, and those of love in that of reason." Rousseau may have been audacious in his thinking about politics and education, but when it came to women, his ideas were almost aggressively traditional.

In *Vindication*, Wollstonecraft takes pleasure in proving that she is no Sophia, chiding Rousseau for his adolescent fantasy of women in *Emile* and pointing out that such marriages held up by petty games of seduction are, by and large, sad, sorry affairs. She parries, too, his easy assumption that man's dominance over woman is the "order of nature," by pointing out that Eve was formed from Adam's rib, and therefore meant to walk tall by his side, not bend to the yoke at his feet. What kind of man, she asks, would want a woman such as the one Rousseau describes? Only a pitiable creature who "has lost in voluptuous gratifications a taste for more refined enjoyments; never can he have felt the calm satisfaction that refreshes the parched heart, like the silent dew of heaven, of being beloved by one who could understand him." Wollstonecraft goes on to advocate relations between the sexes that value friendship over lust and respect over passion: "It is time to effect a revolution in female manners—time to restore to them their lost dignity—and make them, as a part of the human species, labour by reforming themselves to reform the world."

Critics from her generation to ours have called Wollstonecraft everything from prudish to prurient. To some, her prose reveals an uptight proto-Victorian who would deny women their femininity and castigate men for enjoying erotic pleasure—just another feminist killjoy putting a damper on the sizzle between the sexes. Indeed, in *Vindication*, Wollstonecraft spurns sexual desire in favor of reason, a turn that, upon a cursory reading, while sensible, seems more than a little bleak. Or could it be that by leaving those ineffable qualities of sexual desire and love on the sidelines, where the reader may muse on them privately, Wollstonecraft succeeds in elevating the cooperative nature of marriage, one that emphasizes a foundation of respect and intimacy? *Vindication* is a narrowly focused polemic, after all, seeking not to cover the whole of experience but rather to provoke and contradict the accepted wisdom.

• • •

Slowly, with T. expertly routing the conversation, the class had come around to seeing Mary Wollstonecraft as a revolutionary in petticoats, but then T. pulled the switch and started playing devil's advocate. "From a modern perspective, however," she said, "Wollstonecraft's ideas appear more conservative than radical." She discussed how Wollstonecraft's tract remains safely within the social paradigms of marriage and motherhood, calling for a revolution in female manners yet stopping short of calling for a total revolution in female *roles*.

Some of the students took the bait, rising to defend Mary Wollstonecraft. "I don't fault women for trying to work to change the system from the inside," interrupted Santhi. "You know, you can still make changes that way, maybe just incremental changes, but changes."

"And, I mean, wasn't she also trying to bring men into the domestic spheres as husbands and fathers?" asked Maria.

"It's more complicated than that," T. said. "Emphasizing the family role of wife and mother tends to negate women's role in the *public* sphere, whereas for men, being a father and husband is seen as a plus in the public sphere. So there is an asymmetry that Wollstonecraft is not recognizing." Despite Wollstonecraft's call for equality, T. pointed out that she did not take issue with a woman's domestic duties: "If marriage be the cement of society, mankind should all be educated after the same model, or the intercourse of the sexes will never deserve the name of fellowship, nor will women ever fulfil the peculiar duties of their sex, till they become enlightened citizens, till they become free by being enabled to earn their own subsistence, independent of men. . . . [N]ay, marriage will never be held sacred till women by being brought up with men, are prepared to be their companions rather than their mistresses." The class was clearly baffled, as it struggled to pin Mary somewhere on the feminist spectrum—was she or wasn't she?

Finally, Rowan, a striking student with a shaved head and eyes the color of dark denim, raised her hand. "I really liked *Vindication,*" she said, shaking her head, the gold hoops hanging from her ears swinging with the movement. "I know Mary Wollstonecraft has been called, like, a hypocrite because of what happened in her personal life. But what bothers me is how certain events come to define who we are in the public eye. I mean, people loved the fact that they could point to Mary Wollstonecraft, and say, 'Look at this crazy feminist. She *still* tried to kill herself over some guy.' But, you know, it just shows that she was human."

I nodded in agreement and smiled encouragingly at Rowan, preparing myself for this turn in the class discussion. I was surprised, though, by T.'s reaction. Usually open to all of the students' comments, here she simply gave a curt nod. "Yes, well," she said, suppressing a flash of irritation, "let's stick to the text, shall we?"

• • •

But isn't challenging destiny about not sticking to the text? I asked myself later as I passed through the college gates. At the top of the stairs to the subway entrance, I stopped to call John.

I heard Sylvia chirping in the background, and he put her on the phone. "Mommy," she said, "I drew an elephant in school today!" I smiled as I listened to her excited little voice recount the details of her day. "When are you coming home, Mommy?"

I told her I wouldn't be home until after she had already gone to sleep.

"But I'm sending you my goodnight kiss now, sweetheart," I said, making a kissing noise into the receiver.

"I miss you, Mommy," she answered. "I'm hugging the phone."

In that moment, backpack heavy on my shoulder, my daughter's voice in my ear, I wondered, *How can we possibly separate a feminist's life from her work?* I, for one, wanted to know the Mary Wollstonecraft behind the page, how she lived her own life against the pull of destiny—not just as a woman but as a daughter, sister, wife, and mother.

And as a woman in love. What Rowan had referred to in class was Wollstonecraft's public and scandalous affair with Gilbert Imlay, which ended in the birth of an illegitimate daughter, Fanny, named after her friend whose death had devastated Wollstonecraft. Two years after she published *A Vindication of the Rights of Woman* at the age of thirty-four, Wollstonecraft fell in love and lost her virginity to Imlay, often portrayed as the man who seduced the mother of feminism and then broke her heart. Also a writer, Imlay published a novel called *The Emigrants* in 1793, in which he tackled the issues of women's education and rape in marriage. The reasons for Wollstonecraft's attraction to this handsome and charismatic American frontiersman, who shared so many of her values, are hardly surprising, and the feeling was clearly mutual. For all his philandering ways, Imlay appears to have cared deeply about Wollstonecraft. As a British citizen living in France during the Reign of Terror of the French Revolution, Wollstonecraft was in some danger, and, concerned for her safety, Imlay pulled some strings with the American ambassador and had her certified as his wife, affording her the protections of U.S. citizenship. She took this generous act as a sign of Imlay's commitment, and not too long after she became pregnant, giving birth to their daughter, Fanny.

Meanwhile, Imlay, true to his reputation for being a womanizer, had taken up with a mistress. When Wollstonecraft found out, she was enraged and threatened to leave Imlay if he didn't give the other women up at once. He refused. After wavering back and forth between making good on her threat and returning to her lover, Wollstonecraft came to the conclusion that Imlay would never be faithful to her, and she ended the relationship. She could not bear sharing him with another woman. Alone, an unwed mother, Wollstonecraft plunged into a deep depression and attempted suicide by jumping into the River Thames. She was fished out of the water and rescued, a distraught Imlay later arriving at the hospital where Wollstonecraft was convalescing, but their relationship was beyond repair. Gradually regaining her strength, Wollstonecraft agreed to go on a journey to Scandinavia in an effort to escape the painful situation with Imlay, and in the process she wrote a book titled *Letters on Sweden, Denmark, and Norway*.

In a roundabout way, this postbreakup trip would bring love into Wollstonecraft's life once more—this time with William Godwin, an English political writer and philosopher, who traveled in the same circles. Godwin, who had read and rather disliked *A Vindication of the Rights of Woman*, was captivated by the narrator of *Letters* and, after reading it, became determined to make Mary's acquaintance. The two fell in love and married, but with a twist on tradition: They kept separate residences. "A husband is a convenient part of the furniture of a house, unless he be a clumsy fixture," Wollstonecraft writes to Godwin. "I wish you, for my soul, to be riveted in my heart; but I do not desire to have you always at my elbow."

Given their respective reputations as social critics, the two made an unlikely couple to wed, a fact that did not go unnoticed by the press. When their union became public, they suffered snubs, jeers, and gossip. The *Times* triumphantly announced that Mr. Godwin, author of a pamphlet against matrimony, had secretly wed "the famous Mrs. Wollstonecraft, who wrote in support of the Rights of Woman." Societal scorn only increased when it became known that Mary had been pregnant when the couple married. Their union lasted less than a year, cut short by tragic circumstance. Wollstonecraft died from a fatal infection contracted during childbirth, leaving Godwin in charge of both Mary's child with Imlay, Fanny, and their newborn daughter, Mary, who, sixteen years later, would elope with the poet Percy Bysshe Shelley and go on to pen the classic *Frankenstein*.

Scholars have long fastened onto Mary Wollstonecraft's life and character, as if they offered up a riddle that needed to be solved. Even today, Wollstonecraft is possibly one of the most celebrated yet also reviled women in history. The persistent objections to Wollstonecraft as a person have long made dents in the significance of her work, which is perhaps why T. was so hesitant to open up the discussion to her private life in class. Gothic novelist Horace Walpole famously referred to Wollstonecraft as a "hyena in petticoats." In 1947 two psychologists, Ferdinand Lundberg and Marynia Farnham, psychoanalyzed the long-deceased Wollstonecraft and determined that she was an "extreme neurotic of a compulsive type" who hated men and used feminism to diminish the male sex; furthermore, they diagnosed the entirety of the feminist movement as a direct outgrowth of Wollstonecraft's pathology. In a 1974 review of a biography of Wollstonecraft, Oxford University professor Richard Cobb described her as "always silly; she was almost always egotistical; and she was generally envious, rancorous, and meddlesome." And as recently as 2000, the *Times Literary Supplement* called Wollstonecraft "little short of monstrous."

Why such hostility for a woman who died more than two hundred years ago? And how could the little shrew her enemies see in her have won the love and admiration of some of the leading male thinkers of her time? So she was moody. So she was judgmental. So she was overbearing. *So what?* Should this render her ideas irrelevant? To young feminists, she may be an inadequate role model, with her overriding emphasis on marriage and motherhood, if not an embarrassing example of a feminist who could not practice what she preached. To her critics, she may represent a misguided and false consciousness. But from where I stood, Wollstonecraft's choices resounded with the lessons I had learned time and again since entering adulthood—life is unpredictable, relationships are complex, and the mind cannot always rule the heart.

As I rode home on the train back to Annapolis that afternoon, I thought back to what T. said about revising our view of the natural order of things, of trying to transform the system, and to me that's exactly what Wollstonecraft did—if not through her words alone, then by the way she approached her life. I thought back to Cynthia Liu's quote in the *New York Times*, in which she matter-of-factly stated that a woman has to choose either motherhood or a career, because she can't be the "best" at both. On the empty train seat next to me, I pictured the misunderstood Wollstonecraft, petticoats and all, shaking her head in disappointment. Two centuries later, and we were still placing career and motherhood in oppositional spheres, whereas Mary herself envisioned men and women living together, learning together, in a humanistic world. For her own part, Wollstonecraft arguably succeeded: Without the benefit of education or the opportunities usually available to men, she became a prominent writer and thinker; she was a single mother at a time when this was cause for disgrace; she married her lover, but demurred from living with him. She committed to career, marriage, and motherhood, but on her own terms.

Mary Wollstonecraft is an imperfect heroine, but I find her all the more compelling for the weaknesses braided into her strengths, the spectacular failures alongside her many triumphs. When Wollstonecraft found herself living her worst fear as an unwed mother, desolate enough to try to take her own life, she nevertheless managed to survive—to *thrive* even, and to love again. She took full charge of her destiny, and in that respect, she was the best inspiration I had come across in a long time, a much needed reminder that rejecting marriage and motherhood was not the only way to be a revolutionary, but simply the most obvious.

Marital Destiny

Delving so deep into the life and loves of Mary Wollstonecraft had encouraged me to step back and take the same biographer's eye to my own life, enlisting my little sister's help in understanding the influence of our family's history. A senior in college, Caroline had flown in from California for her Thanksgiving break, and the night she arrived, we ended up camped out on the couch downstairs, talking for hours.

Despite our eleven-year age difference, we have always been close, drawn together by adversity. Divorce split our family apart when I was thirteen and Caroline was two, with Caroline going to live with my mother, while I stayed with my father, an oncologist. With both our parents working demanding jobs, I spent the first eighteen years of Caroline's life acting more as a parent than a sibling; the role came somewhat naturally to me since I'd spent most of my own childhood parenting myself.

I have a framed photo from when I was about seven years old. There I am sitting on the front stoop of our split-level ranch house, wearing orange corduroy bell-bottoms, grinning widely to reveal my two missing front teeth. A silver house key dangles conspicuously from a string of yarn tied around my neck. That's me: poster child for the "latchkey" generation. After being an only child for more than a decade, I was thrilled when my sister was born and immediately took charge of her care. During my teens, I changed Caroline's diapers and babysat; during my twenties, I stepped in and counseled her through various adolescent traumas; and when she graduated from high school, I flew across the country, nearly seven months pregnant, to watch her walk across the stage and get her diploma while I squatted, proud as any mother hen, on the edge of my stadium bleacher seat—until some kids released a huge helium balloon shaped like a penis in the middle of the ceremony to raucous cheers, and my mother, sitting next to me, spent a good ten minutes squinting up at the sky, asking, "What *is* that? A rocket? A baseball bat? A tuba?" as I dissolved into coughing fits of laughter, like a third grader.

To me, Caroline was always someone to shield from the sharp corners of life, but the terms of our relationship changed as she got older. I had begun to see her not just as my baby sister but as a peer and as a friend. She is an avid traveler—in one year alone she went to Thailand, Egypt, and Greece—but she also spent a year living in an Airstream trailer in the redwood forests of Santa Cruz. She attends concerts by bands I have never heard of, often going alone so she can concentrate on the music. She writes in impossibly small print. She is funny, sensitive, and smart, and as she is my only sibling in a very fractured family tree, I have held fast to her with all my might, and she to me.

That night I quizzed her some more, about her latest boyfriend and her plans for after college, and then she turned quiet. I knew the face. She was deciding whether to say something.

"Shoot," I told her.

"How are *you*?" she asked, lowering her voice. I could see her taking stock of the weight I had lost, the tightness around my jaw. She may have been majoring in neurology, but it didn't take a brain surgeon to figure out that things had not been going smoothly since John and I moved to Annapolis. He had given Caroline a quick hug when we got back from the airport and then vanished, as was his modus operandi these days.

The world may end in fire or it may end in ice, as the poet Robert Frost once mused, and so it goes with marriage. Relations between John and me had been chilling to glacial levels over the past couple of years. I used to joke that, after we got married, the sound of my voice must have risen to an inaudible pitch for John, like a dog whistle to human ears. It was sort of funny, at first. It was funny, until it wasn't. Sometimes I would have to repeat myself three or four times before John would reply with a preoccupied, "What?" Eventually, I stopped talking. He retreated into his work, and I retreated period. We talked about Sylvia and little else. We no longer looked each other in the eye. The causes and symptoms of what seemed our impending marital breakdown were, I suppose, more intricate than that, but a few years into marriage and parenthood, and we had both grown distant and resentful, each of us bearing a thousand tiny wounds.

As a result, the rising tension in our lovely Victorian house was becoming as much a part of the furnishings as the antique mahogany dining table or the barrister bookshelves. Unable to bear the suffocating atmosphere, I would slip out many evenings under the guise of walking the dog and end up standing on a street corner, cradling my cell phone as I confided my unhappiness to my closest friends. At one point that summer, the hostility skimming underneath our silence erupted during a dinner party with our neighbors, as John and I sniped at each other across the table, our tongues loosened by wine and the illicit thrill of an audience. Afterward, as our guests scurried home, I actually threatened to leave him, and in that moment, standing there in our dining room with my fists clenched at my side, I meant it. He knew it, and I knew it. That scared us enough to call a temporary truce, and so for the past few months we had been interacting with a practiced civility.

But all this was too much to say to my sister right now, the day before Thanksgiving. And so, instead, I sighed. "I'm okay," I said. "Sometimes it's tough, you know?"

Caroline understood perfectly. "I know," she said. "I'm always here if you want to talk about it."

I smiled at her, realizing that after a lifetime of my protecting her, she was now ready to protect me. And I loved her for it.

• • •

We may tend to wrap marriage in layers of romantic gauze, but from the feminist perspective, John Stuart Mill was on to something back in 1869 when he identified such unions as the primary political experience in which most of us engage as adults. "Whatever the balance, every marriage is based upon some understanding, articulated or not, about the relative importance, the priority of desires, between its two parties," he writes in his essay "The Subjection of Women." If feminists are suspicious of marriage, it's because women historically have come out clutching the short end of the stick. This may not be as true as it once was, but even recent studies show that men reap a host of psychological, physical, and practical benefits from marriage while married women generally suffer a downturn in these same areas.

At any rate, anyone who is married, especially married with children, becomes well acquainted with the concept, if not the art, of compromise. With marriage, as with any committed relationship,

two lives, two homes, two bank accounts—and, thus, two destines—
are joined together. The luckiest of us manage to embark on this
three-legged race without tripping and falling; the rest of us, however,
endure the push and pull, the endless volatile chemistry of "you and
I" to make "we."

And then there are the particular events and forces of our up-
bringing that affect how we go about marriage, guiding our expectations and behavior as spouses. My notions about marriage were no
doubt shaped in part by the events of my childhood. Growing up in
the long shadow cast by my parents' breakup, I was not the most
adept person when it came to this whole marriage business. I was
old enough when my parents divorced to view the proceeding as the
rude unmasking of romantic love, exposing its uglier incarnations,
Anger and Control. But I was also young enough when my mother
packed up her belongings and moved out—taking Caroline with her
and leaving me behind with my father—to translate her exit as aban-
donment with a capital A: She wasn't leaving the marriage; she was
leaving *me*.

Faced with the half-empty rooms of our family home, my father
focused his attention on erasing all remaining traces of our former
life. I watched helplessly as he rearranged what furniture was left
and, in what would be only one of many weekend projects, pulled
up the red plush wall-to-wall carpeting my mother had selected when
we moved into the house. For three months my father laid down tiles
in the family room, his white T-shirt soaked with sweat as he
slathered grout between the cracks with an intensity that frightened
me. He decorated his bedroom walls with sailing photographs and
snaked a hose through the window to fill up his latest purchase, a
water bed. He tore down the cartoon wallpaper that lined Caroline's
old bedroom, wallpaper that I had picked out and helped to paste up
before she was born; in its place, he put up a simple floral pattern
more appropriate for what was to be our new "guest room," although

we rarely had guests. It was just the two of us, living in a house that was forever in a state of repair.

All these changes, as the ties to my past were cut one by one, made me feel as if I were fast receding into the distance. At thirteen, I still believed there was a safety in objects, that they at least represented concrete markers of my history, my identity, my place. I clung to what little I could, saving every letter and memento. When I fell for my first boyfriend at the age of fourteen, I fell *hard*. We dated for almost four years, breaking up and making up with alarming frequency, but like most teenage dramas, it was a delicious kind of hell. When we broke up for the last time, just a few weeks before our senior prom, I cried as if my world had shattered. In a way, it had. I had failed at love.

With my parents' divorce and my own teenage heartbreak, I resolved never to get hurt again. I left my leafy Washington, D.C., suburb and first went as far away as I could to California, then came back east to New York City, where I pierced my nose, donned a pair of Doc Martens, and exercised girl power, breaking a few hearts of my own. My friends and I banded together in singles solidarity: Who needed men? Love, we agreed, was for suckers.

But then things changed. My friends slowly paired off, and eventually, so did I. I met John when I was twenty-four, and although he was only four years older, he already owned a successful Internet company that he had founded with two MIT friends just as the dotcom boom was booming. I was impressed by how much he had accomplished at such a young age. I was even more impressed by his maturity. My last boyfriend had talked about taking a road trip to photograph people's Elvis tattoos. John talked about the benefits of buying an apartment versus renting. Not only did John and I go out on dates, but I would go so far as to say he *courted* me, sending me flowers at the office and bearing gifts when he met my parents. We went out to restaurants, Broadway plays, art museum openings.

On Sundays, we made a habit of going to the Grange Hall to read the paper over brunch—he always beginning with the business section and I the book review—trading articles back and forth over our eggs and coffee. A blond, blue-eyed boy from Long Island whose parents were not only still married but *happily* married, he was a wonder to me—calm, confident, and in control; he was a man with roots, someone who set goals with every expectation that he would meet them, and with him I felt safer and more stable than I had with anyone else before. Sitting on a park bench in Union Square early on in our relationship, he suddenly leaned in and put his palm on my cheek. "I don't want to be some guy in your life," he said. "I want to be *the* guy." No commitment games here. John wanted to get married and have a family, I'll admit the idea no longer terrified me. I convinced myself, with all the arrogance of youth, that I could navigate the wilds of marriage with more grace and agility than my parents had.

The truth was, I had no blueprint for how a healthy marriage should be, and over the years, as the infractions and disappointments accumulated, I felt as if the shelter of our union had begun to tip precariously, until every molecule of my body was screaming, "Run!" But I didn't run, at least not in any definitive way, unsure whether the voice in my head was real or just my "issues" talking. I had enough self-awareness to recognize my defensive tendency to shut down when I sensed I was about to find myself in a pile of emotional rubble, and that was exactly what had happened in my marriage: I was there in body, but had departed in spirit. John, meanwhile, with his laserlike concentration on work, was not exactly at his most observant. By the time John did notice, our relationship had, in my mind, already reached a critical condition. At that point, I wouldn't have known how to get back in, even if I'd wanted to, and I didn't know anymore that I wanted to.

I was not alone in my uncertainty. All around me, relationships that had crested on a wave of lavish white weddings a few years before were now slowly dissolving into an ocean of regret. My misery had a lot of company. I spent hours talking to my friends, debating back and forth: Should we stay or should we go? As I listened, the phone line between us heavy with confusion and despair, I couldn't help flashing back to their weddings, many still fresh in my memory, as well as back to my own. I remembered shopping for wedding and bridesmaids dresses; visiting caterers to pick halibut or salmon, buttercream frosting or whipped; listening to wedding toasts, from the comical to the poignant. One husband had wiped a tear from his eye as he spoke of his love for his new bride. Two years later, he could barely remember to buy her a birthday card. I remembered our giddiness as John and I drove back into Manhattan after our wedding reception out on Long Island, windows rolled down to let in the night air. We had not laughed like that in a long time.

It was in this frame of mind that I picked up Kate Chopin's classic novella, *The Awakening*. With some trepidation, I opened its pages, not sure how I would react this time around to the story of a woman who rejects an unsatisfying marriage to pursue her own passions. I soon discovered that *The Awakening* was like literary crack for the disgruntled wife, addictive, dangerous, and capable of leaving behind a nasty hangover.

Exhibit A: me.

The Awakening

"What time is it?" John grumbled, peering at me in the dim light of our bedroom. It was well past midnight, and I was sitting up in bed, furtively hunched over the book, reading by the faint glow of a book light. Once I had started Chopin's book, I had hardly been able to put it down. The story ambushed my thoughts, as any truly engaging story does, so that even as I lay in bed and closed my eyes to go to sleep, my mind darted out of slumber's reach, back to a sultry summer in Louisiana around the turn of the century; alas, I could do nothing else but surrender, hands groping for the book on my nightstand.

"Sorry. I'm almost done," I whispered. "Go back to sleep." He groaned and flopped over with his back to me, burying his head in his pillow, and this action brought forth a scene I had read earlier in the book. I flipped back to find it. Our heroine, Edna Pontellier, and her husband, Leonce, are arguing over her decision to stay outside and enjoy the moonlight. With rising impatience and irritation, he warns that she will grow cold, that the mosquitoes will devour her, but still she refuses to come in. "This is more than folly," he finally blurts out. "I can't permit you to stay out there all night. You must come in the house instantly."

> With a writhing motion she settled herself more securely in the hammock. She perceived that her will had blazed up, stubborn and resistant. She could not at that moment have done other than denied and resisted. She wondered if her husband had ever spoken to her like that before, and if she had submitted to his command. Of course, she had; she remembered that she had. But she could not realize why or how she should have yielded, feeling as she then did.
>
> "Leonce, go to bed," she said. "I mean to stay out here. I don't wish to go in, and I don't intend to. Don't speak to me like that again; I shall not answer you."

A small matter, certainly, this squabble, but then marriage is filled with such microscopic negotiations and refusals. Leonce does not go to bed but instead joins his wife on the porch in his own act of silent rebellion, propping his slippered feet on the railing. He lights a cigar, drinks a glass of wine, then another. They sit there in silence, the moon low in the night sky, until the first strains of dawn break through the darkness: a nuptial game of chicken. Finally, ready for bed, Edna rises from the hammock, teetering unsteadily on her feet.

"Are you coming in, Leonce?" she asked turning her face toward her husband.

"Yes, dear," he answered, with a glance following a misty puff of smoke. "Just as soon as I have finished my cigar."

A brilliant scene, so astute in its depiction of intimate relationships that I could not help supposing it was an actual interaction Chopin had pilfered from her own experience. Beside me, John was snoring again, sound asleep.

Just until the end of this chapter, I told myself with the arch finesse of an addict, but then (oh, what's a few more pages?), really, with so few pages left—it was only a novella, after all—I might as well read to the end. Part of me wanted to finish the last page of Chopin's story if only to release myself from its narcotic hold.

With *The Awakening*, Chopin reminds us that stifling marriages are nothing new; many women's destinies have long been stamped into darkness, their identities lost once they enter the role of wife, but here she offers another version of that same old story. Told over the course of nine months—the span of one character's pregnancy—Chopin tells of how Edna Pontellier transforms herself from dutiful mother and high-society wife into a creative, independent "New Woman." These dramatic changes in Edna's life are set into motion when she meets the dashing Robert Lebrun during a languorous summer vacationing on Grand Isle, a seaside resort frequented by the New Orleans elite. Until then, Edna had been content enough in her marriage to Leonce, a rather dull but loving man, though she has never been one of the "mother-women," like her pregnant friend Madame Ratignolle, who flock to the beach that summer. "It was easy to know them," writes Chopin, "fluttered about with extended, protected wings, when any harm, real or imaginary, threatened their precious brood. They were women who idolized their children, worshipped their husbands, and esteemed it a holy privilege to efface themselves as individuals and grow wings as ministering angels."

Unable to fully submerge her destiny into marriage and motherhood, Edna holds sacred a part of herself. She mentions in passing to Madame Ratignolle that she would never sacrifice herself for her children, and in the heated argument that follows, Edna further explains, "I would give up the unessential; I would give my money, I would give my life for my children; but I wouldn't give myself." This seems to satisfy her friend, who can think of nothing greater than giving one's own life for one's children; she does not understand that Edna "apprehended instinctively the dual life—that outward existence which conforms, the inward life that questions." Unlike Madame Ratignolle, who has fused her life with those of her husband and children, Edna contends that "fate had not fitted her" to be a wife and mother. Rather, fate has other plans for her, bringing into her life a rousing affair that inflames her already defiant nature with the heat of desire.

Back in New Orleans, Edna becomes a woman driven primarily by her own passions. She no longer sees her stuffy high-society friends, cultivating instead new friends who are artists and iconoclasts. She devotes herself to painting, and when her husband, Leonce, and their two sons go abroad, she moves out of the family estate and rents a house around the corner that she affectionately refers to as the "pigeon house." Her husband, rattled by what he considers her strange behavior, consults a local doctor, who advises him, "Don't bother her, and don't let her bother you. Woman, my dear friend, is a very peculiar and delicate organism—a sensitive and highly organized woman such as I know Mrs. Pontellier to be, is especially peculiar. It would require an inspired psychologist to deal successfully with them." He goes on to say that Leonce should wait for Edna to come to her senses.

Chopin gives the reader no easy out. Leonce is neither thug nor scoundrel. If he were, we could attribute Edna's discontent to her husband, not to her own desires. But Leonce loves Edna; he fell in love with her the first time he saw her, with her yellow-brown hair; her strong, shapely hands; her quick, bright eyes. Although in love with someone else at the time, Edna was flattered by such absolute devotion. "Her marriage to Leonce Pontellier was purely an accident," writes Chopin, "in this respect resembling many other marriages which masquerade as the decrees of Fate." After awakening to her place in the world, Edna feels no rancor toward her husband but a growing fondness. She simply longs to give her heart freely.

But when the object of her affection, Robert, returns from an extended trip to Mexico, he avoids calling on Edna, who has been anxiously waiting to see him. At last, he comes by to visit. She is near bursting with love at the sight of him, but he is reserved. He wants to marry Edna, he announces, but since she is already married to another, their love is doomed and they must remain apart, whereupon, in some of the greatest feminist lines of literature, Edna declares, "You have been a very, very foolish boy, wasting your time dreaming of impossible things when you speak of Mr. Pontellier setting me free! I am no longer one of Mr. Pontellier's possessions to dispose of or not. I give myself where I choose. If he were to say, 'Here, Robert, take her and be happy; she is yours,' I should laugh at you both."

Their conversation is cut off prematurely when Edna is called away to help birth Madame Ratignolle's fourth child, and by the time she has returned, breathless, full of expectation, Robert is gone. He has left her only with a short note that reads, "I love you. Good-by— because I love you." Despondent, Edna stays up all night, watching the darkness lighten to dawn. In the morning, she goes to the water's edge, takes off her clothes, and, with her nakedness illuminated by the sun, steps into the water. She swims, arms pumping, toward the horizon. She does not look back. A bird with a broken wing circles above her. She swims until "the shore was behind her, and her strength was gone." And that's the end.

I closed the book and snapped off the light. The hour was late. I shut my eyes and willed myself to sleep—not the easiest thing to do when you have just finished a book called *The Awakening*. After a few minutes, I gave up, turning over onto my back to stare up into the darkness. What was the moral of *The Awakening*, anyway? The story doesn't have a happy ending, the insinuation being that Edna swam herself to oblivion. Or maybe, I thought hopefully, she just went for a post breakup swim and came back to shore, ready to get on with her life. Who was I kidding? Suicide, not liberation, wins the popular vote of literary critics. In bed I turned back over onto my stomach, wondering how to cast my vote and whether my answer would reveal anything about my own marital destiny.

• • •

If I was looking for solace, I would have to wait. T. had paired *The Awakening* with another novella, *The Yellow Wallpaper*, by Charlotte Perkins Gilman. Together, they were a doozy—a one-two punch of feminist negativity. In the former, the heroine commits suicide (maybe); in the latter, she goes mad (maybe). Both novellas warn that the typical destiny of women—marriage and motherhood—comes laden with great personal risk, especially for women who suppress their individual spirits once they become part of a couple.

Like Chopin, Gilman was also writing at the turn of the nineteenth century, but where Chopin buried her feminist themes in her fiction, Gilman, in contrast, was more overtly political. Born in 1860, Gilman wrote prodigiously in both her nonfiction and her fiction about work, marriage, and motherhood, urging women to achieve economic independence. During her lifetime, she published hundreds of stories and poems and more than a dozen books, including the fanciful *Her-*

land, about a utopia made up entirely of women. She is probably best known, though, for *The Yellow Wallpaper*, which came out in 1892, around the same time as *The Awakening*, and it's this Gothic story I recalled best from my undergraduate days.

The Yellow Wallpaper, much like *The Awakening*, took on an added resonance when I read it—and not because the husband in the story also happens to be named John. In this novella, the story's narrator, a young, nameless woman who has recently given birth, slowly descends into madness during a three-month stay at a colonial mansion. While she claims to feel physically ill—so ill that she has left her newborn baby in another woman's care—her husband and her brother, both physicians, dismiss her sickness as merely a run-of-the-mill case of nervous depression and slight hysteria, ordering a treatment of salts, tonics, and a regimen of exercise.

"John does not know how much I really suffer," the narrator writes of her husband. "He knows there is no reason to suffer, and that satisfies him." Much to her chagrin, she is "absolutely forbidden" from engaging in her work as a writer or in any other intellectual stimulation. Secretly, though, she continues to write, spending much of her time hidden away in the bedroom she shares with her husband on the top floor of the house, a large, airy room suffused with sunshine that was probably once the nursery, for there are bars on the windows and "rings and things" in the walls. But the room offers little haven, for the walls are covered in an "almost revolting" yellow-patterned wallpaper that rankles the narrator to distraction.

This yellow wallpaper becomes the central theme of the story, morphing from an object of disgust to one of fascination and, finally, obsession. "It is dull enough to confuse the eye in following, pronounced enough to constantly irritate and provoke study, and when you follow the lame uncertain curves for a little distance they suddenly commit suicide—plunge off at outrageous angles, destroy themselves in unheard of contradictions." She begs her husband to repaper the walls or, at the very least, let them use another room as their bedroom, but he refuses to give in to her "whim," as she herself calls it. She remains mostly alone, staring at the wallpaper day and night, determined "to follow that pointless pattern to some sort of a conclusion."

Out of the pattern's chaos, the shape of a woman trapped behind bars begins to emerge, but only after nightfall. In the moonlight, the narrator sees the paper shimmer and shake, as the woman in the wallpaper tries to escape; by sunlight, the wallpaper is subdued and still. The narrator comes up with a theory that the woman escapes from the wallpaper during the day and "creeps" around. She starts to see the woman's spectral figure roaming on the house grounds. "It must be very humiliating to be caught creeping by daylight!" she confesses. "I always lock the door when I creep by daylight."

On the day before she and her husband are to leave the house, the narrator tries to help the woman in the wallpaper escape, clawing off yards of paper from the wall. She locks herself in the bedroom, throwing the key out the window into the garden. In her manic state, she sees, through the windows, creeping women everywhere. "I wonder if they all come out of that wall-paper as I did?" she asks, for the first time identifying herself with the woman in the wallpaper. Her husband comes home and pounds on the door, imploring her to open up, or, he says in warning, he will be compelled to knock it down with an ax. She directs him to the key outside, and when he enters the room, he is shocked to find his wife creeping along the floor. "I've got out at last," she cries, ". . . and I've pulled off most of the paper, so you can't put me back again!" In the final scene, her husband faints at the sight of his wife gone mad, "so that I had to creep over him every time!" The syntax Gilman employs for this last line in the story leaves the ending intentionally vague, implying that the narrator circled around that room for hours, maybe days, or even years, before escaping, if indeed she ever does.

• • •

The endings of both novellas confound, and, in class, we vigorously discussed the various ways to interpret them: Are *The Awakening* and *The Yellow Wallpaper* ultimately stories of hope or of doom?

"Think about why these authors chose to end their stories this way," T. said. "Did they mean to leave the endings ambiguous in order to give the reader a chance to come to his or her own conclusions?" She fixed her gaze on us. "Come on, guys, what do you think? Does Edna kill herself? Does the narrator in *The Yellow Wallpaper* go mad?"

"*I* thought so—on both counts," said Yvonne. "I don't think we can look at these endings as positive. Sure, Edna made empowered choices, but what does it mean if her spiritual awakening is incompatible with real life? She has this great awakening, you know? But then, no one's there to support her, and, in the end, she's too exhausted to save herself. And the narrator in *The Yellow Wallpaper*, I mean—she descends into madness, ripping at wallpaper and chewing on her bedposts."

"*Has* she truly gone mad?" T. asked. "Or is she really free and liberated and just deemed mad by this society? And what do you think: Does the husband faint, or has she killed him?" The class tittered, and T. smiled. "I kind of think she killed him. Maybe the ultimate triumph, though, is that she killed this embodiment of patriarchy."

"How can you call it a triumphant ending when she's still in the room and she's still, you know, going around and around the room in circles?" Yvonne asked. "John's still *there*, and she has to creep over him every time. Couldn't that also mean the patriarchy will always be there—even though he fainted, or died, or whatever? So there's always going to be that extra effort needed to go forward."

"Men are oppressed by not having an equal partner, right?" Rowan asked, jumping into the conversation. "So when John fainted—it's like he's sunk down to her level. Besides, maybe her craziness is not necessarily so bad. I mean, I believe in letting yourself go crazy—

you know, the cultivated kind of craziness—and I actually think that happened to a *lot* of women back then. For some women, it was a way to gain freedom. You know—you could get married, join a convent," she paused here and fluttered her fingers in the air, "or just go *crazy*."

"God, how depressing," said Maria. "I mean—*nice choices*. Plus, the husbands are so patronizing. They treat their wives like little girls, like they're pacifying them, while the women have to be all like, 'Oh, he treats me so well, so why am I feeling like this?'"

From the corner, Samantha's hand floated into the air, and all eyes turned to her. She had always appeared to be listening intently, a look of concentration on her face, but she had never contributed to the conversation before. On the first day of class, she had confessed that her reasons for taking the class were fairly straightforward. "I want to learn more about women's issues," she said, "but honestly, I'm pretty happy with my life." I found out later that she came from an Orthodox Jewish family and had a fiancé, a Columbia student, whom she planned to marry as soon as they graduated from college. A diamond engagement ring glittered from her finger.

"In *The Awakening*, she married her husband when she didn't even love him, and that wasn't very nice." Samantha's voice had a slight nervous quaver as she spoke. "And in *The Yellow Wallpaper*, I think, okay, the course of action that the husband chose may not have been the best for his wife, but he was trying to help as much as he could, and, I don't know—maybe trying to be a good husband. He's not individually oppressive, and he's also been shaped by the social realm he's living in."

The class seemed to collectively stiffen.

"But it was men who were defining women's roles," T. answered guardedly.

Samantha's cheeks pinkened, but she refused to give up. "But men were not defining women's roles as *individuals*," she said, her voice gathering in strength.

Samantha had a point. If men, too, are products of the culture, how culpable *are* they really? And how complicit might women be in their own imprisonment?

Asking myself these questions was akin to a minor insurgency. As an undergraduate, *The Yellow Wallpaper* had served as an indictment of a society that infantilized women and then vamped up such oppression as concern. Going back to the story now, I still felt angered by the severe limitations placed upon women during Gilman's lifetime, but at the same time, the landscape of absolutes that once dominated my thinking had been rubbed down by experience. Years later, I picked up on intricacies in the story that I missed the first time around. The more I considered the narrator in *The Yellow Wallpaper*, the more I became fascinated by the inconsistencies in her character. She is a bundle of contradictions, impossible to disentangle: She hates the wallpaper but cannot stop studying it. She is desperate to leave the house and then desperate not to leave. She wants to help the shadow woman in the wall escape and then remarks that she will tie her up if she tries to get away. Has she truly escaped in the end or merely become her own warden?

Hold on a minute, my younger self butted in. Please don't tell me that you are actually blaming the *victim* here?

I thought about this. No, I decided, blaming the victim was too stark a statement, too pat a response to my raising the complexities of the story—certainly, Gilman *was* a victim of her culture. *The Yellow Wallpaper* is a fictionalized account of Gilman's very real nervous breakdown toward the end of her first marriage. As with many Victorian women who displayed general signs of psychological distress—insomnia, loss of appetite, agitation, irritability, headaches—Gilman was branded a hysteric and subjected to treatment. Derived from the Greek word *hysterikos*, which means "of the womb," hysteria, as a diagnosed condition, grew from the ancient Egyptian belief that the uterus roamed free within a woman's body, and when it took flight, rising up to press against the lungs and other internal organs, the result was shortness of breath, chest pains, and other physical symptoms. In the 1880s, as they became further corseted in cultural expectations of chastity and naïveté, women were increasingly identified as hysterics. I would guess this was not a coincidence.

The hysteria movement was steered by French neurologist Jean-Martin Charcot and his friend Josef Breuer, a Viennese internist. Having become famous for hypnotizing women into a hysterical state in front of his colleagues in order to study the results, Charcot promoted hypnosis as a cure for hysteria, though he was later charged with coaching his patients on how to act hysterical. Charcot had a great influence on the young Sigmund Freud, who opened his practice in Vienna in 1886. Freud, Charcot, and a host of male doctors classified female depression and anxiety as pathological; some of the more extreme treatments for hysteria—electrotherapy, hydrotherapy, and cauterized clitorises, to name a few—bordered on torture. But for the most part, hysterics were viewed as self-indulgent hypochondriacs suffering from a moral disorder, their care falling into the province of neurologists and psychiatrists who typically prescribed marriage and pregnancy as the cure.

For Charlotte Perkins Gilman, however, these domestic pursuits were most likely the cause of her breakdown. Gilman's father, who came from the illustrious Beecher family, had abandoned his wife and children shortly after Gilman's birth, and she grew up in an impoverished household, changing residences nineteen times in almost as many years. Without their father's support and supervision, she and her brother were treated like charity cases and virtually ignored. To her everlasting embarrassment, Gilman received only four years of formal schooling, which only further alienated her from the rest of the well-educated and accomplished Beechers—a clan that included Harriet Beecher Stowe, author of *Uncle Tom's Cabin*, who was Gilman's great aunt. After such a gloomy home life, the intelligent and willful Gilman, like Mary Wollstonecraft before her, made an ardent vow never to marry so that she might fully dedicate herself to social causes. Then she fell in love.

Enter Charles Walter Stetson, a charming young artist whom Gilman met at the age of twenty-one. He romanced her with flattering intensity, and a prolonged courtship ensued. Stetson proposed and Gilman agonized, unable to shake her reservations about their relationship. For two years, Stetson wheedled and entreated, and Gilman rebuffed and resisted, until, buckling under the weight of his demands and her growing self-doubts, she reluctantly accepted his hand in marriage. Within weeks of becoming a wife, Gilman became pregnant and nine months later gave birth to a daughter, Katharine.

As it turns out, Gilman was right to have misgivings about marrying Stetson. Her husband's avant-garde vocation as an artist belied his more traditional attitudes toward marriage. From the outset of their union Gilman was miserable, as he prodded her into the conventional roles of wife and mother. For the next few years of their marriage, she suffered from debilitating bouts of depression, finally checking into a sanitarium in Philadelphia, where she was diagnosed with exhaustion of the nerves and hysteria. Under the care of Dr. Silas Weir Mitchell, a well-known specialist of the "female condition," Gilman was submitted to the "rest cure," a controversial treatment that included enforced bed rest, overfeeding, and massage. Weir, believing that higher education and excessive intellectual stimulation caused women emotional and physical strain, forbade such activity. In her autobiography, Gilman describes the doctor's orders after she was declared "cured" and sent home: "Live as domestic a life as possible. Have your child with you all the time. (Be it remarked that if I did but dress the baby it left me shaking and crying—certainly for her, to say nothing of the effect on me.) Lie down an hour after each meal. Have but two hours intellectual life a day. And never touch pen, brush or pencil as far from a healthy companionship long as you live."

The treatment and Weir's subsequent instructions succeeded only in driving Gilman deeper into despair. Imagine that. As she writes in her autobiography, "[I] came perilously close to losing my mind. The mental agony grew so unbearable that I would sit blankly moving my head from side to side. . . . I would crawl into remote closets and under beds—to hide from the grinding pressure of that distress."

On the brink of collapse, Gilman finally raised the nerve to defy her doctor's authority and supposed expertise and, more dramatically, to rebel against societal mores by leaving Stetson in 1888. Bringing baby Katharine with her, Gilman moved to California to pursue her ambitions of becoming an activist and writer. Stetson subsequently filed for divorce on the grounds of desertion, and news of it appeared in several newspapers, including a full-page article in the *Examiner* that ran under the headline "Should Literary Women Marry?"

In the years that followed, Gilman garnered some literary acclaim, but could not earn enough money to save her from the responsibilities and financial strain of single motherhood. In a decision that would again shock nineteenth-century society, she sent nine-year-old Katharine back to live with Stetson, who had since remarried one of Gilman's best friends, believing that they could provide her daughter with a more stable home. Gilman continued to maintain close contact with Katharine, but her grief and guilt over relinquishing custody— not to mention the public contempt she endured as a result—would haunt Gilman for the rest of her days. In her autobiography, she describes blowing kisses and waving good-bye to her golden-haired daughter as the train pulled out of the station to make its cross-country journey, taking Katharine back east to live with her father. "That was thirty years ago," Gilman writes. "I have to stop typing and cry as I tell about it. There were years, years, when I could never see a mother and child together without crying, or even a picture of them."

• • •

It's easy to distill Gilman's life into a slogan about women's oppression in marriage and the liberation that awaits them when they escape. By now my generation comes to marriage already knowing it is a benighted institution. We didn't need feminism to tell us this. But we are not all mired in cynicism when it comes to marriage; or, rather, we eagerly pull ourselves onto rafts of hope. Although the stigma of being single is diminishing, with more people choosing to live alone than ever before, many of us continue to be drawn into matrimony, bonds and all, because we crave the comfort, the stability, the support. We not only want a hand to hold through this life, but also want public affirmation of our relationships. This desire has not changed. What has changed are the social, political, and economic forces that once made it difficult, if not impossible, for a woman to leave an unhappy marriage. For some, like Gilman, the consequences were almost unbearable. She had to give up her daughter. Many divorced women from that era suffered the same fate. Of course, the emotional cost when a family splits up will never go away. Something irrevocable is lost when a marriage ends, but something can be gained, too. I have talked my friends through many tearstained nights after they divorced their husbands, and then seen many of them flourish in ways they or I couldn't have predicted. Many of them still mourn the demise of their marriages, even as they have found love again, a better love. Ultimately, slogans are ineffective, because there is always more to any life story: new perspectives, different angles, contrary truths.

Gilman's story is more than that of a woman who notoriously shot to fame after liberating herself from a repressive marriage. Her resistance to marriage, and the hardships of her first union, did not prevent Gilman from marrying again. At the age of thirty-nine, she wed her first cousin George Houghton Gilman, a gentle and steadfast man who affectionately accepted her as she was, depressive tendencies, blazing ambitions, and all. "If this were a novel," she writes, ". . . here's the happy ending."

Wait, marriage—Gilman's happy ending? And if this is so, why don't we hear more about it? Happy endings tend to lack the sensational sway of unhappy ones, which explains why the scandal surrounding her first marriage would trump the satisfaction she derived from her second in the public telling. But I believe there is a useful lesson to be learned from considering both of Gilman's marriages in concert: Whom a woman selects as a spouse can profoundly alter the course of her life. The feminist analysis of marriage sometimes fails to acknowledge this truth when it conceives of marriage as a form of repression. Too rarely are women taught to distinguish between the destructive, the merely serviceable, and the sublime relationship. Not even Gilman, for all her apprehensions about marriage, swore it off entirely, but learned to trust the instincts she had ignored when she married Stetson. In her second husband, she found a partner who didn't box her in but brought out her best self. It was during her second marriage that Gilman published the bulk of her oeuvre and wrote, edited, and distributed her own magazine, the *Forerunner*, all with G. H. Gilman at her side. The two of them stayed together for more than thirty years, until his death in 1934. A year after her husband passed away, Gilman, a vocal advocate of euthanasia, committed suicide by chloroform, preferring death to the late stages of breast cancer. Even into death, she did not go easily.

· · ·

Reading *The Yellow Wallpaper* and understanding how much of the story reflected Gilman's personal experience, I began to see a tale of two Charlottes—both of them depressed and oppressed, and both of them poised at a crossroads in their lives. The fictional Charlotte finds release in madness, creeping around her bedroom in endless circles. "My shoulder just fits in that long smooch in the wall, so I cannot lose my way," she says. The real Charlotte leaves the room, wallpaper and all, and walks out the door, heading out west to follow her lifelong dream, even though taking control of her own destiny brought with it many hardships and difficult choices.

What would I do in Gilman's same situation? This question lingered in the following weeks, as I hugged my daughter close to say good night, my fingers running through the softness of her hair; as I sat up in my attic office to write, staring at the Victorian wallpaper on the walls; as I tossed in bed, thinking ahead to the direction I wanted my life to take. Gilman and I may have lived in radically different eras, yet we shared many of the same struggles in defining ourselves, and knowing this was somewhat reassuring. When I sat in my attic office, my world seemingly winnowed down to the four walls of my Victorian house, Gilman was there with me, and so were Wollstonecraft and Chopin, all of them guiding me to a place beyond. These women had the insight to recognize the nature of their unhappiness and the courage to change their lives, despite the serious obstacles they confronted. And they were passing their strength to me.

Coming Home

My weekly train rides afforded me precious time to think for long stretches about all the issues raised by class, before I got caught up once again in the daily activities of home. I will confess, too, that I took delight in the opportunity to travel light—no strollers, no snacks, no toys. Sometimes I would bring a book along, but it almost always rested on my lap, unopened; my iPod, too, stayed hidden away in my bag, powered off. Mostly I stared out the window, letting my mind wander.

One afternoon late in the semester, as the train barreled south from New York to Baltimore's Penn Station, a plaintive voice sounded in my head: *I am going in circles*. The scenery rushed by my window—the same tall buildings and urban office parks, framed and studded by trees the color of fire, as they slowly gave way to the approaching winter, and trees already bare. I sat and listened to the rhythm of the train wheels. Chug-chug, chug-chug—the steady rhythm soon transposing itself into words: *Why not? Why not New York?*

Well, the why not was easy. We had recently finished a major renovation of our house. Sylvia had been admitted to one of the neighborhood's best preschools. We had established a life in Annapolis. New York was expensive and crowded and dirty, and I could go on. There were a thousand reasons to stay, except one. After almost four years, I still didn't feel at home. I wanted to go back to New York. I missed the energy and opportunity of the city. I missed my friends, my community. I thought about Wollstonecraft, alone and pregnant, slowly rebuilding her life as a Victorian woman with few resources at her disposal. I thought about Kate Chopin, who managed to support six children with her writing after her husband died, a challenging feat in my century, let alone hers. And what about Gilman, also poor and self-taught, striking out west to become a writer? And I was worried about . . . what, exactly? *Real estate?*

• • •

When I arrived home from the train station that night, I found John on the couch in the living room, working on his computer. The dinner dishes were in the sink. Sylvia had already been put to bed. John looked up at me when I walked through the door and smiled hello.

I slipped off my shoes by the door, set down my backpack in the hallway, and crossed the room to sit next to him on the couch.

"I've been thinking we should move back to New York," I said. We had wistfully talked about moving back to the city before, but never with any real seriousness. I could tell he was about to shrug it off, but then he looked up and saw from my face that this time I was serious. He put aside his computer. "I think it would be good for us," I added.

Together, we went through all the same arguments I had raised to myself on the train. We deliberated over selling the house, finding a new preschool for Sylvia, moving from a house into an apartment in the city. We talked about job possibilities and how to make ends meet financially.

"Are you sure about this?" John asked.

I nodded.

He reached over and gave me a hug. "Okay." He put his computer back on his lap and clicked the document he was working on closed. "Let's try to figure out how we would do it."

This was the John I loved.

For the next couple of hours, we sat together shoulder to shoulder in front of John's laptop, researching neighborhoods, preschools, and apartment prices in the city. As he Googled, I offered up a running stream of exclamations—"Hey! What about this place?" or "How about a bilingual preschool?"—and made notes, writing down a list of phone numbers to call in the morning. The forced smiles were forgotten. We were a team again. While John crunched numbers and figured out our budget, I went onto the porch with my cell phone and sat down on the white wicker bench to call Nina, hoping she would still be up. The night was cool, soundless. Nina picked up the phone on the third ring.

"I think we're going to sell the house and move back to the city," I said a bit feverishly. "Is that *crazy*?"

I could hear her breath whistle through her teeth as she exhaled. "Not at all, honey," she said, as if she had been expecting this news for a while. "I think you're just waking up from that hibernation you've been in for the last few years and finally coming home."

• • •

The rest of the semester sped by, and before I knew it, we were at the last day of class. To celebrate, T. brought in a treat called Fantasy Fudge, a disgustingly delicious confection made with Hershey's chocolate and marshmallow fluff. As we indulged in sweets, the chocolate melting from the warmth of our fingers, T. closed out the semester by giving us a pep talk. "How do we maneuver a spiritual triumph without social defeat?" she asked the class. "By living our lives and showing that we are *contesting* these definitions. There's still a lot of work to be done—even today—but there is hope. I don't want anyone to leave here without remembering that." We broke out into wild applause.

After class, a group of students gathered around T. to say goodbye, and I joined them, waiting patiently until the crowd had thinned. "I just wanted to tell you how much I enjoyed your class," I said when I finally reached her. "Thank you again for letting me sit in on the class. I learned so much."

"I'm so glad," T. said. "You know, it's funny. When I first started teaching this class, I thought that the older books wouldn't be as interesting, but now I almost prefer them. They're still so relevant."

"I know!" I said, nodding. Then, impulsively, I stood up on my tiptoes and gave her a hug. She hugged me back, and we said our final farewells.

Downstairs in the building's lobby, I peered out the glass front doors. The holiday celebration was about to begin: My mother and Caroline were flying in from California that evening; tomorrow morning my in-laws were driving down from Long Island. We had

Christmas cards to write, cookies to bake, a tree to decorate. Then, as we were still digesting our Christmas dinner, John and I would descend straight into moving madness. But for now, I pushed aside those thoughts of all that needed to be done. Instead, in this space between class and the outside world, I took a few moments to reflect. Revisiting the texts of first-wave feminism, I had discovered—or perhaps *remembered* is the better word—that destiny can be a creative act. But the early feminists also showed me that creating one's destiny is only the beginning; living with it, day in and day out, is quite another.

I reflexively tightened my scarf around my neck in preparation for the cold before stepping outside. The trees on campus twinkled in the waning light, white Christmas lights strung throughout their bare branches. Not too far along the path, I passed by Rowan, who was sitting on a bench, a burning cigarette held between the bare fingers peeking out of her fingerless gloves. Smoke mingled with her frozen breath.

"See you next semester?" she called out.

"Absolutely!" I called back and then headed for home.

PART III
DIVISIONS

The right attitude is: *"pour faire une omelette il faut casser des oeufs."*
—SIGMUND FREUD, *Dora*

("to make an omelette, you have to break some eggs")

A Room of One's Own

The decision to move back to New York City, in some ways, was the hardest part. Once the process was in motion, the rest fell into place rather beautifully. We not only received an offer on our house soon after putting it up for sale but also managed to enroll Sylvia in a preschool in Brooklyn midyear and find a two-bedroom apartment a couple of blocks away. It was almost *too* perfect. During an exploratory visit to the city, John and I had walked into a school that happened to have a student exactly Sylvia's age moving out of town, and that same afternoon we signed a lease for a pet-friendly prewar apartment, with decent light, a separate dining room and living room facing a quiet courtyard, and a small office for me off the kitchen— my New York City friends were in awe of our good fortune. The universe, it seemed, was giving us its blessing.

Even so, moving is labeled as one of life's most stressful events for a reason. As the first order of business, John and I had to whittle down our belongings to fit into our new and much smaller quarters, and we spent many sweaty hours hauling pieces of antique furniture to the street curb, where they mysteriously vanished so fast I had to assume the street scavengers had put out an APB on our house; I gave my father my Cuisinart and crepe maker since I didn't have enough cupboard or counter space for them in our new galley kitchen; we sold all of our baby paraphernalia to a neighbor who was expecting her first child and donated piles of toys, books, and clothes to the Salvation Army. What was left, we packed in cardboard boxes and sent ahead of us in a moving van.

Finally, the house was empty, and I ambled through its rooms one last time with a stitch of sadness. We had refinished these floors, chipped away the peeling paint, and labored to make this house a home, but it had never quite felt like ours to keep. Before we moved in, an inspector came to take us through the house. He was a local man, with skin leathered by saltwater and sun, and as we crouched in the basement to examine the old boiler, he had patted it like a faithful horse and said to us, "You never own a house like this, you know. You just take care of it until the next person comes along."

Our time here was done. We packed up the car, strapped Sylvia into her booster seat, and took one last look. The house was bathed in pink light as the sun dipped behind it into the water, the windows shining bright with the reflection, and my gaze traveled up to the small window in the attic. As we pulled away down the street, I kept my head turned so I could watch the house until it disappeared out of sight. Then I faced forward.

• • •

And like that, we were New Yorkers again, and when you live in New York, unless you happen to be fabulously rich or incredibly lucky, you adapt to living in small spaces. Perhaps because we knew exactly what we were getting into by moving back to the city, the transition from three-story Victorian house to two-bedroom apartment was not as painful as it could have been. Besides there were all the glorious perks. I did not miss having to get in the car to drive Sylvia to school every morning or to buy a carton of milk at the supermarket; I didn't even miss all the extra rooms with their multiplying dust bunnies or the backyard with its weeds that, overnight it seemed, would rise to bean-stalk proportions.

Our first weekend back in the city, John, Sylvia, and I took an afternoon stroll down the promenade in Brooklyn Heights, taking in its arresting view of Manhattan and the Brooklyn Bridge, the steel and glass cityscape etched indelibly into the blue sky. The wind whipped around us, laced with the chill of winter, and I had this funny image that we had just landed in Oz, that, even as we walked, we were moving from black-and-white into brilliant color. The dog sniffed the air, enlivened by so many scents, her tail wagging furiously behind her, while Sylvia ran in circles around us, her arms spread airplane style, and then screeched to a halt right in front of me, her eyes shining. "I *love* New York!" she exclaimed. I laughed and bent down to give her a kiss on the head. Annapolis seemed a million miles away, almost as if we'd never left the city at all.

Still, the reality of living in under 1,200 square feet was that John and I were now forced to occupy the same orbit, whether jockeying each other for the one shower or bumping into each other in our narrow kitchen while I made breakfast and he brewed the coffee. Privacy became a quaint notion of the past.

"Sorry, Mom," John said, as he bumped into me in the hallway, as we rushed to get Sylvia off to school. Again when he knocked into me in the kitchen, as I was scrubbing the coffee maker. And again, when he barged into the bathroom, as I was brushing my teeth.

"Okay," I garbled through a mouth full of toothpaste, waving my toothbrush at him, "this has got to stop. And I'm not your mom." He knew this drove me crazy.

"Yeah, Daddy," Sylvia piped in. "She's my mom."

"Did you hear 'mom'?" he said, raising his eyebrows. "I said *mon*— sorry, *mon*."

I couldn't help myself. I started laughing, flecks of toothpaste spraying on the bathroom mirror.

My sense of humor, however, did not always rise up so readily. Every sound, every conversation, every tap of the keyboard reverberated throughout the entire apartment. Add to this mix a very loquacious four year old and a beagle with baying in her blood, and our home often seemed more asylum, of the lunatic variety, than refuge.

All this might have been tolerable, except that the apartment was also where I worked—and where John worked, too, at least for our first few months back in the city. The effect was an increase in what I can only describe as mental noise, the clanking of too many fragmented ideas, too many interrupted thoughts. Torn between the stresses of working freelance and the demands of family life, I was fast turning into the caricature of the absentminded mother—constantly forgetting my keys, double-booking appointments, losing the thread of my sentences. Out of necessity, I took to writing lengthy to-do lists and Post-it reminders, which I would invariably misplace. I strode purposefully into rooms, only to halt suddenly, midstep, because—damned if I could even remember why . . . At times, caught up in the chaotic twirl of daily life, I would grope blindly for stillness, for that proverbial eye of the storm, if only for the chance to breathe. No wonder so many mothers start meditating and doing yoga.

With the move, I had missed the first day of Fem Texts and fallen behind on my reading assignment, which was, rather perfectly, Virginia Woolf's *Room of One's Own*. The book—an extended essay, really—is based on two lectures Woolf gave at Cambridge University in 1928. Expanded and published in October 1929, around the time the Great Depression was sweeping across the world, *A Room of One's Own* makes the apparently simple case that in order to write fiction, a woman must have a room and an income of five hundred pounds a year, no strings attached. Then, working backward from this basic proposition, Woolf weaves a sparkling literary cape for the age-old feminist arguments in favor of economic autonomy and equal opportunity for women.

In one of her most memorable illustrations from the book, Woolf imagines that Shakespeare had an equally talented sister, Judith, who, because she is a woman, is undone by her own genius. Deprived of the same education as her brother, her gifts remain locked up inside, discouraged, even as her mind and hands are busied with other tasks, such as mending the stockings and minding the stew. Her father promises her in marriage to the son of a neighbor, a dull wool stapler, and when she protests, he beats her. He later tries to ply her with promises of beads and fine petticoats, but Judith doesn't care about these things. She runs away to London, carried off by her dreams, the humming of her own gifts. Once in the city, she knocks on the stage door of a theater, looking for work. The men who answer laugh in her face, the spittle of their hilarity wet on her cheek. She has nowhere to go to improve her craft, no support for her genius. Finally, the actor-manager of the theater takes pity on her. His pity leads to her pregnancy, and so—"who shall measure the heat and violence of the poet's heart when caught and tangled in a woman's body?"—the young Judith kills herself on an icy night and now lies buried in an anonymous grave at some crossroads where tour buses stop outside the Elephant and Castle.

At the conclusion of *A Room of One's Own*, Woolf reminds the reader of Shakespeare's imagined sister and the responsibility her "lost fate" places on the modern woman. She writes:

> Now my belief is that this poet who never wrote a word and was buried at the crossroads still lives. She lives in you and in me, and in many other women who are not here tonight, for they are washing up the dishes and putting the children to bed. But she lives; for great poets do not die; they are continuing presences; they need only the opportunity to walk among us in the flesh. This

opportunity, as I think, it is now coming within your power to give her. For my belief is that if we live another century or so—I am talking of the common life which is the real life and not of the little separate lives which we live as individuals—and have five hundred a year each of us and rooms of our own; if we have the habit of freedom and the courage to write exactly what we think; if we escape a little from the common sitting room and see human beings not always in their relation to each other but in relation to reality; and the sky, too, and the trees or whatever it may be in themselves; if we look past Milton's bogey, for no human being should shut out the view; if we face the fact, for it is a fact, that there is no arm to cling to, but that we go along and that our relation is to the world of reality and not only to the world of men and women, then the opportunity will come and the dead poet who was Shakespeare's sister will put on the body which she has so often laid down.

These words, when I read them, lodge in my throat. Woolf prophesied that within the next century Shakespeare's sister would live again, embodied by a new generation of women. Woolf herself would not live nearly so long. Twelve years after *A Room of One's Own* was published, she filled her coat pockets with stones, waded into the River Ouse, and drowned herself. By then, World War II had invaded her daily life with its threat of destruction. Bombs blasted her London home and library to rubble.

She had finished a novel, but despair hovered. "I feel certain that I am going mad again," she wrote to her husband, Leonard, on the morning of her suicide, "and I shan't recover this time." For most of her life, Woolf had suffered from episodes of mental illness and violent mood swings that battered her health and relationships, but also infused her writing with radiant insight. In *A Room of One's Own*, she contemplates the "severances and oppositions in the mind," which has "no single state of being." She writes: "Clearly the mind is always altering its focus, and bringing the world into different perspectives. But some of these states of mind seem, even if adopted spontaneously, to be less comfortable than others. In order to keep oneself continuing in them one is unconsciously holding something back, and gradually the repression becomes an effort."

This observation is reflected in her fiction as well. Pick up any one of Woolf's novels: Her prose is frenetic, an exercise in the anarchic wanderings of the mind, thought stumbling over thought, facts and ideas contradicting each other. Woolf writes of a mind divided against itself, ever struggling to coalesce a sense of self from all the bits and pieces of thought, experience, emotion.

Crowded into an urban apartment, working to regain my professional footing, keeping watch of a young child, I thought about Virginia Woolf's conditions for female creativity. If I had the money—five hundred pounds converted into U.S. currency and adjusted for inflation, of course—and a room of my own, which I sort of had here by the kitchen, was that really all it would take? My daughter pounded on the door of my home office. "Mommy? Mommy? Mommy?" I stopped typing, the words of the sentence I had been writing now scattered, the muse frightened away. I swung open the door in a motion of irritation. And there stood my daughter, holding out to me a piece of paper with a poem she had written, her expression serious and proud.

"Mommy," she said, "I wrote this for you."

The Second Sex

I was desperate for a break, so when John decided to take Sylvia to her grandparents on Long Island for the weekend, I seized my chance, insisting the two of them go on without me since I had *tons* of reading to catch up on for class. The hour of frenzy leading up to their departure included only two minor meltdowns—one over my absolute cap of five stuffed animals, and the other over the fact that I would not be going, too. At last, the car was packed, and the key already in the ignition, when Sylvia announced, "I'm thirsty." I looked at John, and he sighed.

"Did you pack any snacks?" I asked.

"No," he said, rolling his eyes. "Whatever. We can get something on the way."

"I'm thirsty," Sylvia said again.

I ran back upstairs and threw a juice box, crackers, and a cheese stick into a plastic bag. Sylvia was sobbing by the time I returned, realizing once again, during my absence, that I wouldn't be coming with them. John was drumming his fingers on the steering wheel.

"But *Mommy*," she cried, "I'm going to *miss* you."

I wavered. I could easily run back upstairs, grab some clothes, and hop into the car with them. My armpits were damp, despite the chill. But, for Christ's sake—it was one weekend. I was desperately looking forward to a couple of days of solitude.

I resolutely gave Sylvia a hug and kiss, wiping away her tears—feeling guilty, just not guilty enough. John started the engine, and I waved good-bye wildly as they drove down the street. When the car turned the corner, I breathed a sigh of relief, sauntered back up the stairs and went into the apartment, closing the door behind me. I stood there in the foyer for a moment, trying to rid myself of the feeling that something was not quite right. Then it hit me.

Silence.

I had forgotten the sound—that faint, high-pitched whir that captures one's ear when you're alone in the quiet. It had been long enough since I had been this immersed in solitude that I almost didn't recognize it. At first the absence of the familiar noise and routine was in itself a diversion, and I lost hours to puttering and daydreaming. But the day stretched before me lavishly, with only the week's reading, *The Second Sex*—splayed open on the coffee table, its pages worn and marked up with notes I took as a teenager—waiting for my attention. Its author, Simone de Beauvoir, stared up at me from the tattered cover, a slightly amused crinkle at the corner of her eye. I had kept this book with me over the years, carrying it from dorm room to dorm room, one home to another, but hadn't opened its pages in more than a decade. Now I picked it off the coffee table and held it in my outstretched hands, staring at Simone, as if we were about to start a conversation.

I was a bit enamored of Beauvoir after I read *The Second Sex* as an undergraduate. She was not only brilliant but, from what I saw of her, glamorous, too—always stylishly dressed, with her hair pinned up in a chignon. She lived in hotels and worked in smoky Parisian cafés, where she produced memoirs, novels, travelogues, and books on philosophy, all published to critical acclaim. Unapologetically independent, Beauvoir, perhaps, was one of the most famous unmarried women in history, though that's not to say she was unloved. Her lifelong affair with Jean-Paul Sartre and her tempestuous tryst with American author Nelson Algren are legendary. As a college student trying to find her way, Beauvoir was a most appealing guide.

Holding the very same copy of the book I had held as an undergraduate, I suddenly felt unmoored from time and place. An image of who I was back then flashed in front of me. My hair was long, down to the middle of my back, and always mussed. (I used to say that any fledgling corporate aspirations I might have had fell apart with my hair, which, despite my best efforts, refused to behave.) Back then I usually dressed in thrift store apparel—vintage dresses, clunky black boots, plaid flannel shirts. A tiny opal pierced my nose, and the only makeup I wore was a dark, purplish red lipstick. Summers

I worked overseas—Italy, Ecuador, Costa Rica—because living in a foreign land made me feel present in a way I couldn't explain.

During those years, my strongest tie to home was my college boyfriend. He was also my best friend. We spent afternoons at Film Forum, an art house theater in Greenwich Village, where we held hands and watched foreign films in its lopsided cavern of a screening room. Subway cars intermittently rumbled beneath our seats. Afterward, we sat in cafés, talking for hours over espresso and cigarettes. He gave me novels, inscribing cryptic symbols on the title pages that only I would understand. I gave him advice on his film projects. He read my short stories and admired my paintings. We moved into a studio apartment together after graduation, as if our future together was a matter of course beyond discussion; marriage was incidental, unnecessary. We were unconventional, we told ourselves. We were artists.

And then, things changed. I started working full-time, earning a steady paycheck and investing in a 401(k) plan, while he was still working late into the night to launch his career as a filmmaker. I pulled the opal out of my nose, and the hole quickly closed up, leaving behind barely a trace, not even a scar. He watched and shook his head as I stood in front of the streaked mirror in our bathroom, trying to tame my hair with various expensive gels and creams. The funky secondhand clothes were folded up and put into storage in the far reaches of my closet and eventually returned to Goodwill. Instead, I wore fitted suits with skirts that grazed the tops of my knees. I traded in my Doc Martens for more delicate high heels. I no longer had the freedom to go to movies in the afternoon, but, then, neither did he, and besides, usually now when we did go to see the latest Mike Leigh movie or Hitchcock revival on a Friday or Saturday night, I fell asleep in the darkness of the theater.

Soon the moments we shared together were occasional and rushed. Often he was gone, traveling. A few days before we were to move into a new apartment, he unceremoniously announced that he had to leave for the summer to edit a film in Los Angeles. I was livid, and in the weeks that followed continued to fume, as I packed up all our belongings and moved into our new apartment by myself. I had not signed up to be this woman, always waiting, always holding down the fort. When he called, I did not pick up the phone. Later I told him this *thing* between us was not going to work. He argued that we could make it work. As artists, we could arrange our lives however we wanted. No, I told him, over the thousands of miles that separated us, I don't have the heart to be that kind of artist, if I was an artist at all. I wanted someone I could count on to be there. I did not want to be alone. There were tears, there were recriminations, and then it was over.

In my mind, this was the fork in the road where Beauvoir and I must have diverged so many years ago.

Simone de Beauvoir had deliberately picked her solitary life of freedom, knowing that for all its advantages, there would be a high price to pay; that she was, in effect, condemning herself to a life of aloneness. I, on the other hand, chose a more oft-traveled path—the one that would eventually lead to marriage and motherhood—surely knowing, too, that for all their rewards, something would have to be sacrificed in the trade. I used to tell this story of settling down as one of also growing up, of leaving my impetuous younger self behind to become a responsible adult. But somewhere in the back of my mind, I suppose I had always wondered whether I was merely acting on too much fear and too little faith.

I stared at Beauvoir, and she stared back at me, her gaze at once challenging and inviting, and at last, I dug into *The Second Sex*.

• • •

"For a long time I have hesitated to write a book on woman," Beauvoir states in the introduction. "The subject is irritating, especially to women; and it is not new. Enough ink has been spilled in the quarreling over feminism, now practically over, and perhaps we should say no more about it." She then goes on to spill an impressive amount of ink to precisely the opposite effect. In more than seven hundred pages of painstaking analysis, Beauvoir sets out to prove that femininity is not a biological destiny, as we have so often been told, but rather a social fabrication—a shroud women slip on, whether by choice or under duress. Indeed, it is not without a touch of irony that *The Second Sex* is often called the "bible" of feminism's second wave, since Beauvoir methodically assails the supposition of sex as destiny.

When the first volume of *The Second Sex* was published in France in 1949, Beauvoir was breaking a relative silence on the subject that had prevailed in the stunned wake of World War II. After French women achieved the right to vote in 1945—a full quarter century after the United States Congress narrowly passed a constitutional amendment granting women suffrage—it was widely assumed that feminism had achieved its goal; the struggle was over! Then *The Second Sex* landed in bookstores, selling 22,000 copies in its first week. Some of the book's sales could be attributed to its immediate notoriety. The press pilloried Beauvoir for her frank discussions of female sexuality, contraception, abortion, marriage, and motherhood, all of which scandalized not a few French readers. "Unsatisfied, frigid, priapic, nymphomaniac, lesbian, a hundred times aborted," Beauvoir reported in her journal. "I was everything, even an unmarried mother" (which she wasn't). Three years later, Blanche Knopf, wife of publisher Alfred Knopf, brought a translated and abridged version of *The Second Sex* across the Atlantic to the United States, where it eventually became a mainstay of college curricula across the country.

As for me, *The Second Sex* entered my life at a fortuitous time. I had just transferred to Barnard, lured partly by New York City, yes, but also because I specifically wanted to attend a liberal arts college for women. Even at the time, it seemed to me a strange longing; unlike some of the women around me, who gravitated toward Barnard with sharply articulated beliefs about feminism, I had not grown up in a particularly gendered household. I remember one friend, already accepted as a senior into an accelerated graduate program in the School of International and Public Affairs at Columbia, whose father dismissed her many accomplishments when she returned home over spring break, advising her instead not to gain too much weight or no one would marry her—this said as he slumped in his easy chair in front of the television, stuffing forkfuls of the dinner her mother had made for him into his mouth. My friend clenched her fists, a look of pure rage crossing her face, as she recounted the story. Listening to her, I felt a somewhat perplexed anger on her behalf, because her fury was not my own. If anything, my experience had been the inverse of hers—it was my father who always cooked dinner, who always told me not to get hung up on appearance, who always lectured me to do well in school.

Growing up, I was raised solidly in the "you can do anything" camp. My father was finishing up medical school and my mother her Ph.D. when I arrived on the scene, the three of us living in graduate student housing in San Diego. It was the early 1970s, and my parents were both twenty-five, young enough to have been suitably saturated in the counterculture of the '60s. As far as I can remember, being a girl was a mere characteristic, like having brown hair and brown eyes. According to family lore, once, when I was about three or four years old, I insisted on competing in a contest with the neighborhood boys to see who could pee the farthest. I may have lost, but from what I hear, my perseverance was admirable. Afternoons were spent running around the neighborhood with the other kids, climbing trees, or digging up earthworms and putting them in my pocket, much to my parents' disgust upon turning them out of my pockets in the laundry room. On weekends, my father recruited me to hand him tools as he tinkered with his old yellow Volkswagen or we would set up the card table so we could build model airplanes together. My mother, in stereotypical Asian fashion, set exacting standards for academic performance and regularly challenged me to beat her at games and puzzles. In my eyes, my parents were equals both at home and in the outside world—after all, I spent just as much time with my mother in her lab as I did with my father in his.

My mother rarely played the gender card, perhaps because she was trying to succeed in a male-dominated field, and therefore didn't want to bring too much attention to herself as a woman. She certainly has never called herself a feminist. If anything, my father would probably win the title. He went on a one-man crusade to protect me from cultural programming as soon as I hit puberty. At an eighth-grade slumber party at my house, a friend brought over a videotape of the R-rated teen-raunch film *Porky's*, and as we sat around the TV set giggling, my father strode into the room, confiscated the movie from the VCR, and called me upstairs for a talk. Sitting me down on the couch in the living room, he told me that the film objectified women—he actually used the word *objectified*— and that he was disappointed I didn't have more respect for myself. Mortified, I spent the entire conversation staring down at the freshly painted toenails on my bare feet.

Later, when I was struggling with calculus in tenth grade, he brought home books with titles like *Overcoming Math Anxiety* and *Girls Can Do Math!* "Dad," I rolled my eyes, "most of the best students in my class *are* girls."

"Just don't get distracted by boys," he said. "Focus on your studies."

I never really thought of sex or gender as a possible constraint until I entered college and was exposed to women's studies classes. The effect was revelatory, then—not, as with so many of my classmates, because the material spoke to what I already knew but rather because it illuminated what I *hadn't* known. This whole spotlight on women's lives in itself seemed new to me. From the age of thirteen, when my parents divorced, I had lived with my father. With no mother or older sister in the house to counsel me through the female experience, I existed in what was effectively a man's world, which affected my conception of self in deeper ways than not knowing how to use a blow dryer or apply makeup. When I left home and got my first small taste of independence, I felt the growing need to reconnect with my sex—to find out what it meant to be a woman, to broker some type of balance between selfhood and womanhood. Having spent years disregarding my femaleness, I suddenly had the sense that it might not be so irrelevant after all. As Beauvoir's states as her reason for writing *The Second Sex*, I, too, wanted to "explain myself to myself."

Beauvoir takes on this task by beginning at the beginning. Starting with the question "What is a woman?" she covers an impressive range of sources, sifting through history, biology, literature, and philosophy in search of an answer. Her basic yet radical idea that "one is not born, but rather becomes, a woman" revolutionized our thinking about the sexes. This process of becoming a woman, Beauvoir explains, does not happen without consequences; it creates internal gaps and fissures, relegating each woman to an inner battle between her self and this other being, the fabricated eternal feminine—the Eve cursed by God and forced to surrender herself. A woman, according to Beauvoir, is "defined and differentiated with reference to man, not he with reference to her; she is the incidental, the inessential as opposed to the essential. He is the Subject, he is the Absolute—she is the Other." Since man's role as a human being fits with his destiny as man, he suffers no similar division of self. Men can have their cake and eat it, too, while women—we women—fret over the calories in each hard-won bite.

Beauvoir is tough, incisive, sharp—never shying away from baring her intellectual chops or biting when necessary. As I read, savoring

my last hours of solitude before John and Sylvia arrived back home,
I was awestruck all over again.

• • •

And then, *slap*. I was sitting in our new classroom a few days later—
a small, stuffy room tucked away at the back of Wollman Library—
when *The Second Sex* landed on the table in front of me, startling
me to attention. Folders and notebooks followed, as Professor L. emptied out the rest of her tote bag in a flurry of activity. Compared to
T.'s cool composure, Professor L. was tense, kinetic, a spring to T.'s
Slinky. She emitted that distinctly frazzled quality of a mother who
has two preschool-age children, which, in fact, she did. When she
announced this as an aside early on in class, I located a kink of disappointment in myself; Professor L. was too familiar, I thought—too
much like me and any number of the moms I knew—whereas T.
somehow better fitted the image of "feminist" I already had in my
mind's eye. I reproached myself for this ridiculous thought, as if there
were such a thing as the archetypal or ideal feminist, except maybe
to those who aren't feminists.

"Eat," Professor L. commanded, handing over a bag of pretzels,
which the class dutifully passed around. "We need to figure out a
snack schedule. This class is too long not to have some food, so here's
a sign-up sheet. We'll take turns bringing in snacks." She slid a piece
of paper to the student next to her. "Healthy food, though, please. Try
not to bring in cookies. Oh—any allergies?" One student raised her
hand and reported her allergy. "*Corn* syrup?" Professor L. repeated.
"That's a new one. Okay, everyone hear that? Nothing with corn
syrup." That pretty much wiped out 95 percent of snacks, I thought.

After we went around the table, briefly introducing ourselves,
Professor L. opened up the class discussion. "Think about how you
define feminism," she urged us. "What does it mean to be a feminist
now, and where is the center of the movement, or is it just a lot of

feminist subcultures out there?" But before anyone could venture an answer, Professor L. continued by answering her own question, a habit I would become used to over the next few months. "The problem is that the concerns of the subculture are too specific to have meaning to the general public. Feminism has been taken over by theory-headed academics and is spoken of in such an arcane language that it is rendered less visible, less accessible, and less relevant." She took a deep breath and crunched loudly on a pretzel. Boy, this woman could talk *fast*.

"I worked at a McDonald's in high school back in Minnesota," said Dani, "and 98 percent of the workers there were women. But when I said I was a feminist, they looked at me funny. And these are the women who need feminism *most*. Meanwhile, there were two men who worked there. They were both managers—and total drunks. . . ."

"My roommate always says she's not a 'feminist,' she's just *feisty*," added Leila. "That way she gets to be feisty, but still 'lovable,' you know?"

"Oh, *I* know," said Professor L.

"It's all about semantics," said Catherine. "I once had a class where every person before speaking would say, 'I don't want to sound like a feminist, but . . .' The teacher finally got so frustrated that one day she just walked out of class."

"Oh, yeah, been there." Professor L. shook her head. "But let's not forget some of the failures of feminists, though, okay? Because, at the risk of turning it around and flagellating feminists for a while, what we haven't been asking, and what we *need* to ask is: *How* can we combat the stereotypes? *How* can we make it more relevant? How can we address the failure to reach beyond the *middle class*, especially the *white* middle class?"

Without missing a beat, Professor L. reached across the table and picked up the copy of *The Second Sex* she had flung on the table at the beginning of class. I sat back in my chair, cradling my own copy between my palms.

"Let's start with this," she said, waving the book in the air. "So what's her agenda here, huh? What's Beauvoir setting out to do? To whom is she addressing this dry-as-dust academic text?"

Professor L. dropped the book back down on the table as if she couldn't get rid of it fast enough.

Dry as dust? Simone de Beauvoir?

Over the next two hours, a Beauvoir came into being very different from mine. This Beauvoir is condescending toward women, oozing dislike for her own sex, even disgust; she is too "male identified," too harsh, and, worse, hypocritical. She defends lesbianism as neither a perversion nor a curse of fate, but then refuses to fess up to her own lesbian affairs. And why does she remove herself so completely from the text? By occupying the position of neutral intellectual, isn't she denying her womanhood and setting herself apart? She flaunts her knowledge, writing arrogantly from a position of privilege, loosely throwing around the term *woman* without acknowledging the difference in experience between, say, a black woman and a white one; as for her comparison of women to slaves and Jews, well, that's plain offensive. Then, as if her full frontal attack on femininity isn't enough, she has to go and accuse women of being complicit in their own subordination, when she herself accepted a backseat in her relationship with Sartre. In short, she doesn't want women to be women. *Whoa,* I thought, completely disoriented.

Toward the end of class, Professor L. relented. "Okay, okay, so this book may have been boring, tendentious, and even repugnant in parts, but I guess we have to remember that it was an important conceptual building block," she said. I recognized her tone. It's autopilot—the same preoccupied tone I use when I'm talking about one thing while thinking of something else, like the pile of things I need to do in the dwindling hours of the day. "Beauvoir emphasized the constructed nature of gender," Professor L. continued, her eye glancing up to the clock. "Her own life was a process of breaking away from the assumptions of femininity. As an existentialist, she saw the individual as an agent of social change."

"That's what I don't understand—but how?" asked Karen. "How can *I* be an agent of social change?"

Professor L. blinked, as if momentarily pulled from a trance, and then looked at Karen as if the answer were obvious. "Well, you can look around and say, 'This is not *me*, this is *crap*.'"

I watched as the woman next to me scrawled those exact words on the margin of a piece of paper—THIS IS NOT ME, THIS IS CRAP—and then underlined them. Twice.

• • •

The classroom indictment of Beauvoir—that she was too cold, too disapproving, too intellectual—left me confused and off-balance. It also struck me as somewhat unfair, reminding me of a conversation I often have with my friend Kristen, a Hollywood screenwriter. One of Kristen's major frustrations on the job is that almost all her fictional female characters are hamstrung by their need to be "likable" and "relatable." It's a razor's edge. They have to be smart but not intimidating, sexy but not slutty, funny but in a *cute* way (and, as Leila in class said, one could add feisty but not feminist to this impossible list). No room for complex characters, or women who express rage, or who have interests outside of dating, losing weight, and shopping. I don't know how often Kristen and I have lamented this state of affairs, she shaking her mass of curly hair and I occasionally reduced to swearing. We regularly recited our own version of the mantra—"This is not me, this is crap"—but sometimes the words are easier said than turned into action.

The tightrope act to be likable is by no means limited to creating characters for the screen; women in the real world are often strapped with the very same requirements. For all our talk of "girl power" and egalitarianism in school, once women leave the captivity of campus to enter the wild world of work and relationships, they often find that the rules of engagement have changed, with unfortunate results for the so-called fairer sex. Many women, caught in the "nice" trap, find themselves passed over for promotions, their achievements over-looked. Only one year out of college, men already make 20 percent more in weekly pay than their female coworkers, at least in part be-cause men are often not afraid of making salary demands; they "know their worth," as they say, while, as a culture, we generally sneer at strong women who ask for what they want, painting them as modern-day Mary Wollstonecrafts—mannish, prudish, predatory. In fact, an astonishingly similar array of descriptions, as Naomi Wolf has pointed out, was used to smear both Wollstonecraft and Hillary Clinton, even though they lived in different *centuries*, for heaven's sake. Through-out the ages, and despite whatever social progress we have made, our put-downs of powerful women have become infuriatingly pre-dictable. Had my Fem Texts class—composed of all women, I might add—really faulted Beauvoir for not being feminine enough? For being too *intellectual*?

"Okay, my dear, sounds like you need a break," Jenny said, after I had given her an earful of my frustration. "Come out and see a movie with me after Sylvia goes to bed, something fun and mindless."

We decided on a Jennifer Aniston flick called *The Breakup*, which she starred in with her then real-life boyfriend, Vince Vaughn. Bad move. A fairly uninspired movie about the end of a relationship, *The Breakup* elicited in me what can only be called a violent reaction. The premise of the film is this: After a couple breaks up, each tries to get the other to move out of their shared slick Chicago condo by any means necessary, except that Aniston's character actually wants Vaughn back—and that's where the film lost me, because I could not for the life of me figure out *why*. Maybe it was when Vaughn's Gary invites strippers over to the apartment he shares with his ex so she can catch him staring lasciviously at a near-naked woman gyrating in front of him, or maybe it was when Aniston's Brooke parades naked through the living room after getting the "Telly Savalas" bikini wax in an effort to flame her ex's desire—take your pick. Whatever the reason, I started talking back to the screen, continuing my commentary for the rest of the film like some petulant Greek chorus of one, while Jenny elbowed me in the arm. The film's only redeeming quality was that in the end, Gary and Brooke remained split up. (Jenny claimed that the woman sitting on the other side of me was crying during the final scene, though I chose not to believe her.)

In what kind of messed-up world would Aniston's character, a beautiful and successful woman working at an art gallery, tie herself into knots after breaking up with her fat, lazy, foul, inconsiderate, video-playing, beer-drinking boyfriend? The basis of the whole movie was absurd, *wasn't it*? But then, suddenly, I saw them everywhere—in movies, on television, and, yes, in real life—these attractive, accomplished women trying so desperately to win over or keep these schlubs (and I mean *schlubs*), as if they were lucky to have a man, *any* man.

"What is going on?" I asked my sister, Caroline, who, at 22 years old, was far more in tune with the current ethos of the dating scene than I.

"I don't know," she sighed, "but it's true. I have some amazing friends who go out with guys who are really nothing special and don't even treat them well."

"Listen, don't ever lower your standards," I said. "If a guy doesn't treat you well, dump him. Don't rationalize his behavior. Zero tolerance!"

I later tested out my "zero tolerance" battle cry with a friend when she called on me to share her latest relationship woes. After a string of bad boyfriends, she had at last met someone through an online dating site whom she liked, *really* liked. They had been dating for a couple of months, and already there was talk of moving in together. But over glasses of wine at an outdoor café, she told me that they were now on the verge of breaking up.

"Why?" I asked, genuinely surprised. A teacher who worked with troubled teens as well as an accomplished guitarist, the guy had sounded like a dream.

Her face crumpled. "I was using his computer and found out that he never took down his profile. I took mine down weeks ago." Her voice dropped to a ragged whisper. "And he's also posted sex ads on craigslist."

"My god, I'm so sorry," I said.

"It's just . . ." she said, her voice trailing.

"What?"

"He was so upset when I confronted him, and he took down his profile right then . . . and believe me, I was pissed. I gave him a hard time."

"No," I said, shaking my head. "Don't even think it. He's trouble."

"I know. I'm ending it." She took a sip of wine and sighed. "You're so lucky you don't have to worry about dating."

I played with my napkin, not sure what to say. I know she wanted to get married. I know she wanted to have a baby. We had talked about this more often in recent years. The passing years worried her, the fact that her fertility was not forever.

"Sweetie, you deserve so much better, and you will find it," I said.

"I'm ending it," she repeated, more firmly this time, but I could hear the disappointment in her voice. And she did end it, although she later confessed to me that she saw him a few more times, ever hopeful, the possibilities of love puncturing even the best of intentions.

• • •

Countless pages have been written on the motivations of a woman in love. Love is the great chameleon, performing as lock and key, at once murder and sacrifice. In the *Second Sex*, Beauvoir honed in on the social conditioning that trains a woman how to be in love. "Men have vied with one another in proclaiming that love is woman's supreme accomplishment," she writes. Nietzsche said love makes women more feminine. Balzac went further, claiming that "man's life is fame, woman's life is love. Woman is man's equal only when she makes her life a perpetual offering, as that of man is perpetual action." To which, Beauvoir squares her shoulders in defiance and declares, "On the day when it will be possible for woman to love not in her weakness but in her strength, not to escape herself but to find herself, not to abase herself but to assert herself—on that day love will become for her, as for man, a source of life and not of mortal danger." Her words are inspiring. But then what is strength and what is weakness can become jumbled in matters of the heart.

Beauvoir herself has been denounced for her relationship with Sartre, their love affair a thorn in feminism's side. To me, however, they are one of history's most fascinating couples; they had a bond that went beyond the duty of marriage. Despite the criticisms of their arrangement, and there are many, Sartre and Beauvoir loved each other, and to someone from Generation Divorce, this seems a rather vital point. Their names are linked in the public imagination, just as their bodies share a grave in Paris.

Wanting to learn more about the relationship between Beauvoir and Sartre, I picked up Hazel Rowley's biography of their relationship, *Tête-à-Tête*. Rowley has a novelist's eye for detail, and she starts her story of their love affair with how Beauvoir and Sartre met as students in Paris in 1929. Beauvoir was a husky-voiced and frighteningly articulate twenty-one year old attending the Sorbonne, Sartre a short, pockmarked twenty-four year old with a wandering eye, literally and figuratively, who presented an altogether unattractive physical package made up for apparently by a certain charisma. Together, they were beauty and the beast. Both were studying for the *aggregation*, the grueling examination for a career in the French school system— Sartre for the second time around, after failing the exam the summer before, Beauvoir for the first.

Intrigued by a talk Beauvoir had given in class on the German philosopher Leibniz, Sartre determined to meet this elegant, clever blonde. Though Beauvoir was, at least initially, more interested in Sartre's handsome friend Rene Maheu, Sartre eventually captivated her with his verve, imagination, and wit. They talked late into the night at bars and cafés, while preparing for their oral exams, and soon became inseparable; intellectually, they were equals, although Beauvoir arguably had an edge on him. At the *aggregation*, Sartre barely captured the top prize, with Beauvoir behind him by two points as the runner-up, an especially impressive score since Beauvoir had been studying philosophy for only three years. Sartre, on the other hand, had benefited from seven years of study in a more rigorous program and was taking the exam for the second time. It would later come to light that the jury had chosen Sartre over Beauvoir only after much debate and deliberation, finally picking Sartre because, as a man, he somehow seemed more deserving of the glory. In this instance at least, Simone de Beauvoir was, indeed, the second sex.

The summer following the *aggregation*, Sartre visited Beauvoir during her family's vacation to the country, and the two of them spent lazy afternoons lying next to each other on the grass, fantasizing about their futures—the adventures they would have, the books they would write. They swore they would not be confined to nine-to-five jobs, or the social straitjackets of marriage and children. They would embrace freedom and take responsibility for their own futures, no matter how difficult or frightening. This belief—that life has no predetermined purpose or meaning, that our reality is created entirely through our individual choices—was to become the foundation of the theory of existentialism, a philosophical school of thought centered on the principle that "existence precedes essence," for which Sartre is best known.

Sartre applied his views on freedom to his relationship with Beauvoir, too. While he believed they were "two of a kind," sharing an "essential" love, he had no intention of remaining monogamous, and he told her so in no uncertain terms. He suggested instead that they continue to experience the possibilities for growth and pleasure in "contingent" relationships with other people—he fully expected her to take other lovers as well—yet their intimate relationship with each other would remain paramount; they had to promise to share every secret, every thought, every fear. That was the deal, and it was one they more or less kept throughout their lives.

In 1990, after her death, Beauvoir's letters to Sartre were published in their entirety. Neither censored nor edited, the couple's correspondence reveals a portrait of their polyamorous pact that is none too flattering. Beauvoir and Sartre not only discussed the calculated nature of their respective seductions but scrupulously described every detail. On occasion, they even shared the lovers themselves—generally young, impressionable women, whom they would then gossip about, often cruelly.

What arises from these letters is a petty, mean-spirited Beauvoir, and in the aftermath of the publication, her naysayers vociferously attacked both Beauvoir and her relationship with Sartre. In a 2005 *New Yorker* essay, cheekily titled "Stand by Your Man," literary critic Louis Menand uses his review of Rowley's *Tête-à-Tête* to offer his own opinions about Beauvoir's motives for engaging in such an unseemly agreement. After dismissing the theory that their relationship was a "partnership of equals," he briefly considers the possibility that Beauvoir was, in fact, the engineer of the whole thing, but discards that theory, too. His last theory—that it was a "traditional sexist arrangement" in which the woman grudgingly accepts her man's philandering—prevails. "Beauvoir was formidable, but she was not made of ice," he concludes. "Though her affairs, for the most part, were love affairs, it is plain from almost every page she wrote that she would have given them all up if she could have had Sartre for herself alone."

Rowley is miffed by Menand's conclusion, as am I, and she steps up to refute it directly in print. "Beauvoir was a strong woman who made some courageous and radical choices," she writes. "I do not see her living in [Sartre's] shadow . . . not at all. I find this attitude patronizing and sexist."

In Rowley's book, my Beauvoir is partially redeemed. To judge her by conventional standards, as Rowley points out, is to completely ignore the existential underpinnings that shaped her life: she considered the fortunes of an individual in terms of not happiness but liberty. Never guided by this goal of monogamous union, Sartre and Beauvoir instead struggled to maintain their freedom against the emotional tides of love and sex. By her own account, Beauvoir at times missed Sartre so desperately that she sank into despair. *Of course* she felt anger and jealousy over Sartre's lovers, which probably gave rise to moments when she wanted Sartre all to herself, as Menand and others contend. But we know she also felt passion— even love—for other men, and perhaps women, too. Most of all, we know that she tried to live her life according to the philosophical principles in which she believed, even at the price of loneliness. "In what a 'desert world' I walk," she writes in her journal, "so arid, with the only oases my intermittent esteem for myself." To make the claim, then, that all she ever really wanted was Sartre's sexual devotion, that she was merely living her life at his direction, *is* sexist.

On the contrary, I think Beauvoir looked to the pain and pleasure of her experiences for the creative force necessary for her writing, which, in reality, was her first love—before Sartre. Maybe this was the real pact she made, and she made it with herself.

• • •

If I was not the same starry-eyed reader I once had been, I still admired Beauvoir. Even after she had been so brutally excoriated in class, I was not prepared to renounce her. After class one afternoon, I walked over to the Hungarian Pastry Shop on Amsterdam Avenue, my favorite hangout as an undergraduate, and where I passed many an afternoon smoking cigarettes and taking advantage of the free coffee refills. The café had hardly changed since then. The same antique sconce lamps dotted the walls, infusing the narrow room with their dim, yellow light. Scruffy-looking students camped out at the wooden tables staring at their laptops, surrounded by piles of books. Only the eye-watering haze of smoke had long since dispersed with the city's no-smoking regulations.

At the sight, I again experienced emotional whiplash. Ever since I had moved back to the city, the accidental sight of a friend's old apartment building, as I turned down a street with my daughter chattering at my side, or the brief glimpse of an empty storefront where a favorite restaurant used to operate all at once opened up a window into my memory, the past flickering across my current life. Suddenly, I wondered if my recent fixation on Simone had less to do with her and more to do with me, trying to resolve a self divided between past and present.

"Stephanie?" called out a voice, breaking me from my reverie. I looked up and spotted a young waitress, rail thin and wearing a T-shirt so worn, it was almost diaphanous. A tribal tattoo crawled up the pale underside of her forearm. I waved her over to my table, and she walked gingerly, balancing my cappuccino in one hand and croissant in the other.

Once fortified, I braced myself for whatever remarks Beauvoir might make in her critique of both marriage and motherhood, opening *The Second Sex* to those chapters, which, curiously enough, had not been assigned in class. As I expected, she approached both institutions without any sentimentality. "No doubt marriage [for men] can afford certain material and sexual conveniences: it frees the individual from loneliness, it establishes him securely in space and time by giving

him a home and children; it is a definitive fulfillment of his existence," she writes. Marriage for men is a means to an end. But for
women, marriage is itself seen as destiny's peak. Marriage may provide economic insurance, an easy retreat, a standing Friday-night
date, but ultimately, Beauvoir concludes, most marriages end with
two lonely people locked in misery: "A thousand evenings of vague
small talk, blank silences, yawning over the newspaper, retiring at
bedtime!" To an existentialist, marriage, with its promise of commitment to one partner till death do us part, represents nothing more
or less than a hidden trap. "For me a choice is never made, it is always being made," says Beauvoir. "The horror of the definitive choice
is that it engages not only the self of today, but that of tomorrow,
which is why basically marriage is immoral."

Motherhood fares a little better in Beauvoir's estimation. Without
an *essential* definition of woman, or, for that matter, man, there can
be no such thing as the *natural* mother. Having children, she believes,
is a chosen duty, not a physiological destiny or a privileged accomplishment. "To be sure, the child is an enterprise to which one can
validly devote oneself; but it represents a ready-made justification
no more than any other enterprise does; and it must be desired for
its own sake, not for hypothetical benefits," she writes. I pondered
this idea for a while, her words seeming particular prescient of today's
popular culture, with its constant magazine headlines trumpeting
the celebrity mom and how "motherhood *changed* my life"—but not
her body evidently, given the equal number of headlines devoted to
how she got bikini-ready within weeks of giving birth. To go by these
magazines at least, a baby appears to be the newest fashion accessory.
For Beauvoir, however, motherhood should not really be about the
mother at all: "To have a child is to undertake a solemn obligation,"
she states. "If the mother shirks this duty subsequently, she commits
an offense against an existent, an independent human being."

I stared out the window, the glass mottled by the reflection of
people and lights within the pastry shop. Sitting there in Beauvoir's

milieu—alone, in a dark café, lost in a book—I examined my life through Beauvoir's gimlet eye. I saw the trips not taken, the flirtations not followed up on, the adventures not experienced; I saw the many moments of my life claimed by others, the nights making dinner, kissing knees, rubbing foreheads, soaping behind the ears, walking the dog, doing the dishes; I saw the novels interrupted, the museum exhibits missed, the sleepless nights, the fights, the frustrations, the laundry, the birthday parties, the time spent worrying about this, worrying about that. Such restrictions compelled by the responsibilities of family life are nothing new, but the ache of missed opportunities felt exceptionally sharp and undeniable at that moment.

It was time to go. I packed up my belongings, leaving an extra tip for my waitress on the table, and then took the subway from the Upper West Side back to Brooklyn to pick Sylvia up from school. As soon as she caught sight of me, she squealed and torpedoed herself into my arms. Kneeling on the blacktop, with my daughter's small arms wrapped around my neck, I realized that while part of me appreciated the freedom Beauvoir symbolizes—and probably always will—there was another side that Beauvoir did not recognize. Where Beauvoir saw marriage, and to some extent motherhood, as the ambush of a woman's future self, an irrevocable choice, it could also serve as an umbrella for a potentially vast array of smaller choices by which we continue to define who we are and how we will play these roles.

Holding my daughter's small hand in my own as we made our way home, I experienced the sudden release of this insight. To say that motherhood had changed me was not entirely accurate; rather, motherhood was always changing me, challenging me. Author Rachel Cusk observes in her memoir of motherhood, *A Life's Work* that after she had children, she was never quite herself with them, but neither was she quite herself *without* them. As mothers, we learn to dwell in this divide.

The Feminine Mystique

....

Beginning with *The Second Sex*, the second half of Fem Texts opened up to a fast changing world for women. Most of the issues that had occupied pre–World War II feminists, such as access to education and suffrage, had been achieved. "Rosie the Riveter" was a cultural icon and stood for the masses of American women who flooded the workforce during the war. Two female writers—Virginia Woolf and Simone de Beauvoir—had muscled entry into the male-dominated Western canon. Yet some things had not changed. At every turn, I heard echoes of the same issues that continue to engage us today, heard them as if caught in a sound chamber. Or a time warp.

In *The Second Sex*, for instance, Beauvoir notes the following about the debate between feminists and antifeminists: "The latter assert that the emancipated women of today succeed in doing nothing of importance in the world and that furthermore they have difficulty in achieving their own equilibrium. The former exaggerate the results obtained by professional women and are blind to their confusion. There is no good reason, as a matter of fact to say that they are on the wrong road; and still it is certain that they are not tranquilly installed in their new realm; as yet they are only halfway there." As I read this passage, I nodded in assent, until my bobbing head slowed, stopped, and tilted to the side. Wait a second, I had to remind myself, Beauvoir wrote those words in *1949*, before the rise of suburban sprawl, Woodstock, the civil rights movement, second- *and* third-wave feminism. . . . She was almost as old as my *great-grandmother*.

I was somewhat comforted when Professor L. made a similar gaffe the day we turned to Betty Friedan's *Feminine Mystique*, the mass-market best-seller that spoke to millions of housewives around the country when it was published in 1963—and the book that had awakened my desire to take Fem Texts again.

"I'm curious," Professor L. asked the class. "Did most of your moms read this book?"

"My *grandma* read this book," volunteered Lucy. "This would have been way too outdated for my mom."

Professor L. shook her head. "My God, you're right," she said. "You guys are so *young*. Well, did anyone relate to it, or did you all find that it was dated, too?"

"I actually thought it was frighteningly modern," said Mandy. The oldest of five children who grew up with a stay-at-home mother, Mandy had signed up for Fem Texts on little more than a whim, she had admitted, and approached the material with a lively inquisitiveness, asking questions without even a hint of self-consciousness. "I mean, now it seems like we have the same housewife ideal Friedan talked about—just with the added pressure to have a career."

"My mom always worked more than my dad," said Lucy. "I thought this book was really interesting because I had never been exposed to any of these ideas before."

"Not where I come from," said Catherine, who came from Nevada. "There was a *big* pull for women to stay at home."

As I listened to their comments, it was clear that a half century later, even this new generation is not yet "tranquilly installed" in the realm of equality.

The Feminine Mystique, probably the best-known "feminist text" to date, shook up the placid calm of 1950s conformity and heralded the next coming wave of feminism. Originally intending to write an article titled "The Togetherness Woman," Friedan conducted a fifteen-year follow-up with her classmates from Smith College. She found from the questionnaires pouring in that a disturbing number of white upper-middle-class women—the wives of successful husbands and the mothers of "perfect" children—were not "together" at all, but, in fact, unhinged by a kind of despair. Knowing with a reporter's instincts that she was on to something, Friedan, a suburban housewife herself, spent the next five years researching and writing

The Feminine Mystique, hiring babysitters a couple of days during the week to watch her three children.

While Friedan's book helped to spark another revolution, much of what she was saying—basically an updated appeal that "women are people, too"—had been said before. Building on the ideas of Wollstonecraft, Gilman, and Beauvoir before her, Friedan encouraged women to unequivocally reject the housewife ideal as well as other canned images of femininity. But Friedan framed the issue of a woman's identity differently from her predecessors. Whereas Beauvoir examined the work of such writers and thinkers as Nietzsche, Hegel, and Stendhal, Friedan drew upon more accessible sources, hitting the streets of the suburbs, pen and pad in hand, and interviewing scores of real-life housewives. She looked, too, at how popular culture, marketers, educators, and the media—women's magazines in particular—all conspired to push traditional forms of femininity on impressionable young women before they had a solid sense of their own identity. If Beauvoir turned to history and philosophy to understand herself, Friedan dipped into the annals of psychoanalysis, popularizing some of its revelations, so that as many women as possible could understand themselves.

Friedan believed that the "feminine mystique"—a term she coined for the cultural belief that women could find true happiness only by fulfilling their femininity as wives and mothers—had succeeded in scaring women away from pursuing careers by convincing them that ambition was a poison that would turn them into shriveled old maids. Both anecdotal and empirical evidence appeared to back up her proposition. By the mid-1950s, 60 percent of college women were dropping out to get married, and Friedan saw that her peers—the well-educated, the privileged—had bought into the mystique, abandoning their schoolgirl dreams of becoming doctors or artists in order to get married and have babies. Years later, however, alone in their spotless kitchens in their suburban homes, these same women were suffering from withdrawal. "When motherhood, a fulfillment held sacred down the ages, is defined as a total way of life, must women themselves deny the world and future open to them?" Friedan asks. "Or does the denial of that world force them to make motherhood a total way of life? The line between mystique and reality dissolves; real women embody the split in the image." More practical than philosophical, Friedan set out to heal this inner divide.

For all of Friedan's caveats that "it would be quite wrong for me to offer any woman easy how-to answers to this problem," the book nevertheless promotes a simple plan: Women need to get an education and then get a job, whereupon everything will click into place. Women themselves will be happier, resulting in happier husbands and children. Household chores will diminish, if only because, their minds occupied by loftier goals, women won't care so much about keeping house; and if they do, they can always hire someone else to clean their homes for them. "In actual fact, it is not as difficult as the feminine mystique implies, to combine marriage and motherhood, and even the kind of lifelong personal purpose that once was called 'career,'" writes Friedan. "It merely takes a new life plan—in terms of one's whole life as a woman."

Friedan's diagnosis and prescription struck a chord with the female public. The book sold more than 3 million copies and mobilized many women to change their lives. Friedan herself went on to become a founding member of the National Organization for Women, divorced her husband in 1969, and fled the suburbs for a high-rise condo in New York City. "I couldn't keep living my schizophrenic life," she admits in the book's epilogue, "leading other women out of the wilderness while holding on to a marriage that destroyed my self-respect." Although the book came out almost a half century ago, the reverberations of the explosion of the feminine mystique can still be felt today; seldom is there a discussion of the work-family divide without mention of Friedan's name, which means we hear her name *a lot*.

Nevertheless, Friedan's legacy remains an embattled one. In the years that followed publication of *The Feminine Mystique*, Friedan gained a reputation for being abrasive, arrogant, and homophobic. She was criticized for targeting her book at a very limited group of women— white, educated, upper-middle class—without acknowledging that her assumptions might not apply to all women. But beyond the evident charges of racism and classism, the students in Fem Texts also took issue with her solution to the feminine mystique itself.

"I'm sorry—I have to say this," burst out Nora, an older student, and mother, in her early thirties who had dropped out of school and was now returning to get her degree. "At times, this book made me really mad. It even made me cry, because it's *hard*. It's *so* hard." Her voice trembled. "My daughter is sick right now, but I have to be here, and it's so hard. My mother's taking care of her, but it's not the same. It's just not the same." Nora waved her copy of *The Feminine Mystique* in the air. "She doesn't address any of that."

Professor L. clucked her tongue and pointed to the cell phone sitting in front of her on the table. "One of my kids is sick, too," she said sympathetically. "So I have my phone out, just in case I need to make a quick exit. It *is* hard."

By now, the rest of the class had turned somber, a little freaked out by this small peek into the realities of motherhood. Lucia, one of the quieter students, raised her hand and explained that her mother was a nanny, who later started her own housecleaning business. She worked long hours and was often exhausted by the time she came home at night. "I saw her struggle with how to have a career and still have a family. I feel like I have to choose," she said. "I talk about that with my friends all the time. It's just not as easy as it was promised to be."

What women didn't know then about the difficulties of balancing a career and a family, we know only too well now. The air in the classroom was heavy with this knowledge.

Daughter of the Revolution

....

My mother had never felt the need to open the pages of *The Feminine Mystique* to give voice to her experience. She had never stayed at home, stewing with the resentment of dreams lost, pinning her hopes on her daughters like so many ornate brooches that had already gone out of style. She is a Phi Beta Kappa college graduate with a Ph.D. in molecular biology who had already risen to the top of her field by the time I was a teenager. So when I read *The Feminine Mystique* in the early 1990s, I read it with a college student's cool detachment. I did not personally recognize this mystique described by Friedan, not in myself and definitely not in my mother. My life outside the home had begun when I was around one month old and my mother went back to work. From then on, I had babysitters ranging in age and experience, from college students to senior citizens to neighborhood stay-at-home moms who watched me along with their own children. I adored some of these babysitters, was indifferent to others, and felt mistreated by one or two.

This constant separation from my parents affected me in obvious and not so obvious ways. My father tells me that once, when I was around a year old, my mother went away for two weeks, and for days after she returned I refused to look at her. I cannot speak of the price my parents paid, leaving me in the care of strangers, only mine: the mysterious fevers that took hold whenever one of them went away on a business trip, the sound of my own footsteps entering a silent house after school, the loneliness I felt starring in my elementary school play, knowing as I sang "Kumbaya" on stage, that my parents were not sitting in the crowded audience because both had to work. Backstage, a neighbor gave me a flower plucked from the bouquet she had brought her own child.

At the same time, I was proud of my mother, of both my parents. They were doing such important things; they were *saving lives*. At the age of two, I was enrolled at the on-site preschool at the National Institutes of Health in Bethesda, Maryland, where my mother worked, and I can recall how special I felt, holding my mother's hand as we walked across the NIH campus. I was part of her other world, only a short walk from the lab where she spent those long hours away from me, while I played with the children of her colleagues. It was the closest I had come, in my short life, to a sense of community. Since I was only the next building over, my mother would stop by to visit during lunch, and, on my fourth birthday, she surprised me by bringing in a cake glowing with candles and decorated with a smiling clown's face on top. My happiness that day has forever engraved the event in my memory.

As soon as I started attending the local elementary school, the time I spent with my mother was drastically reduced. No more morning car rides or midday visits. I took to walking myself to and from school, the house key dangling from my neck. Sometimes I would spend the afternoons playing with my friends until my parents came home from work; other times I would plop myself belly down on the floor in front of our thirteen-inch television to watch old reruns of *Leave it to Beaver* or *The Brady Bunch*, spellbound by all that I seemed to be missing, even as I knew that the yearning for such a family life was fanciful. I could wish and dream, but my mother was never going to be June Cleaver or Carol Brady, not even if she tried to play the part, wrapped an apron around her waist, and met me at the door with a plate of freshly baked chocolate chip cookies. My mother was the one who, bearish from being cooped up in the house for even a few weeks after I was born, cut her maternity leave short so she could return to the lab. "And I was glad she did," said my father. "I would come home at night, and she would slam a dinner plate in front of me. I thought she was going to take my head off."

I do not think I exaggerate when I say my mother loved her career more than she loved her role as a mother, and part of me doesn't begrudge her for that. I have seen the way she radiates when she's in front of an audience, displaying her considerable expertise—the way her voice turns into a melody, strong and confident—and I know that she's much more comfortable in this identity she has worked so hard to build than she ever could have been in a kitchen or a PTA meeting or lying on the floor stacking blocks with a toddler for hours on end. This is who she is, and I love and respect her for it. But despite the enormous admiration I have for my mother and all her accomplishments, another part of me continues to mourn a lost childhood, the one in which I stand on the stage, star of my school play, and peer out into the audience, this time to find my mother's face smiling back at me.

• • •

My mother was in the delivery room when I gave birth to Sylvia. She had already been in New York City for two weeks, waiting impatiently for her first grandchild's imminent arrival. Her flight was due to leave the next morning by the time I finally went into labor. As I lay in the hospital bed, teeth bared and groaning from contractions, my mother paced around the room, barking at the attending nurses. "My daughter's in pain," she roared. "Do. Something."

"Mom, it's okay," I told her, after one of the nurses curtly informed us that the anesthesiologist was busy and would be with us as soon as he could. We were obviously not winning any friends. "Maybe you should go to the gift shop," I suggested. "Get some snacks."

For the next few hours, as the contractions built up in intensity, my mother rubbed my arm and tucked me in when my teeth started to chatter uncontrollably from the epidural. She read me articles from the magazines she had purchased at the gift shop to entertain me, although I can't recollect a single story she recited. When at last it was time to push, my mother held one of my thighs pressed against her, John held the other, and I pushed to their chorus of encouragement. After Sylvia was born, my mother held her wet, wrinkled body wrapped in a blanket, as John cut the umbilical cord. I lifted my head, craning my neck to see the slick black hair on the back of my baby's head and my mother's face grinning down at her. She stayed with me until the close of visiting hours that night. Before her flight the next morning, she took a taxi to Chinatown and brought back to the hospital several takeout containers of almond tea, one of my favorites, and pig-knuckle soup, which the Chinese believe helps a woman to replenish her strength after giving birth. I had tears in my eyes when she left to fly back to California. Our relationship had started to change in that delivery room, as I became a mother and she a grandmother, causing a powerful shift in the tectonic plates of our family.

Since becoming a mother, I have found that I understand my own mother both more and less. In those moments in which I have been caught up in my work, I have felt the similar rush of ambition to succeed professionally in the larger world, even if at the expense of disappointing my daughter. I have experienced firsthand the limitless need of young children for their parents, and as a result, have been able to forgive the infliction of some of my childhood wounds. Yet I have also buckled under my daughter's expectant gaze, setting aside assignments and obligations to read her a book or listen to the latest song she has made up. I have constantly reminded myself of the way young children see the world in only primary colors. For all the practical reasons underlying my decision to work as a freelance writer rather than return to a full-time job, there was clearly an emotional rationale as well. Haunted by my parents' relative absence during my childhood, I wanted the flexibility to be there for my own daughter, especially during her early years.

What I neither wanted nor expected, though, was to end up identifying so strongly with the women of *The Feminine Mystique*, as I had when I first retrieved the book at the bookstore in Annapolis. Anecdotes from Friedan's interviewees, such as the following from a Nebraska housewife with three children and a Ph.D. in anthropology (my college major, no less), came dangerously close to describing my own life:

> A film made of any typical morning in my house would look like an old Marx Brothers' comedy. I wash the dishes, rush the older children off to school, dash out in the yard to cultivate the chrysanthemums, run back in to make a phone call about a committee meeting, help the youngest child build a blockhouse, spend fifteen minutes skimming the newspapers so I can be well-informed, then scamper down to the washing machines where my thrice-weekly laundry includes enough clothes to keep a primitive village going for an entire year. By noon I'm ready for a padded cell.

At that point in my life, *The Feminine Mystique* felt like an indictment. But reading the book surrounded by women almost half my age, I once again saw the book's divergences from my own story rather than the similarities. Although Friedan's "feminine mystique" imposed many traditional notions of marriage and motherhood on white upper-middle-class women that remain in effect today, the mystique was also the product of a very particular type of '50s conformity. The malaise Friedan writes about, this "problem that has no name," hung over the neighborhoods of that era like so much suburban smog, while underneath simmered acres of discontent. Men, too, did not surface from their suburban housing developments unscathed, as borne out by numerous chronicles of their restlessness in the fiction of that time, from Sloan Wilson's *Man in the Grey Flannel Suit* to Richard Yates's *Revolutionary Road*. Today we are not afflicted with exactly the same problems. Just as women no longer wait at the kitchen window for their husbands to return home from the big city, an icy gin cocktail in hand and a hot dinner on the table, most men no longer remove themselves entirely from domestic affairs and keep their children at arm's length.

In many ways, my life with John looked nothing like that 1950s world Friedan describes. He wanted to be an involved parent, as much as I did, to walk his daughter to school in the mornings, attend her school performances, and participate in her parent-teacher conferences. Nevertheless, this shared desire manifested in different ways as we negotiated our careers. I may not have been commuting to and from an office, but I also could not devote hours to elaborate craft projects or volunteering at my child's school. Without the validation of either working or stay-at-home mom, I felt lost in a limbo beyond recognition. As a freelance writer, I had joined the growing but still, for the most part, invisible ranks of work-at-home moms.

When Sylvia was around two, we enrolled her at a local preschool for half the day, and with my mornings free, I was ready to apply for a job outside the home. I was burned out from pitching articles, waiting for paychecks, and paying for my own health insurance. Worn down from the instability and isolation, I craved the camaraderie of coworkers—even, yes, a squabble or two set off by office politics would be a refreshing change from the hum of my own internal dialogues. More concretely, though, my savings account was running low. I had waitressed in college and worked to support myself ever since graduation, and although I was bringing in some money from freelancing, the sporadic pay was hardly a substantial contribution to the household funds. I hated not having a regular income and frankly was terrified that one day I would be unable to support myself if this kept up; the thought of being financially dependent on John, or anyone else, filled me with dread and a fair bit of shame.

So I churned out cover letters and résumés, optimistic I would be able to find something. I had jumped off the job track for a couple of years, but I had a master's degree and years of work experience. As weeks, then months, passed without any viable job options opening up, and the money in the bank account continued to dwindle, my panic rose in equal measure. Anxiety whipped around in the pit of my stomach like a live wire, sparking and wild. At night, I would lie awake in bed, suspended by worry over what I began to call the "yawning abyss" of my future career prospects. Beyond my fear of becoming a barista was the sickening suspicion that all my hard work throughout college, the workplace, and graduate school had come to this: I had made the wrong choices and slid down to the last rung of the ladder. Meanwhile, I watched myself transform into some sort of pre-Friedan housewife: cranky, irritable, and suddenly, compulsively, neurotic about Swiffing the floors.

Part of the problem was my chosen profession. A computer engineer, John worked in a high-income field in which jobs were practically dropping into his lap; employers *wooed* him. My field, on the other hand, was "creative," which meant coveted, overcrowded, and low paying. To make a fraction of his salary, I would have to work twice as many hours, and with a child, I didn't have twice the hours to give. I could already make out the lay of the land. As our financial needs increased, John would work more, and I would shoulder the brunt of the child care, along with the domestic chores, and then what? What happened when our daughter left home and went to college? I would be even older, even less employable. Determined not to let this happen to me, I began to take on more and more freelance projects, branching out into editing and teaching, until there I was, working almost twelve hours a day, trapped in a freelancers' ghetto in which I could never say no.

• • •

From there, I found myself sitting at the kitchen table in my mother's house in California, talking on my cell phone as I furiously typed on my laptop. It was the day after Thanksgiving, and I had been up since six o'clock in the morning. Scattered across the center island counter lay the detritus of last night's dinner—crusted plates and utensils, untouched. The house was quiet other than my murmurs into the receiver and the click of my computer keys. John returned with Sylvia from the backyard.

"Mama, Mama, look what I *found*," she cried, bounding across the living room toward me. "I have a pet snail!" She proffered her small hand, shoving it gently in front of my face. I stared at the small mushroom-colored snail that slid across her palm, leaving the faintest trail of slime, and smiled, a bit desperately. The phone sat precariously wedged between ear and shoulder as I cupped the mouthpiece, still typing.

"That's great, sweetie," I whispered.

I was interviewing a human rights lawyer whom I had been trying to reach for the past two days for an article on forced marriage. The assignment had come unexpectedly, right before Thanksgiving, a last-minute message left on my machine by a magazine editor. Her voice in the message was tense, apologetic. She needed the article as a replacement for another article that fell through; there was no wiggle room with the deadline. I had less than a week. And so I had spent my holiday doing research, reading reports, phoning experts, writing drafts, and talking to my editor, often after we had each put our respective children to bed.

I learned about nine-year-old girls, only a few years older than my own daughter, married off to sixty-year-old men, taken away from their families, pulled out of school, raped, beaten, abused. I learned how many become pregnant and suffer severe health complications because they are simply too young, their bodies too small, their bones fragile as a baby bird's. I learned that mothers and fathers wish this bleak fate on their daughters because it is tradition, because they view the female sex as property, but also because this is the best way to ensure that their children will actually eat, have shelter, survive. The lawyer told me stories, as I absently combed through Sylvia's hair with my fingers, trying to tame the mess of golden locks she refused to cut; she pulled away but continued to talk about her snail, petting the shell lovingly. Either she didn't realize—or didn't care—that I was on the phone, and why should she? She was five years old.

"I'm going to name him Louie," Sylvia was telling me, as she tried to pull herself back onto my lap. I made pleading gestures to John, and he came over, glaring. This was not the Thanksgiving break he had in mind when we flew six hours across the country. I had barely left the house since we arrived, remaining at a code-red stress level, while he had spent the past few days taking care of Sylvia and talking to my family. His eyes narrowed into a mutinous look.

"Please," I mouthed.

"Come on, Sylvia," he said a bit too loudly. "Let's go find Louie something to eat." He grabbed the newspaper and glared at me again before stomping out the back door.

"Mommy, you're *always* working," complained Sylvia before following her father out the door.

I apologized into the phone for the interruption and finished up the interview, feeling a set of tiny spikes of tension form along my back, each one furiously waving its own flag: guilt, frustration, anger, exhaustion. I pressed my fingers into my temples. I needed to do more research. I needed to make more phone calls. I needed to finish this article. My breath was sour from two cups of coffee, and my stomach clenched from too much caffeine, too little sleep. Sylvia's muffled shrieks of delight floated through the window; the sprinklers had switched on, which never ceased to amuse her. The sky was blue, "like a perfect piece of blue paper," as Sylvia had described it that morning.

She poked her head through the back door. "Mommy, *please* come outside. I want to show you something." She paused. "You're not going to, are you, Mommy?"

Something about the resignation in her voice reminded me of myself as a child, wheedling my own mother. I sighed and pushed my chair back from the table. "Oh, what the hell," I thought. I was going to help find that damned snail some food, even if I had to stay up the whole of the next night to get my work done, which, of course, was what I ended up doing.

Later, at around two in the morning, as I was typing away on my computer again at the kitchen table, my mother wandered downstairs in her silk pajamas, her slippered feet padding across the marble floor. She looked at me with eyes half-closed with sleep. "You're still up," she mumbled. "You want a cup of tea?"

"Sure, thanks." I did not stop typing.

She banged around in the kitchen, filling the teapot with water, putting it on the flame, and then foraging through the cupboard for some biscuits until the ready whistle of the pot pierced the quiet. Then she carried over two cups of tea and sat down next to me at the table. She watched me for a moment. "Poor Sylvie," she sighed.

"Huh?" I asked, not really paying attention.

"She's on vacation, and she doesn't get to see much of her mom." She took a sip of tea and flipped through the stack of newspapers on the table.

I stopped typing. I rubbed my eyes, which were burning from exhaustion. Was she kidding? *My mother* was saying this? I could almost taste the resentment rising in my throat.

"What do you mean?" I asked, my voice crouching dangerously low.

"I just think it's sad for her, that's all," she said, looking down at the paper. "I know she misses you."

I was preparing my verbal strike when, suddenly, my belligerence drained away. I realized that we were not really talking about Sylvia but about me, and this was my mother's indirect way of apologizing for all those moments she missed during my childhood.

I took a sip of tea. "She knows I miss her, too," I said, and my mother stayed with me, quietly reading the newspaper, until I had finished my article and at last could go with her upstairs and crawl into bed.

Who Has Time for "Happy"?

The article I was working on during Thanksgiving was handed in on time and eventually published, and, seeing my words in print, I did feel a sense of accomplishment, of satisfaction, of relief. Sylvia pulled the magazine down from the rack at the supermarket, eyes wide. Later, she reported to her friends proudly that her mommy was a writer and that she wanted to be a writer, too. When I pick her up from school, her teachers always remark on her love of reading and telling stories. She comes home with books she has made in school. For now, at least, I dare to believe I have managed to stitch together an Amazing Technicolor Dreamcoat of identity—mother *and* writer.

These are the good moments, but there are also the bad ones, and the entire spectrum arching between. Moments when my temper flares, so swift and bright, I scare even myself. Sometimes, feeling overextended, I am prone to snap. Maybe Sylvia refuses to put on her shoes when we're already late for school, and I jam her feet in them a little too roughly. Or she starts whining for a cupcake when she has just had a box of animal crackers, and I lash out in disproportionate anger. Or she accidentally spills a sticky glass of juice across the brand-new dining room table, and I send her to her room in a rage. I can feel this hulking restiveness beneath my skin that I try with all my might to restrain. Parenthood is rife with these little fits of fury, these powerful eruptions of frustration, and to keep them at bay, I constantly search to find the right balance of responsibility to my child and responsibility to myself: This, after all, was the most important message of *The Feminine Mystique*, and it's one I have taken to heart.

Nevertheless, two or three generations later, I also see how Friedan's message, while liberating to so many women, unintentionally placed us in a theoretical quicksand from which we have been flailing wildly to escape ever since. "The feminine mystique says that the highest value and the only commitment for women is the fulfillment of their own femininity," says Friedan, countering this with the argument that women be allowed to fulfill themselves, not just as women but, more important, as human beings. In the decades that followed *The Feminine Mystique*, these common refrains— *fulfillment, satisfaction, happiness*—have dictated the debate about the work-family divide, although these prismatic words lack any definitive meaning.

As Beauvoir notes in *The Second Sex*, "It is not too clear just what the word 'happy' really means, and still less what true values it may mask. There is no possibility of measuring the happiness of others, and it is always easy to describe as happy the situation in which one wishes to place them." To compare work and motherhood in terms of satisfaction and fulfillment is a similarly specious endeavor, for they are plainly not the same kind of experience. Seeing my name in print cannot possibly be compared with seeing my daughter's dance performance at school—not because one is necessarily better or more important, but because they are so very different and serve such different needs. Any mother knows this, even if some media pundits would seem stubbornly determined not to acknowledge this crucial distinction with their relentless coverage of the Mommy Wars.

Today, women suffer less from Friedan's mystique than from another kind of problem—a problem that has *too* many names. We have been dissecting the feminine mystique, and its progeny, for going on five decades now and have become only too well versed in all the ways in which we can't Have It All, the limits that career and children place on us, the reality that, in the end, something has got to give. Indeed, surveys dating back to the 1970s show that more and more women are reporting they are unhappy, while men, on the contrary, are becoming happier, much to our confusion and consternation. We have come up with a host of culprits to blame for women's persistent unhappiness, ranging from anxiety and consumerism to guilt and second shifts. The result? A raging case of "issue fatigue," as one critic put it. The feminine mystique has become the feminine *critique*, and while, yes, it is perhaps somewhat reassuring to realize that we are not alone but part of a genderwide crisis, the old adage "misery loves company" takes us only so far when we are, in the end, still miserable. If Friedan's specter was the 1950s "happy housewife" pictured in glossy magazine advertisements, ours is surely the '80s "supermom," now lying crumpled on the floor from too much cultural kryptonite. And in her wake enters a decidedly less glamorous antihero: the mother who is always reaching to make ends meet, always harried, always frazzled, and always—always—coming up a little short.

• • •

This much, however, is unmistakable. For all its effervescent joys, there's no denying that motherhood substantially affects a woman's earning potential, although few people want to hear it. We prefer to paint motherhood as art, separate from the world of commerce. Talking about lost wages, opportunity costs, rising dependency— these topics threaten to cheapen the experience of parenthood, which is supposed to be selfless, transcendental, *meaningful*. Former

economics reporter and author Ann Crittenden once calculated that
a woman who has one child loses about a million dollars in lifetime
earnings. Obviously, men pay a price, too, whether they scale back
on work to spend more time with their families or work longer hours
at the expense of emotional ties with their spouse and children. But
even as more men participate in parenthood, there remains the expectation that women alone must confront the question of whether
to continue working after a child, while the man is usually expected
to pick up the financial slack. Everyone asked my husband when he
planned to go back to the office; only a few people asked me. Raising
a child is vital work, but apparently it is still women's work.

Whenever a feminist writer tries to undrape the motherhood mystique, whether Friedan or, more recently, Linda Hirshman, who wrote
a modern-day manifesto called *Get to Work*, she is usually hit with
the same accusation of rending apart the fabric of society. Even today,
with so many women succeeding in the workplace, the idea of the
professional working mom threatens. In a scathing appraisal of Hirshman's book, *New York Times* columnist David Brooks quotes
Hirshman as saying, "The family—with its repetitious, socially invisible, physical tasks—is a necessary part of life, but it allows fewer
opportunities for full flourishing than public spheres like the market
or the government." Au contraire, scolds Brooks. Work is mostly
drudge, "just ask an associate at a law firm," he suggests; genuine
joy and flourishing are, rather, to be found in the home, where parents (read: mothers) have the actual power to bolster their children's
IQ and well-being as our next generation of citizens. Brooks conveniently adds that men and women are "wired differently," with women
being much better at people-related activities, while men are much
better at abstract concepts.

For all his talk that Hirshman's manifesto is a throwback to 1975
time-warp feminism, Brooks's piece reads like 1949 sexist propaganda
encouraging women to sublimate their own ambitions for a larger

cause. It's the old "great men have great mothers" routine, and when I happened upon his column, I was disappointed at this lost chance to move the conversation in a more positive direction. Brooks could easily have taken the opportunity to talk about the importance of parenthood and adapting the workplace to be more receptive to the demands placed on both men *and* women, instead of grinding the same old sexist saws: *kinder, kuche, kirche.* "Power is in the kitchen," he writes, concluding with what seems a slightly halfhearted (and certainly backhanded) progressivism: "The problem is not the women who stay there, but the men who leave."

If only Brooks had sat down with Terry Martin Hekker, a grandmother who happened to contribute a "Modern Love" column to the very same edition of the Sunday *Times* in which his column appeared, the two of them could have had an illuminating powwow about work and motherhood. As Brooks gushes about mothers remaining in the kitchen, Hekker exhorts women to get the hell out. Interestingly, though, Hekker is no disciple of the second-wave feminism Brooks attacked, but was one of its outspoken opponents back in the 1970s. In a *New York Times* editorial in defense of housewives like herself, Hekker wrote: "I come from a long line of women, most of them more Edith Bunker than Betty Friedan, who never knew they were unfulfilled. I can't testify that they were happy, but they were cheerful. And if they lacked 'meaningful relationships,' they cherished relations who meant something. They took pride in a clean, comfortable home and satisfaction in serving a good meal because no one had explained that the only work worth doing is that for which you get paid."

Hekker's editorial led to a book, aptly titled *Ever Since Adam and Eve*, as well as a round on the talk-show circuit. But that was then. Fast-forward more than thirty years later, and Hekker's husband has run off with a younger woman, leaving her with only a paltry alimony, set to expire in four years, as payment for the decades of her adult life she devoted to caring for their home and five children. In her sixties, alone, with few marketable skills, Hekker has to hock her engagement ring to keep a roof over her head, while her ex takes his new girlfriend to Cancun. When Hekker files her tax return, she finds out she qualifies for food stamps. She decides to request an increase in her maintenance, only to have the judge tell her to stop complaining and start applying to job-training programs. At her age and without any prior work experience, Hekker comes to the brutal realization that her career options are rather limited; motherhood, however valued by our society, is neither paid work nor deemed worthy enough to put on a résumé, and divorced older women like Hekker are one of the most poverty-stricken groups in America. "My anachronistic book was written while I was in a successful marriage that I expected would go on forever," Hekker writes. "Sadly, it now has little relevance for modern women, except perhaps as a cautionary tale: never its intended purpose." To borrow from Beauvoir, Hekker was a feminist not born but made by unfortunate experience.

• • •

If studies show that women are not as "happy" as in the days before Betty Friedan, then perhaps the results say less about women's happiness and more about how we frame the terms of the debate. To focus on the drop in personal levels of happiness among women as a societal benchmark only blinds us to where we are today. Few of us would want to return to the era of *Mad Men*. Rather, we should take these feelings of dissatisfaction and, instead of looking back at the past with misplaced nostalgia, look forward to what types of laws and policies might realistically help to improve women's and men's lives in the present. Besides, isn't discontent the mother of change? It certainly was for the feminists who emerged in the wake of Friedan.

The Dialectic of Sex

When Brooks invokes 1970s feminism, he is essentially taking a cheap shot, but it is a strategic one. He knows that many of his readers will react just as intended to his provocations, instantly accosted with images of barreling, braless women covered in body hair. Strangely, this ghoul of the 1970s feminist persists in defining feminism into the oughts. Every Fem Texts class I took—despite whatever far-flung differences in style and tone might later surface—began in pretty much the same way. The professor would ask us to summon in our minds a "feminist," conjuring up all our worst stereotypes, and we would go around the table trying to exorcise her hovering presence.

If Virginia Woolf spoke of waging war against the Angel in the House, we as a class on feminism had to contend with the hairy, man-hating lesbian in the room. You know, *her*. The woman who cries feminist to cover the fact that no man would want her, that squat and humorless woman who is bitterly destined for spinsterhood, the woman who doesn't just burn her bra but builds a raging bonfire in her backyard. Not that any of us were *that* kind of feminist—a few students were even a little iffy as to whether they were feminists at all. Did such feminists even exist in the twenty-first century? Had they ever existed? As two of my professors were quick to point out, women never actually publicly burned their bras in protest, but the image, too good for the media to pass up, soon became iconic.

What is true is that for a period of time during the tumultuous 1960s and '70s—after the widespread flogging of the feminine mystique, and during the civil rights movement, the Vietnam War, Watergate—a relatively small number of women were very publicly and vociferously *pissed off*. Their eyes had been opened, their consciousness raised, and they did not want to play nice anymore;

moreover, they didn't have to. All around them, the neat facade of
fifties conformity was dissolving into a messy cross-hatching of
divisions—black and white, young and old, men and women—not
to mention all the variations *within* these groups. A new generation
was developing the vocabulary to articulate realities that had been
hitherto hidden. Racism. Sexism. Patriarchy. Oppression. In the
midst of this growing political awareness, women started to stand up
and speak out. This wasn't Betty Friedan's elite brand of feminism,
either, but something bolder, wilder, *radical*. These women didn't
just want to tweak the system, like the women who had come before
them; they wanted to rip it apart, and the extreme, as they say, always
makes an impression.

Some of the ideas of the radical second wavers can seem positively
outlandish, viewed from our retrospective perch here at the dawn of
the twenty-first century, and even occasionally a bit sci-fi scary. At
the end of her 1970 best-seller, *The Dialectic of Sex: The Case for
Feminist Revolution*, radical feminist Shulamith Firestone goes so
far as to map out a strategy for societal upheaval, complete with
charts and diagrams. Firestone, who famously described childbirth
as akin to "shitting a pumpkin," believed that in order to achieve
true equality between the sexes, we would have to explode the nu-
clear family unit; this was the only way to reverse centuries of gender
discrimination. Her plan relied on freeing women from the "tyranny
of their reproductive biology" by means of artificial reproduction in
a lab. Children would no longer really "belong" to anyone, and the
ties of blood would dissolve, leaving people to choose their own
"households," in which chores like cooking and child rearing, would
be shared evenly. Marriage and monogamy would become obsolete,
sexual relations would be undertaken solely for pleasure, and eventually our sexist culture as we know it would disappear. No more
Vera Wang, or, for that matter, Liz Lange. Firestone was right about
the mainstreaming of artificial reproductive technology, though

clearly none of her other predictions came to pass. If anything, we seem to have become only more wedding and baby obsessed since the days of *The Dialectic of Sex*.

I wasn't yet born when Firestone's book was published, but that doesn't exempt me from a twinge of nostalgia at her talk of communes and free love. I may shave my legs and use deodorant, but I have a spark of the hippie in me. Professor L.'s eyes got a little misty, too, as we talked about radical feminism.

"Are there any left?" she cried out to the class, pounding her fist on the table. "Do *any* of you consider yourselves radical feminists?"

Her gaze swept around the room, and one or two very tentative hands went up. "Well, what was wrong with them, then?" she demanded.

As we began to close in on *The Dialectic of Sex*, I imagined us encircling a small, wounded, alien-like creature, each of us taking a turn to curiously poke at it with a long stick. And, sure enough, up rose the voices of dissent from the class.

"To hate childbirth is to hate a fundamental piece of your history!"

"There are lots of women who *love* being pregnant!"

"My mom always said she would rather be pregnant than go to the dentist!"

"When I think about society raising children, I think of public school versus private school!"

"It's so much better to have individualized attention!"

"We are never going to eradicate the family!"

"I *like* my father!"

"She's too radical. It's just not effective!"

"Too unrealistic!"

"Too alienating!"

"Too angry!"

Professor L. listened to the chorus of student responses, her eyes darting from one face to another.

"Okay—hold on a second," she said, the sound of challenge in her voice, "Did anyone like the anger? I *like* the idea of being angry and not just pandering for social change."

I admit that I, too, found something energizing about Firestone's unapologetic feminist fervor, her clarity of vision. And although I also agreed with many of my fellow students' reservations, I could not help but think we were missing a crucial point in our discussion of radical feminism. "Cybernetic socialism," as Firestone calls it, may seem hokey today, but *The Dialectic of Sex* was an outgrowth of a particular moment, an idealistic time fueled by hope and outrage. This was not some fringe tract sold on street corners but a book published by a major publisher. Despite its Marxist analysis and its anti-love, antimarriage, antiestablishment stance, *The Dialectic of Sex* became a central text of second-wave feminism that has been reprinted a dozen times, selling many thousands of copies. Too often, in our age of cooperation and compromise, we focus only on the destructive aspects of the anger that blazed behind the words and ideas of radical feminism—how it divided the nation and the family into his and hers—while forgetting what was created, the opportunities that radical feminism blasted open for women. Anger, after all, leads to action, while ambiguity tends to lead only to confusion.

"I guess anger can be useful," conceded Sarah, a moment earlier one of the more vehement critics of radical feminist tactics. "But only sometimes," she added quickly.

Professor L. and I exchanged glances, a brief but shared recognition that we stood on one side of this generation gap and the rest of the class on the other.

• • •

Radical is derived from the Latin word for *root* and denotes an unsparing examination of the bases of certain entrenched beliefs and behaviors in the interest of uprooting them. When conservatives talk about radical feminists, they usually fail to acknowledge that these women were radical *for a reason*. Their anger did not just materialize from the ether. It came from lived experience. When she wrote her book, Firestone's rage was real. The day before Richard Nixon's inauguration in 1969—and a year before *The Dialectic of Sex* was published—Firestone and Marilyn Salzman Webb, a veteran of the activist group Students for a Democratic Society, attended a "counterinauguration" and rally against the Vietnam War in Washington, D.C. They had been invited by the rally's organizers to speak about the still nascent women's liberation movement. In her chronicle of that era, *The World Split Open*, historian Ruth Rosen describes what happened after the two women climbed onto the stage:

> Webb, who had remained within the Left, began her speech by declaring, "We as women are oppressed. We, as women [who] are supposedly the most privileged in this society, are mutilated as human beings so that we will learn to function within the capitalist system." Suddenly, pandemonium broke out below the stage. Webb plunged on, denouncing a system that treated women as objects and property. To her horror, she watched as "fist fights broke out. Men yelled things like 'Fuck her! Take her off the stage! Rape her in a back alley!' Shouts followed, like 'Take it off!'" . . . Firestone, who had already given up on the Left, strode on the stage to condemn men as well as capitalism. "Let's start talking about where we live, baby," she shouted. "Because we women often have to wonder if you mean what you say about revolution or whether you just want more power for yourselves." The largely male crowd booed and shouted obscenities.

Note that this was no Sojourner Truth facing an angry tribunal of white preachers to ask, "Ain't I a woman?" Webb was giving a political speech to a group of ostensibly like-minded liberal individuals fighting to change the system.

In one particularly telling anecdote, a group of women wrote a paper about the lack of leadership roles for women in the civil rights group Student Nonviolent Coordinating Committee, to which Stokely Carmichael famously retorted that women's only position in the civil rights movement was "prone." Women who took offense were chided for being too strident and lacking a sense of humor. But Carmichael's joke caught on and was repeated over and over again, until whatever lighthearted tone the comment originally may have had was completely lost and instead became something ominous. Tensions increased between men and women in the movement, and tempers rose, fueling feminism's turn to the extreme.

Like any movement, the brief and fiery reign of radical feminism had its share of fanatics to support the stereotype. Valerie Solanas, for instance, one author of the arguably satirical *SCUM* (Society for Cutting Up Men) *Manifesto* calling for the "gendercide" of all men, shot and stalked artist Andy Warhol. In general, though, women were looking to express a justified anger. They had joined the civil rights movement, giddy for a real social revolution, only to find themselves marginalized and betrayed by misogyny. Of course, since ancient times, women have been the targets of discrimination and denigration—and, indeed, still are—but these women perceived a historical moment in which it was incumbent upon them to stand up and protest. The moment did not last long, but its reputation of infamy certainly has—which speaks volumes to our cultural discomfort with rebellious women.

In a rather grim epilogue to the radical feminist movement of the early '70s, a few of its central actors later drifted into obscurity or madness. After the publication of *The Dialectic of Sex*, Firestone, only twenty-five years old when she wrote the book, virtually disappeared and spent time going in and out of psychiatric hospitals.

Solanas, too, ended up battling mental illness, after serving prison time for her attempted murder of Warhol. Some radical feminists shifted into cultural feminism, trading politics for spirituality, and a celebration of the ways in which women are different from—and superior—to men. Others, like writer and activist Gloria Steinem and Robin Morgan, former editor in chief of *Ms.* magazine, carried on the good fight. Many more, I suspect, simply gave up calling themselves feminists at all. By the 1980s, the backlash, so superbly chronicled by journalist Susan Faludi in her book of the same title, was in full swing, while *feminism*—the simple notion that women ought to define their own destinies—had once again become a bad word.

• • •

Entering college in 1989, the age of Political Correctness, I stepped into a small revolutionary wing in the culture wars. In those days, women were *wimmin*, history was *herstory*, and college students across the country hung in effigy the formerly revered "dead white males." I had classmates who openly refused to read anything from the Western canon in defiance of the patriarchy. Sympathetic to the cause, I nevertheless declined from joining their ranks in this particular fight—as a book lover, how could I do otherwise? But I did agree with bringing more diversity and awareness to the curriculum. Land mines created by language were scattered across campuses, and when they detonated, the result was a fracturing, a shattering. Campuses polarized along PC lines. Sometimes, one side went too far, prosecuting harmless speech as if it were a lethal weapon openly brandished; sometimes, the other side did the same, purposely using speech that was hateful in an attempt to incite and enrage. We were breaking the rules and trying to come up with new ones, with varying success. The cold war had ended, MTV was rocking the vote, and, as a generation, we were politicized, buffing the ideas of '60s and '70s radicalism to once again deal with the overlapping issues of race, class, and gender. We recognized that there were very real inequities in the system, but the Berlin Wall had fallen, so maybe, we believed, other walls could, too.

The summer before my junior year of college, my friend Barbara, who was interning on Capitol Hill, called me from the office phone during her lunch break. "Thurgood Marshall is retiring," she whispered.

I was sitting on my father's beige sectional couch, twisting the phone cord around my fingers as she filled me in, my stomach curling as the reality set in that one of the last liberal Supreme Court justices was making an exit, and President Bush, No. 41, a self-anointed champion of "family values," would be choosing the next nominee.

A couple of months later, as the Senate grilled the contender for Marshall's seat, Clarence Thomas, amid charges of sexual harassment, the curl in my stomach unrolled into fury. And I wasn't alone. Crowding around the TV set in the corner of the student lounge, my fellow dorm mates and I were at once transfixed and horrified by the Senate hearings. One of his former colleagues, Anita Hill, had accused Thomas of inappropriate behavior, describing how he regularly made sexual overtures, brought pornography into the office, and, most memorably, joked about finding a pubic hair on his soda can. The anecdotes were bizarre, but the anger they stirred was in earnest. Thomas famously raged that he was a victim of a "high-tech lynching for uppity blacks," while Hill was also publicly smeared, labeled by then conservative journalist David Brock as "a little nutty and a little slutty." Sex and race crossed swords. Those of us who supported Hill wrongly reassured ourselves that surely Thomas would not be confirmed to the Supreme Court.

When he was, rather than throwing their arms up in disgust and defeat, many women were galvanized. Issues affecting women—from rape on campus to representation in Congress—came to the surface of everyday conversation. Women were getting radical again, taking to the streets in protest. Another presidential election was around the corner, bringing the promise of a new generation in the White House with nominee Bill Clinton and Hillary Rodham Clinton; these were not the stodgy blue-blood Bushes, with Bush Sr. marveling at the newfangled technology at grocery stores, as the first lady volunteered her thoughts on skirt hemlines (*not* above the knee, in case you're wondering). Both graduates of Yale Law School, where they had first met, the Clintons were, in comparison, young and eloquent. Clinton showed up on MTV and played his saxophone for the late-night audience of *The Arsenio Hall Show*. Young people registered to vote in droves. On election night in 1992, I was coming home from dinner with my boyfriend when a fellow subway passenger announced that Clinton had eked out a victory. The crowd in the Ninety-sixth Street subway station let out a collective whoop, and my boyfriend and I hugged each other on the platform, our relief almost palpable.

Yet the new era was a strange one. One moment I was watching the Clarence Thomas confirmation hearings, filled with ire, and the next moment, it seems, I was watching *Ally McBeal*, full of irony. By the time I graduated from college, feminism was imperiled. Pundits everywhere were ringing its death knell, claiming we were now post-feminists (or even post-postfeminists), lipstick feminists, "not a feminist, *but*" feminists: Pick your poison. I was too preoccupied to notice. I was working, dating, and contemplating starting a family. As other responsibilities started to build up, feminism began to seem more and more like a younger woman's battle anyway, one who read magazines like *Bitch* or *Cunt* and had multiple tattoos webbing her skin. I may have still called myself a feminist, but I was no longer sure what that meant.

Where had all the anger gone—and not just my own? Looking around me, I could see little sign of the righteous indignation I remembered from my own undergraduate days among the students in Fem Texts. The passage of time may have blurred my vision, but, for the most part, these young women seemed more resigned, more tentative, more conflicted than I had been at their age—not because they didn't wince at the bruises of injustice due to their sex but because the battlefield, if you could call it that, had transformed. In the past few decades, women have made incredible strides in the government and the workplace, yet, for many women, not as much has changed on the domestic front.

If the personal is political, then the political, too, has become personal. Women wrangle for equality mainly in the skirmishes of everyday life, at home and in the workplace. These fights take place mostly in the trenches, as we go into hand-to-hand combat over pay raises and flex time with bosses or embark on the perennial campaign to get a partner or spouse to pitch in more with the child care and chores. These are not sexy issues. By the end of what sociologist Arlie Hochschild calls the "second shift," when the children are asleep and the dishes are drying in the rack, most of us are too exhausted to rally for any chest-thumping, big-picture causes, nor would we know where to begin. By deputizing the individual woman as the primary agent of change, liberal feminism failed to fully weigh the burden of such a profound responsibility, perhaps at the expense of the fight for broader social change. No wonder radical feminists like Firestone wanted to implode the system from the inside out.

How Does a Feminist Do Laundry?

When John moved into my West Village apartment, bringing in tow an antique dresser, a couple of boxes, and a full laundry bag, the last thing on my mind was how we would split up the household chores. We were young and in love. We spent the weekend unpacking his belongings, lining up his toiletries next to mine on the bathroom sink, jubilant over how exciting it was to be in "our" home. It was an excitement that bathed even the most mundane tasks in a magical glow—grocery shopping, doing dishes, vacuum cleaning; every chore was fun, because we were doing it *together*, as a couple. But at some point, real life started to elbow itself into our domestic bliss. I was only twenty-four years old, and John was twenty-eight. Work consumed both of us, and by the time we reunited in our apartment every evening, we were both pretty much pooped.

Soon, a routine had ensnared us. Living alone, I had never watched television, but now it seemed the TV was *always* on, a third presence in our already crowded apartment. John would walk through the door after work, kicking off his shoes near the door, and collapse on our one couch. One click of the remote, and the sound of a laugh track dominated the room. I let it slide, understanding that this was his form of unwinding. With John lounging against one arm of the couch, I scrunched up against the other, trying to concentrate on whatever manuscript I was reading. Relationships were about compromise, right? Eventually, though, I started to call into question the mechanics of this so-called act of compromise. When John left his pizza boxes with several mangled slices on the coffee table, I deposited them in the garbage, asking him, "Sweetheart, could you please throw away your pizza boxes when you're finished?" always making sure to keep a honeyed tone in my voice. "Oh, sure," he would answer, nodding absently. "Sorry about that." And he would come over and plant a kiss on my forehead. Yet the pizza boxes still piled up. Once, in an experiment often tried by women everywhere, I let his dirty dishes sit in the sink, monitoring how long it would take him to put sponge to ceramic. (Answer: longer than it took to raise a nice crop of fuzzy green mold and an odor foul enough to make your eyes water.)

It was a balled-up sock, in the end, that pushed me over the edge. Back in his bachelor days, John would bring his dirty clothes to his

corner Laundromat every week, and they would return to him clean
and freshly folded on the very same day. I remember feeling semi-
impressed that he was so organized about it, while I lugged my own
laundry down to the basement every weekend, having to jockey for
a machine and keep watch over my clothes in the dryer. Laundry
had always been a much reviled all-day undertaking for me, but it
got worse after John moved in. Mysteriously, he stopped making trips
to the Laundromat and instead chucked his dirty clothes right into
the ham per with mine. Correction: He threw his dirty clothes near
or on top of the hamper. Somehow, those smelly little critters never
quite made it in, and I would pick them up with thumb and index
finger and plop them into the basket.

"John," I would say, "could you put your clothes in the hamper,
please, and not on the floor?"

Same answer. "Oh, sure. Sorry about that."

Same lack of result.

My irritation soon grew faster than mold on a dirty dish, as all
traces of sweetness curdled to outright bitterness. Not that I didn't
try to share the burden.

"John, could you do the laundry today?" I started to ask every
Sunday morning, my voice sounding brittle even to my own ears.
Engrossed in the Sunday *New York Times*, he would hardly raise his
head, muttering, "Yeah, I'll do it later." Hoping he would get the hint,
I would huff and puff, quietly rearranging the pillows, books, and
stacks of paper around him. I mean, who at twenty-four years old
wants to be a nag? Besides, I was hardly a neat freak, and, as my father will attest, I had at times in my life quite deservingly earned the
title of slob. But regardless of my subtle hints, inevitably, I would end
up doing our shared laundry myself—fuming and cursing under my
breath as I made my way to and from the bowels of our co-op building. Which is exactly what I was doing when, to put it bluntly, I lost
my shit. I had two manuscripts sitting in the apartment that had to
be read by Monday, but instead I was doing laundry—the same laun-

dry *John* had promised to do—because the towels, which he had left in a damp pile on the bathroom floor after showering, now stunk of mildew. Red faced and perspiring, I entered the apartment, arms filled with my third load of laundry, to find John lolling on the couch, chortling at some antic on the TV screen. I was already livid when my eyes landed on the offensive dirty sock balled up on the couch next to him. That did it. I had asked him no fewer than five times to pick up that very sock and put it in the hamper, yet there it contemptuously sat.

All at once the sock became emblematic of all my frustrations. I shot my worst glare in John's direction, but he was oblivious. Trembling now with fury, I dumped the laundry bag out onto the couch, and in his full view, I meticulously separated all his clothes into a pile. Then, with great aplomb, I gathered his clothes in my arms and threw them out the window. Not quite a revolution, but more than a spin dry.

John sat up and stared at me. Now I had his attention. "What did you do that for?" he asked, genuinely befuddled, which served only to enrage me further.

I faced him, arms akimbo. "From now on, do your own fucking laundry!" I barked. Then I spun around and marched into the bedroom, slamming the door behind me. I hurled myself onto the bed, then lay there for a while, staring at the wall. *I can't believe this is happening to me*, I thought to myself, unnerved by the depth and swiftness of my rage—far different from the enabling outrage at gender inequality I had felt in college. Dark, enervating, and quite honestly embarrassing, this was an anger for which I was not prepared. I had read about the oppression of housework, but always thought of it as some other woman's problem—you know, the dowdy hausfrau, not *mine*—and was now somewhat humiliated to find myself whining about dirty dishes and socks.

As I lay on the bed, going over what had just happened, I resolved that this was one battle I could not—or would not—surrender. I got off the bed and shuffled back to the living room. "Sorry I blew up," I apologized to John, who had gathered his clothes from outside and was folding them into a pile. "But I meant what I said. I am not your mother, and I'm not your maid, and if you don't start helping out around the apartment, then," I took a deep breath, "we can't live together."

"I'm sorry, too," he said. "I didn't realize." After that, things around the apartment improved dramatically, and without fail, John started doing his own laundry.

The "laundry incident" happened when John and I were in our twenties and running a household was relatively simple. Once Sylvia was born, though, we had to engage in an entirely new round of negotiations in the Housework Summit, only this time the demands were obviously greater and the stakes higher. We were married. We had a child. We had a house. Almost without realizing, I found myself picking up the baby slack around the house. As a nursing work-at-home mom, it was all too easy to take charge of the additional responsibilities and chores that come with having a baby—the feeding, the diapers, the laundry, the shopping, the nightly bath, the bedtime routine—until it simply became habit. The anger and resentment were still there, but sent underground, as if they had no right to be spoken.

Despite our best intentions, John and I initially divided our labor down classic sexist lines: I washed the dishes, wiped the counter tops, picked up the toys, threw away the rotting food in the fridge, paid the bills, replaced the toilet paper rolls, and the multitude of other necessary, but minor, tasks that can quickly take over the day. John staked out the bigger, rarer, and somewhat "sexier" chores: He took out the trash twice a week, unclogged the drains and gutters when needed, hauled the bulk trash out to the curb once a month, and changed the occasional burned-out lightbulb. I was too exhausted to fight the tide, but not the erosion. Forget about "issue fatigue"; we had a chronic case of "marriage fatigue." Few things will drain the romance out of a union faster than a sink full of dirty dishes waiting to be washed after putting a fidgety toddler to bed, night after night after night. We were so bogged down by the management of daily life that John and I had lost sight of the big picture—each other.

Eventually, John stopped asking about my writing assignments, not even bothering to read my articles when they came out. When he ate cereal in the morning, the sound of crunching reverberating in the silent kitchen, I had to restrain myself from grabbing the bowl away from him and dumping it over his head. I stopped answering when he asked me where to find the soap or toothpaste or Tylenol—and soon I worried the rage was warping me, perhaps permanently. I had always been quick to laugh and couldn't resist a joke, but my face was edging into a default scowl.

• • •

After months of repressed animosity, we decided we needed help. We were still living in Annapolis at the time, and a friend gave me a recommendation for a marriage counselor. That we were voluntarily going to sit in a therapist's office, ready to admit we had a problem, was testament in itself to the direness of our situation. Neither one of us was exactly a prime candidate for counseling. John is more math than verbal, and while close friends might describe me as chatty, therapy definitely wasn't my bag. My dad is from England, and my mom is from China, two cultures typically paired with phrases like "stiff upper lip" and "saving face." We were stoics. "Better to suffer silently" could have been my family's motto. As a child, I could be feverish, vomiting, and shivering with chills, and my father would hand me a couple of baby aspirin. "You'll live," he'd say. And when my sister went to see a psychologist to discuss a rash of panic attacks she experienced during her teens, my mother actually instructed her on the things she *couldn't* talk about.

So sitting next to John on the counselor's couch was like some version of hell to me. I kept my eyes trained forward, on Dr. Batz, a bespectacled man with flecks of gray at his temples and a completely unreadable expression that made me slightly nervous. I noticed my jaw was aching, clenched tight like some sort of steel trap. I tried to relax it.

"So what brings you here?" he asked.

Hoping to collect my thoughts and buy some time, I took a deep breath, exhaled, and forced my shoulders away from the territory of my ears. Dr. Batz leaned back in his leather desk chair and stared at the two of us, waiting with the patience of someone who makes $120 an hour.

"Well," I began, my voice thick. I glanced quickly at John, who was intensely studying his hands. "We need help."

There, I had said it. Dr. Batz nodded, his steady gaze unsettling, reptilian almost. Did the man ever blink? I continued to talk haltingly, plotting out the causes of my dissatisfaction, all the while tracing circles with my fingers on the couch, a tweedy olive-colored monstrosity from the 1970s. The story was one that he must have heard before— two people growing further and further apart, until they're merely rotating around each other, without ever quite connecting. I talked about fleeing New York for the safety and ease of Annapolis, but how the unexpected sense of isolation I felt only increased my need for attention and companionship. Suddenly, I wondered how many couples had sat in this very spot, trying to weave their fraying marriages back together or rip them asunder for good. I wondered how many couples had unleashed their disappointments in this tiny office, sealed away on the first floor of Dr. Batz's three-level colonial home, plucking tissues out of the boxes strategically placed on each end table, even as the domestic life of his family—a wife and two children, judging from the framed photographs on his desk—continued on upstairs.

John remained mute the whole time I was speaking, his blond hair flopped over one eye; I could tell he would have rather been anywhere but where he was. I began to wind my spiel down, and during a lull in my monologue, Dr. Batz finally spoke.

"Does he drink or do drugs?" he asked.

"No," I answered. "Nothing like that."

"Is he physically abusive?"

I shook my head vigorously. "No, of course not."

"Has he been unfaithful?"

"Not that I know of . . . no," I said, increasingly unnerved.

"Is he failing to provide for you and your daughter?"

What the *hell*? My face was hot. "No, he's a great father," I said evenly.

Dr. Batz shrugged. "So what's the problem, then? He seems like a nice, good-looking guy. . . . "

By now, my nervousness had dissipated, and I was officially pissed. "Perhaps a metaphor would help," I said, determined to keep my voice light. Leaning forward, my elbows pressing into my knees, I could practically feel John rolling his eyes. I had often pulled this same metaphor on him during our arguments. "So we have too many books and not enough shelves to put them all on," I said. My hands had left my lap for dramatic emphasis. "But whenever I suggest that we give some of the books away," I waved a hand in John's direction, "he refuses, not because he wants to *read* them, but just because he likes to have them on the shelf. You know what I mean?" I looked Dr. Batz in the eye now, searching for some sign of comprehension, but he remained unresponsive. "Anyway," I continued, "that's what I feel like. I feel like a book on the shelf that he likes to have around but has absolutely no interest in reading."

Dr. Batz's expression finally shifted slightly, and he gave me a bemused smile. "Have you ever seen *Kramer vs. Kramer*?" he asked.

Huh? "Yes," I answered cautiously, derailed by this weird detour. In fact, I distinctly remembered seeing the movie in the theater with my mother when I was around seven years old, around the same age as the boy in the movie. The film made a great impression on me, because at the time I could imagine nothing worse than having to choose between two divorcing parents. "Why?" I asked.

"Oh, it's just you remind me of the Meryl Streep character," he said, "that's all. You should maybe watch it again." He looked down at his watch. "Well, I'm afraid our time is up."

John rocketed off the couch.

Dr. Batz led us to the back door, and John and I followed the stone path that curved around the side of the house, stepping around the ten-speed bicycles strewn across the grass, to the driveway at the front of Dr. Batz's house, where our station wagon was parked. The sunlight was sharp in my eyes, and I welcomed getting under the shade of the car. Strapping the seatbelt across my chest, I thought I caught a glimpse of something in the side view mirror, but it was only my own reflection.

John started chuckling to himself as we pulled out of the driveway. "Really burned you up, that *Kramer vs. Kramer* comment, didn't it?" he said, and then added, "He was totally off base, by the way. I don't think you're Meryl Streep, and I think I know you a little bit better than Dr. Batz."

I smiled back. Then I started to laugh, too.

· · ·

Our next few visits to Dr. Batz had the strange effect of reuniting us against a common enemy. (Could this have been his secret counseling strategy? If so, it worked.) After a few sessions, John and I decided that we no longer needed the costly ministrations of Dr. Batz to help us through this rough patch in our marriage, and, besides, our grievances had been hung up and aired, all before a scrutinizing witness, and for the moment at least we felt lighter, more hopeful. We were excited about our impending move to New York, which also helped keep us on our best behavior. John would solicitously ask about my day and make an effort to unplug himself from his computer in the evenings so we could spend more time together as a family. I held back my snarky comments and recriminations and instead phrased my frustrations in the therapy speak of feelings, not accusations— "When you do this, I feel . . ."—and, attentive of what I was doing, he would respond in kind. And I have to say, for all my resistance, those therapists might be on to something, because things did slowly improve, especially after we moved back to the city.

One Friday night a couple of months after we had moved into our Brooklyn apartment, we stopped in the DVD rental place after dinner, looking for a movie to watch after Sylvia went to bed. Scanning the drama section, I happened upon a copy of *Kramer vs. Kramer*, and unable to resist, I grabbed it off the shelf, waving it at John.

"What do you think?" I raised my eyebrows. "Should we dare?"

"Sure, let's do it," he said.

Later that night, we got under the covers to watch *Kramer vs. Kramer* in our bedroom, and for almost two hours, I watched Dustin Hoffman's character discover the joys of fatherhood—who can forget the iconic French toast scene?—after his wife, my doppelganger, leaves him and their young son to find herself. It's a great film, funny and poignant, and I'll confess that I went through a box of tissues while watching it. But what hits me, beyond Dr. Batz's comparing me to a flaky mom who abandons her child, is that Meryl Streep is only in the movie for about fifteen minutes. Dr. Batz, in his comparison, had not even given me a starring role in my own goddamned drama.

I lay sprawled out next to John, mildly outraged, as the credits scrolled down the screen.

"Now if Dr. Batz had compared you to Dustin Hoffman being a spaz in the kitchen, he would have been on to something," John volunteered.

"What are you talking about?" I slapped him on the arm. "I'm a great cook."

"Remember how I found the oven manual still in your oven after I moved in?"

"That was, like, ten years ago."

"You had been living there for two years and didn't even know the manual was in the oven," he pointed out. "And don't forget the bacon-fat cookies that—"

I gave John a face full of pillow before he could launch into any more descriptions of my cooking calamities, and he responded with a counterattack, and soon all thoughts of Dr. Batz, and his anachronistic associations, had disappeared.

• • •

Over time, both John and I have learned that despite its apparent triviality, squabbling over who does the dishes every night can have serious consequences for a marriage. I have one friend who basically left her husband because, for all his obvious intelligence and advanced degrees, he could not seem to figure out how to hang up his wet bath towels.

"It's only a bath towel," he protested, as she packed her bags. "It's not that big a deal."

Well, yes, a bath towel is no big deal. But as any social scientist can tell you, there are such well-documented phenomena as the "tipping point" and the "aggregation effect," in which even the smallest transgressions—a bath towel here, a dirty sock there—can become magnified into a crime of epic proportions under the right (or wrong) circumstances. A wet bath towel consistently left on the floor over the course of years, seemingly immune to simple requests or angry demands to be picked up, becomes a call to arms in domestic warfare. Second-wave feminists, raised in an era of militant domesticity, knew this implicitly and highlighted the importance of domestic relations right away, putting it smack in the middle of their political agenda.

They understood that housework is largely about power and respect—not all the time, but often enough. Consider the way housework becomes a public slur, a weapon leveled against the woman who enters the public sphere and is told to iron some man's shirt or some other form of "get back in the kitchen, where you belong." While cooking and cleaning can sometimes be soothing, satisfying even, this is not about the triumphs of the occasional spring cleaning or the pleasure of a home-cooked meal; this is about housework being presented as some sort of genetic destiny.

For any woman who has ever felt a similar "domestic rage" and needs to know that she is not alone in her frustration, I recommend she pick up a copy of an essay called "The Politics of Housework" by Pat Mainardi, which was published back in 1970. "Participatory democracy begins at home," Mainardi writes. She goes on to describe how she proposed to her husband that they both share the housework; they both had careers and both paid the bills, so why not? It was only fair. Sure, he agreed good-naturedly. What follows is a hilarious list of all the ways her husband then tries to wriggle out of his duties. Some of my favorite highlights include:

"I don't mind sharing the work, but you'll have to show me how to do it."

Meaning: I ask a lot of questions, and you'll have to show me everything every time I do it because I don't remember so good. Also don't try to sit down and read while I'm doing my jobs because I'm going to annoy the hell out of you until it's easier to do them yourself.

"We have different standards, and why should I have to work to your standards? That's unfair."

Meaning: If I begin to get bugged by the dirt and crap, I will say, "This place sure is a sty" or "How can anyone live like this?" and wait for your reaction.

"I've got nothing against sharing the housework, but you can't make me do it on your schedule."

Meaning: Passive resistance. I'll do it when I damn well please, if at all. If my job is doing dishes, it's easier to do them once a week. If taking out laundry, once a month. If washing the floors, once a year. If you don't like it, do it yourself oftener, and then I won't do it at all.

And so on. But whereas second wavers, like Mainardi, instructed women en masse to question their domestic responsibilities as a political expression of feminism, third wavers and beyond are more circumspect about the issue of housework and less politicized, which perhaps makes sense. Today a woman's domestic prowess is far less tied to her identity, her sense of self, even as we continue to search for solutions to some of the very same issues our mothers faced in the home.

I Want a Wife

When John and I moved back to New York, our work lives underwent a major shift. John, newly entrepreneurial with another Internet company, had shifted into start-up mode. So, at the same time that we were unpacking and adjusting to the move, he was also dealing with meetings, conference calls, finding and renting office space in Manhattan, and all the unexpected crises you have to handle when you set up your own shop. There were the emergency calls at odd hours, when some piece of equipment broke down and he had to go into the office to fix it. Many nights I would wake up to find him next to me in bed on his laptop, his look of concentration visible in the glow of the screen, his bursts of furious typing like a flash rainstorm.

I understood that this all-consuming intensity of purpose was necessary in the early stages of starting a business, and I wanted to be as supportive as possible, but it wasn't always easy. "I feel like we have a third person in our bed," I told him more than once, and took to calling his computer Lola and his iPhone, another constant appendage, Lolita—my wan attempt to find the humor in the situation.

Meanwhile, in addition to teaching and writing, I had started working a regular gig as a freelance editor for an independent British publishing house, which meant that I, too, was setting up the home office, hooking up the printer and fax machine, opening up a FedEx account, and delving into a growing pile of manuscripts. Once John moved into his own office in Manhattan, and with Sylvia in full-day kindergarten and an after-school program until five o'clock, it became easier for me to concentrate on my own work during the day. Still, with the demands of two new jobs, we were really pressed. I was stuck, trying to figure out how to be accommodating of John's work, while not shortchanging my own or compromising the time I spent with Sylvia. So much for the "second shift." I was operating in four shifts, my workday usually ending sometime around two in the morning. I think I was sleeping, on average, about four hours a night, and so was John. This simply was our life, and we got used to it, but it took its toll.

My friend Kristen was astonished to learn this when I called her to complain about my exhaustion, and John's, too. "Really, it's no wonder you guys don't go completely off the deep end," she said. "I can't believe you don't have any help. You need a break, a date night, *something*. I'm getting online right now and sending you some numbers. Hire a regular babysitter, or at least someone to come in and clean the house every week! Believe me, it's money well spent."

She was right, and although such an expense would have been a luxury, it was not totally out of the question. Why didn't I hire some help? Was it from some outdated notion that I should—or could— "do it all"? Was it because I felt like I wasn't bringing in enough money to defend the cost? Was it because I suffered from some sort of liberal guilt and felt that I would be exploiting women who were less fortunate than I? Whatever the reason, my resistance exposed, in part, what has been called feminism's "dirty little secret."

• • •

Nearly a half century after Betty Friedan's prediction that things will seamlessly fall into place once women enter the workplace, the easy existence of the two–wage-earner family has been debunked by nearly every piece of empirical, anecdotal, and statistical evidence. Simply put, two parents cannot have full-time careers yet still enjoy the same perks of coming back to a pin-neat house, well-cared-for children, a healthy and home-cooked meal, and eight hours of sleep each night between freshly laundered sheets, not without someone else taking on some, if not all, of those tasks.

"*I* want a wife," my mother used to joke when I was growing up, swiping from, I later learned, a 1972 article in *Ms.* by Judy Syfers. You know, a "wife"—code word for someone to tend to you, cook your meals, take care of your children, clean the house, and fulfill your sexual needs. "My God," Syfers concludes in her article, "who *wouldn't* want a wife?"

The demand for a "wife" has only grown in recent years, as women have continued to pursue careers outside the home in record numbers, leaving behind the gaping need for help in keeping a family's domestic life running smoothly. Taking Friedan's advice, those with the inclination and the money hire other women to perform the services that were traditionally relegated to the wife—child care and housework. This has been taken to task as feminism for the elite, for it can have the unfortunate effect of resting on the backs of other women, who are not as wealthy or privileged. In the past few decades, the escalating demand for domestic labor has dovetailed nicely with globalization to facilitate a steady stream of third-world women, many of them leaving behind their own young children to come to the United States.

Popular stories like *Mary Poppins* and *The Nanny Diaries* ignore the issues of race and class entwined in the nanny business. Given the dynamics of power in this relationship, a number of women who come to this country are coerced into substandard, or even violent, conditions. Conferred none of the traditional rights of legal spouse, nor, in many cases, the benefits of paid employee, they straddle an ever-so-fine line between insider and outsider within an employer's private life—a virtual stranger, yet privy to the family's innermost workings. At the heart of this fragile arrangement is the triangle formed by the nanny, mother, and child. Working mothers with nannies often navigate a relationship laced with dependency and guilt in which the boundaries of acceptable behavior are fuzzy at best. And then there is always the implicit judgment of the mother as a parent: In Disney's *Mary Poppins*, the mother was a flighty suffragette. In *The Nanny Diaries*, she was a scheming socialite.

Even though both my parents worked full-time, I never had a nanny growing up, but I did have a string of occasional babysitters and various day cares. When I was around ten years old, however, my mother hired a live-in "housekeeper" who cleaned, cooked dinner, and cared for my sister after she was born. She was a middle-aged Chinese woman, and I, rather uncharitably, begrudged her for moving into the bedroom next to mine and taking away my mother's attention with animated conversations I couldn't even understand. My sister, on the other hand, was raised by this woman for most of her childhood and became quite close to her, as if she were another member of our family. When my mother and sister moved across the country to California, they stayed in occasional touch, speaking now and then over the phone, but over the years the calls became more infrequent. Eventually, the calls stopped altogether, and this woman who had raised her from infancy vanished from her life.

The plight of female domestic labor—nannies, maids, and sex workers—was not a major focus when I took Fem Texts in the 1990s, but in the interim, the hiring of such labor has gone increasingly mainstream, driven by the practical and economic realities that exist both here and abroad. Like my sister, several of the students in class had nannies, or grew up with regular household staff, and even if they didn't, popular culture and the media had introduced them to the many fraught issues involved. Before long, the conversation moved into the emotional calculus involved in hiring domestic labor. Even though Professor L. had assigned Barbara Ehrenreich and Arlie Russell Hochschild's *Global Woman*, which discusses in particular the forces of globalization on women workers in the developing world, the conversation had turned local, with Professor L. herself leading the way.

"A friend of mine was just crying the other day because she over-worked her nanny," Professor L. said, "and the nanny quit without notice. She kept saying to me, 'How could she do this to my child? She's supposed to love my child.' And I asked her, 'Why? Why is this woman supposed to love your child?'"

"One of my nannies just walked out without giving notice or anything because my mom dumped so much stuff on her," said Lisa. "She had to, like, scrub the floors—*and* take care of me and my brother."

Professor L. nodded her head. "So often the work is combined," she said, gaining steam. "And let's be clear. We're talking about the lowest forms of housework here, the kind that involves hands and knees and bodily effluvia. It's different from, say, dusting the mantle. This kind of work has never *not* been considered women's work. So it remains a sexist structure as much as it does now a classist one. Rather than force their husbands to do it, women will *pay* other *women* to do it."

"There have to be some disadvantages for the kids," said Mandy, who announced she had never had a nanny. "I mean, I'm sorry, but having a nanny *cannot* be as positive as having your own parents. And there's this thing called love, which complicates the issue."

"I have a confession," said Dani. "I'm getting my mother a maid for Christmas. Oh, God, that sounded awful. What I meant to say is, I'm hiring someone to come in and clean the house for a few months as a treat. Is that wrong?"

Before anyone could respond to Dani's question, Karen jumped in. "I'm not a bad person, but I think this whole antinanny and anti-maid position is sort of like people who say, 'I'm not going to eat meat because I don't believe in the poultry industry.' It's not like it's going to go away, so why *shouldn't* my family hire a maid?"

Professor L. shot Karen a stern look. "But that doesn't mean you have to ignore making possible structural changes to this relationship so that it's fair," she countered.

"Look," Karen said, in an agitated voice, "we had the same woman cleaning our house for years, and we were all really nice to her and paid her well and gave her bonuses and everything. So what's the problem with that? I think, as long as you're *nice* . . ."

"NO!" Professor L. insisted. "Being 'nice' is not enough!"

"Hey—my mother was a nanny, okay?" interjected Lucia, not even bothering to raise her hand, and by now looking completely disgusted with the conversation. She was one out of a mere handful of women of color in the room. "She was *always* complaining about the pay. It was amazing how many people tried to cheat her out of money. And then the condescension . . ."

"Well, yeah, that's wrong—sure," said Karen. "But what if you *don't* do that?"

Class was almost over, and I could see Professor L. straining to draw some sort of larger conclusion from the day's material. "You know, there are better ways to regulate this kind of work that protects women. And I just want to point out that our system is not the only system. Take Sweden, for example. They offer maternity and paternity leave, as well as universal day care. And immigrants are taught language skills and offered opportunities at subsidized education, so they aren't doomed to unskilled jobs. . . ."

Karen frowned and leaned over to whisper something in her girlfriend Anja's ear, and I thought I heard her say something like "Not the Sweden comparison!" but I couldn't be sure. Anja rubbed her shoulder.

"But there's something else to think about, too," Professor L. said, giving us a parting observation. "Remember, child care and housework used to *unify* women. It was important to second-wave feminism as a unifying force. But housework is now a divider by race, class, and immigrant culture. Is it really liberating for women to pursue a 'male pattern of work' if they're simply oppressing others in the process?"

Sexual Politics

. . . .

Indeed, the theme of division among women, rather than unity, had begun to permeate the readings, with more and more issues pitting woman against woman, particularly around the explosive issue of sex. In 1960, the FDA approved the first birth-control pill, which at last gave women a relatively safe and predictable method to control their own fertility. Then came the sexual revolution, which took place not only in the bedroom but in the courtroom as well. In 1965, the Supreme Court ruled that a Connecticut state law banning the sale of contraception to married couples was an unconstitutional invasion into the marital bedroom; a later decision, *Eisenstadt v. Baird*, extended this right to privacy not only to married couples but also to individuals. Finally, in 1973, a slim majority of the Supreme Court's black-robed and all-male justices held that a woman's right to an abortion fell within the penumbra of the right to privacy and was therefore constitutionally protected. This was an enormous win for feminists that altered the politics of reproduction in America.

Yet even while riding high on this victory, the feminist movement as a whole was coming apart. Second-wave feminists splintered into liberal, radical, and cultural feminists with one major rift developing along the fault line of pornography. The goals of women's liberation and the sexual revolution had initially coincided on the issues of legalizing contraception and abortion, temporarily muting any other disagreements and making for some strange bedfellows; Hugh Hefner, the founder of *Playboy*, even helped to fund feminist efforts on these two fronts. By the late 1970s, however, a group of feminists had banded together, including Gloria Steinem, Robin Morgan, and Susan Brownmiller, to actively fight against pornography. The antipornography camp took the position that not only were women degraded by pornography, but such images actually bred violence against women; as Robin Morgan put it, "Pornography is the theory; rape is the practice." At the same time, though, many feminists were encouraging women to explore and express their sexuality, and these activists saw the attack on pornography as predominantly antisex. The media's parroting of comments like "All intercourse is rape," attributed to radical feminist Andrea Dworkin, didn't help. By the time I entered college, the feminist antiporn camp had been well established. My own generation's position was a bit more undecided on the matter.

I first came across pornography when I was in sixth grade, and my best friend showed me her father's secret stash of *Playboy*, which he hid under the bed, along with a dog-eared copy of *The Joy of Sex*. We would spend afternoons lying on the shag rug in her parents' bedroom, flipping through the pictures, covering our faces with our hands to muffle our giggles, always alert for her mother's footsteps in the hallway. Already, at that age, we were beginning to test the line be-tween sexy and sex object, aiming for the former and trying to avoid the latter. The intricacies of sexy were complicated and confusing enough, and this was the early '80s—long before *Jenna Jameson, G-strings*, and *Brazilian bikini waxes* would become household words.

The prospect of entering junior high then—one more stepping-stone closer to adulthood—was at once thrilling and terrifying. I still vividly remember my first day of seventh grade. My palms were sweaty. I kept wiping them across my skirt, hoping not to leave a stain. I had spent hours the night before modeling all the clothes in my closet, searching for the perfect first-day-of-school outfit. I must have twirled in front of the long oval mirror hanging on my wall a hundred times, finally settling on a slouchy mint-green Esprit shirt that hung almost off one shoulder, *Flashdance*-style, a knee-length denim skirt, and high-top Reeboks with fluffy white socks. Come morning, I was regretting my choices. The halls of my new school were tunnel-like, smelling of an eye-stinging mix of ammonia and citrus, and I was surrounded by a crowd of faces—some of them fa-miliar, many of them not. I kept tugging on the shirt, pulling the neckline up to cover my bare shoulder.

Second period. Biology. I took a seat in the second row next to Gina, one of my friends from elementary school. Each of us relieved to rec-ognize a friend, a partner in this sea of strangeness, we claimed two desks right next to each other and compared schedules. I felt better. A few more recognizable faces trickled in, and the room soon filled with a buzz of chatter that immediately came to a stop when the teacher walked through the door. Mr. Lewis was middle-aged and had sunken eyes that were partially hidden behind the smoky lenses of his glasses. Something about his look, the way his eyes roved around the class, made me nervous. And now those blue eyes seemed to be fixed upon me.

"You," he said sharply, his finger pointed straight at me. "Come up, would you?" Exchanging a questioning glance with Gina, I dutifully stood up and walked to the front of the class. But the teacher's eyes were on the move again. "And you." He was now pointing at a boy, Peter, beckoning him forward. Mr. Lewis put his hands on my shoulders, his palms making direct contact with my skin, and propelled me forward, so that I was facing the class—right beside Peter. "What's the difference between these two?"

I shot a look of horror at Gina, who shook her head in sympathy. My whole body was burning as thirty pairs of eyes stared at me; already I could feel a telltale flush spreading across my neck and face.

Gina raised her hand. "Her name is Stephanie," she said boldly, "and his name is Peter." Much later, after taking women's studies classes, I would marvel at this instinct of hers to call out my name; I would also have the language to explain why I felt so defenseless, standing up there in front of my peers, reduced to a set of external characteristics, objectified. But at the time, I, too, reacted on impulse: I walked back to my desk and sat down. "I'm sorry," I said, "but I'm not participating in this. I really don't see the point."

Mr. Lewis raised his eyebrows at me. "Well, then, we can continue with you sitting down."

By the end of class, I was shaking with embarrassment and rage.

For the next three years, Mr. Lewis was my nemesis. Something about my undisguised dislike attracted him. As the faculty sponsor of the cheerleading team, he was constantly surrounded by a cadre of short-skirted girls. Some of them spent hours after school sitting on his lap, whispering in his ear. I was not one of those girls. I didn't inhabit my body that way, as a device, a weapon even. "Talk to me," he would say to us in class. "You can tell me *anything*, things you can't tell your parents. I'll understand." Sometimes, as a joke, he would snap a girl's bra strap.

Once, during class, his hand traveled down the back of my shirt, and I swung around. "*Quit* it, you pervert!" I blurted out, not knowing where I found the courage.

"Do you even know what that means?" he teased.

I whipped back around, hovering protectively over the rubber human heart on my desk and tried to ignore him.

Yet, all around me, girls fell sway to his spell. They talked about how cool he was, how witty and wise. He told them they were beautiful, and their eyes would light up like candles. I thought he was a creep, but I was definitely in the minority.

One afternoon, he sneaked up behind me in the hall. "Do you want to be a cheerleader?" he said in a hushed tone so close to my ear I could feel his breath. "You should try out. I'm one of the judges, you know."

I slammed the locker door. "No, thank you," I said.

With a grin, he suddenly lunged at me, picked me up, and slung me over his shoulder. He was a big man, well over six feet, and I was barely five-foot-four. I pounded on his back, demanding that he put me down, but he refused. The bell rang, and I was flailing wildly, screaming that he was making me late for my next class. Now people were staring. But not in the least bit perturbed, he carried me to my next class and deposited me at the door. I rushed inside. He swiveled his head around the corner and smiled at my Spanish teacher. "My fault she's late," he said, and then winked at me. I felt sick.

When I finally complained to the principal of the school, he told me that I was being "too sensitive." Yes, Mr. Lewis, had an "unusual" teaching style, but it was "incredibly effective." It was a different era. In any case, I let the matter drop and avoided Mr. Lewis as much as possible. Eventually, I moved on, to high school and beyond. Last I heard, Mr. Lewis had been arrested for statutory rape.

In his own inappropriate style, I suppose, Mr. Lewis introduced me to a crude form of sexual politics that has existed since the days of Eve. Along with English, biology, and algebra, then, I learned fast that a woman's body can be her power, but it can also be her downfall—and the shorter the skirt, the longer the fall. I had stepped into the classic female paradox, although, of course, I didn't think of it that way back then—none of us did. The crucible of puberty was no doubt confusing for everyone, male and female, and we were ill-equipped to point out any of these glaring contradictions. But we were quick to judge each other anyway as we scrambled to make up the rules of engagement.

As we got older, the girls got skinnier, slinkier, meaner, while the boys got denser, louder, more obnoxious. One girl I knew in elementary school turned from a sweet, plump kid with glasses into a skeletal teen squeezed into skintight clothes, her lips scarlet, her hair crimped into a perm. She walked alone between classes, eyes straight ahead, as if she couldn't hear the whispered rumors churning around her that she was turning tricks in the school parking lot. I watched her silently and wondered what had happened to her; I still do. No one wanted to be fodder for that kind of gab. Tales of drunken hookups and heated breakups spread through the school's institutional green halls with an almost viral intensity. Some girls were labeled "sluts," disparaged as objects of desire, while other girls were deemed "hot," and celebrated as virtually the same thing—and oh, how thin the line that divided the two. Sex *within* a relationship was acceptable; random sex was not.

But it wasn't usually about the sex, at least not for the girls I knew; sex with high school boys, after all, was not exactly a pleasure cruise. Rather, it was about fun, companionship, camaraderie, drama, intrigue, envy, fitting in, feeling special, and, perhaps most of all, control. Our bodies were simply the means to all this, something to be harnessed. On some basic level, we understood this, even if we couldn't quite articulate it.

• • •

In college, I would soon adopt the language of power, alienation, and objectification to express these processes. While my peers and I were dealing in the adolescent wrangling over sex, feminist principles had been steadily seeping into academia to interrogate even the most common representations of relations between the sexes. Consider the following passage from Henry Miller's *Sexus*:

I would ask her to prepare the bath for me. She would pretend to demur but she would do it just the same. One day, while I was seated in the tub soaping myself, I noticed that she had forgotten the towels. "Ida," I called, "bring me some towels!" She walked into the bathroom and handed me them. She had on a silk bathrobe and a pair of silk hose. As she stooped over the tub to put the towels on the rack her bathrobe slid open. I slid to my knees and buried my head in her muff. It happened so quickly that she didn't have time to rebel or even to pretend to rebel. In a moment I had her in the tub, stockings and all. I slipped the bathrobe off and threw it on the floor. I left the stockings on—it made her more lascivious looking, more the Cranach type. I lay back and pulled her on top of me. She was just like a bitch in heat, biting me all over, panting, gasping, wriggling like a worm on the hook. As we were drying ourselves, she bent over and began nibbling at my prick. I sat on the edge of the tub and she kneeled at my feet gobbling it. After a while I made her stand up, bend over; then I let her have it from the rear. She had a small juicy cunt, which fitted me like a glove. I bit the nape of her neck, the lobes of her ear, the sensitive spot on her shoulder, and as I pulled away I left the mark of my teeth on her beautiful white ass. Not a word spoken.

Kate Millett excerpted this particular passage to open *Sexual Politics*, a book that began as her doctoral dissertation at Columbia University and ended up becoming a best-seller when it was published in 1970. To expose sexism in literature, *Sexual Politics* takes the reader on a methodological tour through the fictional sex lives of a stable of male writers—Henry Miller, Norman Mailer, D. H. Lawrence, and, as counterpoise, the gay former prostitute Jean Genet. These men don't just write about sex, Millett contends; they glorify the male libido, but at the expense of women, who are treated as something less than human. For instance, regarding the Miller passage that acts as prelude to her book, Millett writes: "What the reader is vicariously experiencing at this juncture is a nearly supernatural sense of power—should the reader be male. For the passage is not only a vivacious and imaginative use of circumstance, detail, and context to evoke the excitations of sexual intercourse, it is also a male assertion of dominance over a weak, compliant, and rather unintelligent female. It is a case of sexual politics at the fundamental level of copulation."

In short—and this is the part that seems so accepted today, though back then it was considered a groundbreaking concept—there is a *political aspect to sex*. Obviously, sex and politics have been intertwined since the days of Eve, but never perhaps so overtly as in the recent past. In the 1970s, even as feminism was gaining ground, sex was shoved onto center stage—spotlighted as proof of our liberation as well as of our oppression. And this explicit pairing of sex and politics created a confounding maelstrom from which we are recovering still.

At the time, however, Millett's analysis of the patriarchy through literature was not yet well-trodden territory. Before *Sexual Politics* came out, no one in academia, not even feminist academics, had so thoroughly taken a feminist lens into their studies. The paradigm of aggressive male and submissive female was received as the natural dynamic between the sexes, and therefore rarely contested. Millett dared to ask those questions: How does a *woman* feel as she reads this scene? And if the voiceless, wriggling Ida is the male fantasy, what are the implications of such a fantasy for women?

"How many of us have seen that classic scene in the movies where the guy grabs the girl and she tries to pull away, but then melts in his arms?" asked Anja in class, during our discussion of *Sexual Politics*. "Who wrote that story? I mean—is that sexy? I guess, maybe. But it seems to take away a woman's agency, because, then, how do you say no? I mean, is this story imposed, or is it, like, a genuine feminine desire?"

Another student, Vanessa, languidly recrossed her legs, her long raven hair falling in a wave over one eye. "I guess I see a difference between saying no and not meaning it," she said, slowly, confidently, "and saying no and *meaning* it. Maybe Ida is just having a pleasurable sexual experience without the trappings of romantic love. Maybe by critiquing it as sexist, we're just moving into another realm of right and wrong. I mean, just because social systems create a desire doesn't mean it's not in its way authentic. It's like, why do we always interpret a scene like this as she's giving in to him and he's benefiting from her giving in? Maybe some women don't *want* to give up this ideal of woman because they derive some power from this image."

Did Vanessa just say *no doesn't mean no*? I waited for a swell of protest from my classmates, if not a lone objection. No one argued with her. I suppressed a groan. I could not believe we were back here *again*. Oh, my God, I thought, Mary Wollstonecraft would turn in her grave. If a woman feels a certain power in being sexually attractive, it's also a limited and refracted power, one that forces her to judge herself through the eyes of others; feminists throughout the ages have recognized and dismissed this little PR spin on "female power." The idea that Vanessa imputes such clout to Ida in this particular scene of Henry Miller's *Sexus*, a scene with which Millett chose to open *Sexual Politics* for a reason, struck me as ludicrous: Miller intentionally strips Ida of any voice. Her desires are beside the point. *His* pleasure is paramount, while she is little more than a body to be used. The next pages of Miller's novel only further demonstrate the narrator's relationship with his conquest, with such exchanges as the following:

"You don't really like me, do you?" Ida asks.

"I like this," said I, giving her a stiff jab. "I like your cunt, Ida . . . it's the best thing about you."

No one else in the class appeared fazed by this, which left me flummoxed. Suddenly, the generational distance between X and Y seemed immense. Sitting in the classroom, talking about sex and power, I realized just how much this generation had been steeped in ready sexuality. Although, to be honest, even I had been affected. I may not have scheduled a bikini wax before giving birth or installed a stripper pole in my home, but I had recently gone on a whim to a Saturday-afternoon burlesque dance class, thinking it might provide a bit of wanton fun after a friend of mine had raved about it. But where she had felt sexy, I felt silly. I couldn't skulk out of there fast enough, baseball cap pulled down low on my head, once the nipple tassels came out. What I realized that afternoon was that feeling sexy comes in many forms and registers—and twirling tassels, shimmying hips, and tiny thongs were most definitely not my forte, nor was I going to insist they be.

Still, the pressure to adopt this girl-gone-wild form of sexiness is relentless. Strippers and porn stars are celebrated as role models of female empowerment, goading women to applaud, if not emulate, their style. Journalist Ariel Levy, in her book *Female Chauvinist Pigs*, describes the rise of women who love raunch. Tougher, wiser, and way cooler than her "girly-girl" counterparts, the FCP can happily hang out with the boys, going to strip clubs, reading *Playboy*, and participating in all the other usual rites of objectifying women with the best of her male counterparts. But unlike her male pals, the FCP is both surveyor and surveyed. "The task then is to simultaneously show that you are not the same as the girly-girls in the videos and the Victoria Secret catalogs," writes Levy, "but that you approve of men's appreciation for them, and that possibly you too have some of that same sexy energy and underwear underneath all your aggression and wit. A passion for raunch covers all the bases."

Appearing sexually "liberated," it seems, has become a top priority among many young women. Whereas our most popular *Columbia Spectator* column circa 1991 was an ironic deconstruction of *Beverly Hills 90210*, college newspapers today feature student "sexperts," who graduate and go on to fashion whole careers out of giving sex advice. Young bloggers chronicle the vagaries of their own sex and dating adventures on campus, revealing the intimate, and usually depressing, details of every hookup. This kind of "sexposure" can lead to a honey pot of opportunities: book deals, columns, and media jobs that feed on notoriety. Then again, trading on lewdness has always been a lucrative business. What is new is that some would seem to be embracing it in the name of feminism.

Object Lesson

A woman with impossibly blonde hair and pneumatic breasts was moaning on the screen as she rubbed against her male costar, her bleached hair forming a shocking contrast to his tanned skin as it fanned across his stomach. Soon they were having jackhammer sex. The class twittered in nervous laughter. Most of the women in the class armored themselves with bravado, whispering to each other, and occasionally calling out comments to the screen; others fiddled uncomfortably in their seats, lips pursed. One woman, Eliza, turned tomato red and covered her eyes. "I can't watch," she apologized.

To discuss pornography, we were going straight to the source. Back when I took Fem Texts, which was starting to seem like the Dark Ages, we took a more scholarly approach to pornography. I remember my professor briefly describing, in words not images, certain depictions—a Mapplethorpe print, a *Playboy* spread, a snuff film— while the class debated where to draw the line separating art, or other types of expression, from pornography; discerning that line, however, no longer seemed a point of interest.

Dani had brought in *Strap-on Secretaries* from her own private collection, and much as the title suggests, within the first few min-

utes, the female star of the film had strapped on a dildo and penetrated her male costar from behind. Thankfully, we were spared too
much more. I was starting to feel a little woozy when Professor L.
shut off the film. Around me, the air was almost festive.

Is this empowerment? I asked myself for about the umpteenth
time. *Is this feminism?*

Not a chance, University of Michigan law professor Catherine Mac-
Kinnon, would say. In her slim volume *Only Words*, one of the day's
reading assignments, she argues that pornography should not fall
under the protective veil of free speech. MacKinnon sees pornography
as an extension of actual abuse—the pornographic act, and later the
pornographic material, repeatedly cleaving a woman from her body.
"Soon your experience is not real to you anymore, like a movie you
watch but cannot stop. This is women's version of life imitating art:
your life as the pornographer's text. . . . You learn to leave your body
and create someone else who takes over when you cannot stand it
anymore. You develop a self who is ingratiating and obsequious and
imitative and aggressively passive and silent—you learn, in a word,
femininity." MacKinnon can be a little intense, especially when writing about hot wax poured on nipples, of blood and bondage, and
her words don't have as much relevance in the case of *Strap-on
Secretaries*, since it is the woman in this porn film who wields the
fake penis. But still, whether violent or vanilla, dildo or no, pornography is still objectifying, right?

Dani, the purveyor of *Strap-on Secretaries*, had been itching to
speak ever since the lights came on. "I didn't like MacKinnon at all,
frankly. I mean, the fact is, most women in porn are participating as
consenting adults. So who are we to say that it's wrong? There's a
distinction between fantasy and reality that MacKinnon *completely*
ignores." She paused a moment between thoughts. "All in all, I think
the whole debate is kind of silly. Besides, porn is an economic opportunity for women who might otherwise be flipping burgers at a
minimum wage." A few heads nodded in agreement.

I studied Dani as she spoke. With her shoulder-length hair tied back in a ponytail and tortoiseshell glasses, she had a sort of mod-librarian look; occasionally, she wore plaid skirts with knee-high socks that on her looked more funky than provocative. Most of the time, though, she was dressed in sweats, with a tattered Jansport backpack strapped, either ironically or, perhaps, ergonomically, across both shoulders. She wasn't someone you would peg as owning *Strap-on Secretaries*. So picture my surprise when, during introductions on the first day of class, she announced that she worked as a dominatrix in an S&M den around Times Square for $250 an hour. When the other students heard this, they got excited—$250 an *hour!*—and a couple of them started asking very detailed questions about how to apply and what, exactly, she had to do besides pour herself into black leather. She quickly clarified that a dominatrix was not a prostitute, meaning she never had *sex* with her clients; she merely tortured, whipped, and, when necessary, peed on them. Her parents thought she had a well-stipended internship. She reported all this matter-of-factly, and the class laughed in open admiration.

Then Dani had turned serious. "I just think it's so brave," she said, "that these men—I mean, these are men with families, who have, you know, high-powered jobs—and yet they're taking this *incredible* risk to explore their sexual needs." At this, I almost started cracking up. Off the top of my head I can come up with a few things I think of as brave: taking photographs in a war zone, tackling a mugger holding up an old lady, getting up on stage when you have stage fright. Stopping at a sex joint in Times Square before heading home to your wife and kids in Westchester? Not so much. I waited for someone to disagree, but no one did, at least not aloud. They all had stars in their eyes, it seemed. Dani was a trailblazer, a hero—woman's studies major by day, dominatrix by night—and proud of it. They could not get enough of her tales from the trenches.

"You're a postmodern phenomenon!" exclaimed Professor L. "A women's studies major *and* a dominatrix."

"Weirdly, most of the dominatrices *are* women's studies majors," Dani replied.

Of course they are.

If my classmates were excited to hear about Dani's extracurricular activities, imagine how they engaged in this latest topic. For the next hour, I heard a lot of good things about porn, how it was "opening the channels of communication about sexuality" and "loosening the boundaries of normalcy." What I found interesting, however, was that *not one person* in the class uttered the word *objectification* during the discussion, almost as if objectification were a given, as natural as, say, intercourse itself. In college, my generation couldn't get enough of carving out private spaces and identities, but this generation has grown up in the age of public consumption, in which life can be viewed as one great, long reality-TV show. Their adolescence unfolded on MySpace and Facebook, where they could post photos, comments, even their innermost thoughts and feelings, for anyone to see. Perhaps with so many women today taking the lead in objectifying themselves, cries of objectification no longer carry the same resonance.

Now I've been around enough to know that it's not difficult to present the current porn culture in a positive way: women are co-opting pornography, and just as lesbians repossessed the word *dyke*, they are taking control of the process, strapping on the penis, both metaphorically and literally. But I don't believe it, not in my gut. For all its ubiquity and apparent praises, I simply can't find, in all these pieces of commercialized sex, a picture of empowerment.

"Pornography is not real sex," Professor L. had to remind the class several times when the students crept toward a conflation of the two. "Do we understand that?"

At last, Tamara piped up from the back of the room. A rather gaunt, curly-haired woman, she did not speak too often, but when she did, she always spoke with authority. "I *liked* MacKinnon," she said, her soft voice flecked with steel. "She is complicating the relationship between fantasy and reality." Listening to Tamara speak, her voice resolved, but also defensive, I saw how young women today are faced with a Hobson's choice of sorts—I mean, what woman doesn't want to be considered attractive? But given the current options, at least in this classroom, they could either worship porn stars and strippers in a showy display of their sexual self-confidence or side with the more uptight MacKinnon, who touts porn as sex discrimination. We were reading MacKinnon way back when I took Fem Texts in the '90s, and since then a spate of books had come out critiquing pornography without giving credence to the old antisex and proporn dichotomy— Levy's *Female Chauvinist Pigs*, for one. Where were they?

To make her point, Tamara had done some disturbing research. In *Only Words*, MacKinnon refers to a 1984 *Penthouse* spread in which Asian women were "trussed and hung." One of the models, bound between her legs with a thick rope, appeared to be a child. Not long after this particular issue was published, an eight-year-old Asian girl was found dead in North Carolina, after she had been sexually molested and strung up in a similar fashion, and MacKinnon calls on this incident to support her claim that porn creates a climate in which sexual violence can occur. We had also talked about this very same spread in tones of horror when I was an undergraduate, but I had never seen it. Fumbling with her computer, Tamara proceeded to project the spread onto the very same screen where not long before women with fake breasts were strapping on dildos. The picture came into focus. The scene clearly represented a lynching, the women naked, defenseless, hanging, their expressions blank as death.

The class looked at the images on the screen, darkness obscuring their faces as the computer's fan whirred in the background. Tamara's face was partially illuminated as she stood to the left of the screen, the shadows cutting angles into her cheeks, her eyes wide and expectant.

Then Dani spoke up. "That's really not so bad," she said. "I thought it would actually be worse."

• • •

The ancient Greeks first identified the mind-body problem, and we have been striving to apprehend it ever since. Women have had the hardest time with this divide, their bodies hijacked by popular culture, reshaped, and reflected back to them in a way that often deprives them of voice and desire. The word itself, *pornography*, derived from Greek, means "writing about prostitutes." Notice the word does not convey writing about *sex* per se, but is about those who partake in sex for money. No matter how you dress it up these days, pornography was originally created by and for men as a money-making enterprise. To be sure, many women also benefit financially from the porn industry, but offering up one's body to strangers, feigning sexual pleasure for an hourly wage, is an economic choice that really has nothing to do with female desire.

So how did porn become the embodiment of female empowerment? Obviously, not all pornography is the same. A panoply of porn exists to suit every taste, including the films of self-proclaimed feminist pornographers, like Candida Royale, who cater to a predominantly female audience. I know, too, that some women really enjoy watching porn and incorporating it into their sex lives in pleasurable ways—and more power to them. But I am thinking of the many more women, girls even, who seem to have squeezed themselves into the constrictive definition of *sexy* created by male-driven porn, who have waxed and moaned their ways to fake orgasms in bedrooms across the country, feeling, at best, the ephemeral sense of triumph that someone has found them "hot." I can't help but wonder if the current celebration of porn I saw displayed in the classroom has truly given young women a greater voice in their sexual lives or had the opposite effect.

Porn did not have nearly the same widespread popularity back when I was in college that it does today. I used to hear about occasional get-togethers to watch porn in someone's dorm room, usually hosted by a bunch of philosophy majors intent on deconstructing

Schindler's Fist or *Sperms of Endearment*. I never went to any myself, not to make a statement but simply because such gatherings
didn't interest me. By the time I graduated from college, any hard-
line attitudes toward porn were already softening. Women were
openly rejecting what they saw as the puritanical strain of '70s feminism, and, eager to parade their sexuality, they set out to prove
that women could be just as dirty and desirous as men. This was
not a bad thing, women wanting to take control of their own pleasure. But among the women I knew, I began to notice that those
most concerned with proving how sexy and empowered they were
actually enjoyed sex the least. They were trying so hard to fit this
sexy mold pushed by porn that they never asked themselves what
turns them on.

Genuine sexual desire, the mind-boggling chemistry of it, is messy,
awkward, unscripted, exhilarating, and, in its best moments, a tender
dance of desire. Porn relies on lights, cameras, and artifice. In twenty-
first-century America, however, it seems these distinctions are increasingly blurred, making it ever harder to distinguish between sex
and pornography. MacKinnon denounces the act of pornography as
alienating a woman from her body, so that she experiences what's
happening to her from a distance, as *if* it were on TV. Now it seems
the equation has flipped, so that the experience of sex between two
people may no longer feel right *unless* they have seen the same
moves on TV—or until they have seen their own experiences broad-
cast for everyone else.

The class on pornography left me worried about how the next generations of women—my daughter's generation in particular—will
pilot themselves through a culture that increasingly elevates this
conforming brand of raunchy sexiness above all others. I fear too
many girls and young women will not be able to shoulder the pressure
to play along as blatant sex objects; their own desires will be too confusing, too amorphous, too undeveloped at that age to manage the

role. Already so many girls suffer when faced with disaffection from their own bodies, entering into a battle of abuse with their own flesh, without being further encouraged by our culture to shortchange their talent for tart, all in the name of sex appeal.

For me, Fem Texts with Professor L. ended on this discordant note, and I left the class with the longing for feminism to direct a straighter course, if not for me, then for my daughter. In class, we had talked about the politics of sex, the power of sex, the promises of sex. We had fixated on that long, rattling caboose of implications that trails the physical act, but we had never addressed the passion or pleasure of sex, nor its very heart—desire.

PART IV
DESIRE

And the trouble is, if you don't risk anything, you risk even more.

—ERICA JONG

Fear of Flying

On campus, spring arrived. Bright-green buds burst from the branches of the trees; bodies lounged on the steps of Low Library, spreading onto the grassy lawns separated by brick walkways. Three shirtless boys played Frisbee in the rectangular field across from Butler Library, their T-shirts flying from the waistbands of their shorts so they hung like white cotton tails, their exposed skin still winter pale. A couple smooched on the sidelines, hands roaming each other's bodies, without a shred of self-consciousness. I strolled to class, taking my own sweet time, a warm breeze wrapping around my legs, deliciously bare in the sunshine. All of us seemed to be colluding in a bacchanalian rite brought on by soaring temperatures and the scent of cherry blossoms and lilacs in bloom.

Blame it on spring fever, but instead of reading our next assignment, a philosophical article by French feminist Hélène Cixous, I had gone off syllabus and immersed myself in Erica Jong's *Fear of Flying* instead. I figured it was a groundbreaking feminist classic in its own right, hailed as one of the first erotic novels written by a woman to explore female desire, and besides, in the wake of *Sexual Politics* and all that porn, I needed to detox. I was hankering for the kind of realistic portrayal of life's nuances only fiction can provide.

Published in 1973, *Fear of Flying* introduced Isadora Wing, a heroine who unapologetically takes up the mantle of her own desire—she has affairs, enjoys sex, and, my God, *lives* to tell the tale. With *Fear of Flying*, "feminist" and "funny" were linked, joyfully, in the same sentence, paving the way for more successful and sex-driven, if slightly neurotic, female characters. "See," I reassured myself as I climbed up the three flights of stairs to class, sandals slapping on the linoleum, "I am sticking to my feminist journey, just in my own way." Even so, I slunk into class, wondering if I should at least try to skim Cixous's article before we began.

As I took my seat I noticed that many of the other students were doing exactly that. In addition to suffering from spring fever, we had, I sensed, officially hit the midsemester slump. Over the course of the semester, the fresh faces and stylish clothes had given way to sweat-pants and shorts, as the women came into the classroom, dark circles ringing their eyes, fingers clutching thermoses of coffee—a lifeline to wakefulness. But if anyone could keep us engaged in the discussion, it was Professor H., an English professor who entered college in 1968, right as feminism was gaining momentum on the ground.

Professor H. had conducted all of our class conversations with graceful compassion, encouraging us to continue our weekly discussions outside the classroom—as well as to collaborate with each other on projects and ideas. "I'm a proponent of forming coalitions," she had told us on more than one occasion. For Professor H., feminism was not merely a subject to be studied but a *movement*, in every sense of the word. And she seemed especially determined to help us find a blueprint for living rewarding lives.

Unlike T. and Professor L., both of whom were roughly of my generation, Professor H. was *there* during the 1960s and 1970s. Having actually witnessed some of the events of second-wave feminism that later generations could only read about in books or see dramatized in a TV miniseries, she lacked a certain cynical edge that had sometimes emerged with the other professors. They could rattle off the major points of the decade—the civil rights movement, the Vietnam War, Woodstock—but from across the distance of years, they seemed unable to convey fully that incendiary fusion of anger and hope. Sequestered in our fluorescent-lit classroom, we were performing a clumsy autopsy on a movement we never really knew. What we needed was someone to bring that era to life for us, and Professor H. did exactly that.

Nevertheless, Professor H had her work cut out for her. The course reading had become denser, more abstract, and at times contradictory, and as we wandered deeper into the theoretical hinterlands, even Professor H. was having trouble stirring the class. Earlier waves of feminism had been more uncomplicated in their goals—education, suffrage, economic equality—while later objectives were murkier, more elusive. The radical feminism and liberal feminism of the 1970s had given way to the more recent trends in poststructuralist and postmodern feminisms aimed at parsing women's oppression, and as a result, our discussions were moving further and further away from the experience of everyday life, despite Professor H.'s valiant attempts to bring them together.

This morning, Professor H. was writing the following words on the board:

Phallus   *Phallocentrism*   *Phallogocentrism*

She translated. The *phallus* was the abstract power the penis represents; *phallocentrism* was the cultural cult of the phallus; *phallogocentrism* was the phallus-oriented nature of language itself. In linguistics, there is the "sign," or the written word (for example, *penis*), then the "signifier" (or the actual penis), and finally the "signified" (or the *idea* of the penis). Penises, both literally and figuratively, have been tied directly into feminism's battle to reclaim women's desire ever since Sigmund Freud famously identified the male sex organ as the root of female trouble: *What do women want?* Why, a penis—which, of course, they don't have! Not surprisingly, the casual, unsubstantiated assumption of penis envy has been burning up many feminist academics for, oh, the past hundred years or so.

But not all psychoanalysts subscribed to Freud's theory. One of the most prominent Freud revisionists, French psychoanalyst Jacques Lacan, advocated a more linguistic approach to the cult of the penis. Lacan believed that human beings encounter a deep split when they begin to use language, or, as he describes the process, when they "enter language." The result is a sense of exteriority, or estrangement. Because language is always metaphorical, a gap springs up between expressing a want and receiving its answer, rendering language an inadequate mode of expression. For Lacan, our desire is always for *jouissance*, a term that refers both to orgasm and to a state of blissful, ecstatic union that would complete us by healing the "split" that occurred when we entered language. But this desire is nothing more than wishful thinking. Women don't want an actual penis, as Freud suggests, but want the power that comes along with it—and not just women, but men, too. Men may have penises, but they do not have the *phallus*; none of us really does, leaving us all caught up—men and women both—in a never-ending game of Find the Phallus.

As if all these real and imaginary phalluses filling the room weren't distracting enough, here came Cixous, a poststructuralist feminist, who marked out language itself as a feminist battleground. In her 1975 article "The Laugh of the Medusa" (originally published in French), Cixous exhorts woman to "put herself into the text—as into the world and into history—by her own movement." Her prose is high voltage. She tells women to write, write, write! If women are the dark conti-nent, as Freud once claimed, then we should revel in the power of darkness. If woman is cast as Medusa, as "the supreme talisman who provides the image of castration—associated in the child's mind with the discovery of maternal sexuality—and its denial," as Freud professed, Cixous orders us to take that supposition and turn it on its head: Look at Medusa straight on, and you'll see—she's beautiful, and she's laughing.

"There is something empowering about taking this myth and challenging ourselves to adopt a different interpretation. This applies to language, too—for instance, the word *voler* means both to fly and to steal," said Professor H., getting excited now. "Imagine feminism as the little patches of grass growing in the pavement—if we allow it to grow, then eventually the pavement will crack. This is what Cixous is saying, she's saying, 'Let's change language itself—let's explore the cracks.'" Professor H. paused, deciding on the tack she wanted to take next, as twenty faces stared blankly back at her. "Cixous is urging us to adopt a positive femininity—she's written a type of manifesto here. Basically, she sees inequities embedded in language itself. And so she wants women to write from the body—to reclaim the body and get beyond the reverse discourse. She is saying let's write in white ink, in mother's milk."

Are you kidding? I thought to myself crankily. I was all for coming up with a positive model of femininity—it's what I reentered the gates of my alma mater in search of—but writing in mother's milk . . . What does that even mean?

The windows of the classroom were open, and that seductive breeze wafted in again, heavy with nectar and exhaust. My thoughts started to wander off as I stared out the window. Fanning myself with my notebook, I imagined writing in the translucent ink of mother's milk, my mind tripping over a literal extrapolation of the image. First of all, no one would see it, and second—wouldn't it start to kind of smell bad after a day or two? I scrunched up my nose and suppressed the audible snicker rising to my lips.

Meanwhile, Professor H. was looking at the class hopefully to see if we were getting it, and I really wanted to get it. I sort of adored Professor H. and felt the pressing need to please, which was surely due to my abundant mother issues. Yet I couldn't deny that I was lost; we all were.

As if reading my mind, one student blurted out, "Honestly, the more women's studies classes I take, the more confused I become," and dropped her head in her hands.

Professor H. smiled patiently and rearranged the aquamarine silk scarf tied loosely around her neck. "Well, let's see if we can clear up some of the confusion before the semester ends," she said.

• • •

Over the next few days, I kept trying to read Cixous, but I was having trouble, and not only because the essay itself was abstract and dense, but because life kept getting in the way. I had been determined to continue my normal existence while I took Fem Texts—to traverse the gap between theory and practice, so to speak—yet there always seemed to be some demand or work crisis cropping up that took me away from my reading, right as I was getting comfortable on the couch. I was switching from Cixous to the nightly bedtime ritual, from Freud to food shopping at Trader Joe's. The result was a sort of cognitive dissonance, as I struggled to make the connections. Cixous was pushing me to "fly the coop, take pleasure in jumbling the order of space, in disorienting it, in changing around the furniture, dislocating things and values, breaking them all up, emptying structures, and turning propriety upside down." I could barely get dinner on the table.

That Friday night, Jenny, Tasha, and I made plans to meet at a crowded Soho restaurant. Although we now all lived in the same city, Tasha had an infant and a toddler, and we rarely found the time to get together—just the three of us—without a husband or child in tow. But this was a special occasion. About a year ago, after many months of marriage counseling and several reconciliation attempts, Jenny had decided to separate from her husband. They had been living apart for some time, and today, at last, the divorce had been finalized. Before dinner, Tasha and I had convened to debrief at the bar, while we waited for Jenny to arrive.

"How's she doing?" I asked.

"She sounded okay when I spoke with her, but it's hard to tell."

Right then, Jenny walked through the door. Dressed in black skinny pants and a silk shirt, her hair curled and makeup expertly applied, she looked fantastic. I noticed the two businessmen sitting next to us at the bar turn slightly to stare, their conversation slowing to a near stop. Jenny caught sight of us and flashed us a smile, waving us over to join her.

"Somehow I don't think we have to worry about her," Tasha said, sliding off the bar stool.

Before the breadbasket was even empty, we were giggling like we were in our twenties again, and by the end of the appetizers, the conversation had turned to relationships and sex. Jenny was telling us about a flirtation with a movie producer she had met at a party a couple of weeks ago. They had been in a holding pattern of exchanging coy e-mails for a few days now, and he was pushing for a date. She admitted she was intrigued, but also a bit gun shy after her divorce. "I know I'm the one who left," she said, "but the whole thing has still majorly messed with my self-esteem. I keep wondering if maybe some sexier, better version of me would have been able to convince him not to be such a workaholic."

"No!" Tasha and I cried simultaneously.

"This producer guy sounds promising," said Tasha. "Go out with him and just enjoy yourself—you deserve it! I think it'll be good for you."

"I think I will," Jenny said, then leaned in conspiratorially. "But I have to say, the thought of being naked in front of a new person is terrifying."

Tasha and I nodded, but even though we could understand her hesitation, we egged her on anyway. Jenny was our single alter ego, an adventurer in the realm of sexual possibility.

"What if I'm the last woman with pubic hair?" she asked.

"Let's hope not," said Tasha.

"Seriously," I said, taking a swig of wine. "A zipless fuck. That's what you need."

Jenny shrieked in delight. "Erica Jong! Oh, my God, I remember reading that book in junior high!" She sat back in her chair. "The zipless fuck," she repeated, shaking her head.

I had also read *Fear of Flying* back in junior high. Drawn in by the cover with its naked, shapely torso revealed behind a declining zipper, I had checked the book out of the library one Saturday, probably in search of sex scenes à la Jackie Collins. Was I disappointed when I later scoured the pages under the cover of my duvet. At the age of fourteen, I was not at all prepared for Isadora's circuitous debates over whether to leave her laconic husband for the roguish Adrian Goodlove. (In one of my favorite lines in the book, Isadora explains how it was her husband's quiet nature that first attracted her: "How did I know that a few years later, I'd feel like I was fucking Helen Keller?") For all its vaunted sexuality and the promise of that prurient cover, I soon discovered there was a lot of talk in *Fear of Flying* but not much action.

Reading *Fear of Flying* again twenty years later, however, I was riveted. Isadora's meditations, which expose and examine a modern woman's anxiety over her plenitude of choices, are satisfyingly familiar. *Now* I could relate. As for the zipless fuck, Jong has both less in mind and more in the act she made so famous. The zipless fuck is so named because, joining in an embrace, "zippers fell away like rose petals, underwear blew off in one breath like dandelion fluff. Tongues intertwined and turned liquid. Your whole soul flowed out through your tongue, and into the mouth of your lover." Throughout the novel, the zipless fuck hovers in the background, a restless fantasy in our heroine's imagination, but one that is never consummated. The sex in *Fear of Flying* is, in fact, secondary—metaphorical for a whole landscape of female desire: the longing to fly, to soar, checked only by desire's shadow, which is fear, the consuming dread of coming too close to the sun, like Icarus, then plunging back to earth, bruised and broken. Safer to stay on the ground—but, wait, what if a world of wonder awaits us in the sky? And so 'round and 'round we go, torn in different directions by our conflicting desires.

Tasha had never read *Fear of Flying*, so Jenny and I gave her a quick sketch of the plot. Isadora is a twice-married graduate school dropout—she's sexy, neurotic, intelligent, think version 1.0 of *Sex and the City*'s Carrie Bradshaw. With her writing career stalled and her marriage to a psychoanalyst gone stale, Isadora finds herself attracted to a man she meets while accompanying her husband to a conference in Vienna—home, not coincidentally, of Freud. Soon Isadora is caught between these two men, one of whom surely will lead her into happily ever after, if only she can figure out which one. In truth, Isadora is really wrestling with herself and what kind of life she wants to lead: Upper West Side wife? Bohemian poet? A '70s woman, she understands the folly in waiting for Prince Charming to take her away from the mental spinning in her head, but she can't stop herself. She deliberates between her husband, Bennett, and her lover, Adrian, swinging back and forth like some mad pendulum, and the ending, though ambiguous, shows an Isadora finally facing her uncertainty without fear.

"Sometimes I feel like not all that much has changed for women," Jenny said. She paused. "So I have to tell you guys something."

We looked at her, waiting.

"I'm moving to L.A."

"Wait a minute," I said. "Back up—*what*?"

"I'm going to try to break into TV writing—you know I've always wanted to—and, well, I decided it was now or never. I might be back here in a few months, but I have to at least try."

Tasha put down her glass. "Wow," she said.

"I've realized a lot about myself since the divorce," Jenny said. "I don't really want to get married again, and I don't think I want children, either. I almost talked myself into wanting those things, but I don't . . . I mean, I want relationships, of course, and I love being the fun aunt to my brother's kids—but that life just isn't for me, you know?"

"This calls for more wine," I said, flagging down the waitress. Jenny stood up and stretched. "I'm going to go out for a smoke break."

"I can't believe she's leaving," Tasha said, after she had left the table.

We watched Jenny through the restaurant window, as she borrowed a light from another smoker. She said something to him, and he laughed; then he stepped closer to her, his head tipping toward hers as he spoke, and she threw her head back and laughed, too.

"This might sound crazy," Tasha said, "but you know, I'm a little jealous."

"Yeah," I nodded. "So am I."

• • •

After dinner, Jenny stayed in Manhattan, while Tasha and I took the subway to Brooklyn. Jenny's announcement had put me in a strange mood, and after Tasha and I parted ways on the street, I decided to stop for a frozen yogurt before going home. The place was packed, filled with teenagers and college students swaggering and preening, following the steps of some ravenous mating ritual I had long since forgotten. As I spooned up my frozen yogurt under the glare of the bright lights, while rock music throbbed from the speakers, the thought crossed my mind that I would never again experience that same thrill of discovering the pleasures of sex and intimacy. The insight nearly knocked the breath out of me. I suddenly felt old, invisible to the youthful throng surrounding me, but the moment passed.

To be sure, the physical trials of pregnancy, childbirth, and nursing had changed my relationship to sex, as well as to my own body. Sex, though still important, was no longer the centerpiece of my life the way it had been in my late teens and twenties. Shortly after Sylvia was born, I gave a reading at a bookstore on the Upper West Side. A friend, who was a few years younger than me, came over to say hello and to congratulate me on the birth of my daughter. "Sooooo," she stage-whispered in my ear, "when do you get to have sex again?" She seemed so young, so vibrant, so *concerned*. Her question caught me off guard. "Um, not for a few weeks at least," I said, trying not to shudder. Having sex was about the last thing I wanted to think about in the wake of squeezing out the eight-pound baby I was now nursing several times a day. "Oh," she smiled sympathetically, "That's a *long* time . . ."

Not long enough, I thought.

At the end of the evening, I shared a taxi home with two of John's friends who had come to offer moral support in place of John who was at home watching Sylvia. We piled into the backseat and soon were skidding down a rain-slick Broadway.

"You look great," said Ed, turning toward me. "John said that . . ." His voice trailed off. I spotted Paul, who was sitting between us, elbowing him surreptitiously in the side.

"Said what?" I asked suspiciously, pitching myself forward to look at Ed.

"Dude," muttered Paul, shaking his head, "what were you thinking?"

"Tell me," I demanded.

"Oh, nothing bad," Ed said, backpedaling for dear life. "He just said . . . I don't know, that you looked . . . matronly."

"*What?*" I screeched.

"Maybe that wasn't exactly the word he used," Ed said.

Paul was still shaking his head, whispering, "Dude, shut up, just *shut up.*"

We didn't speak much after that. The taxi dropped me off, and I stormed into the apartment to find John standing in the middle of our living room, Sylvia draped belly down across his forearm, her head in his palm, her skinny arms and legs dangling limply in the air. She was fast asleep. He put a finger to his lips. I tiptoed over, gave Sylvia a kiss on the downy top of her head, and kept my mouth shut.

But a couple of days later, I couldn't hold it back any longer. "Really, John? *Matronly?*"

"But that's not what I said!"

"Oh, then what *did* you say?"

"I said, uh, that you looked like a mom," he said, adding, "Which you *are*. It's a good thing."

I was momentarily confused. John was right—I was a mom, and a nursing mom at that, which meant I had a baby attached to me for most of my waking hours. Never before had I experienced such constant touch, such pressing need; motherhood had vanquished all thoughts of sex, and even the prospect of being sexy, from my mind for the foreseeable future. Despite the media carnival of sexy moms, motherhood and sexual desire, for me at least, seemed like a contradiction in the beginning. For that first year after Sylvia was born, the desire lay mostly buried by the landslide of physical and psychological demands of parenthood. But that didn't mean I wouldn't balk at being told I looked like a mom, at the implied denial of my sexual self. I worried that side of me might disappear forever; to my relief, it didn't. I inhabited my body again as one capable of desire, as desirable, accepting the marks of age and motherhood as beautiful badges of honor. To quote Jong's Isadora, "A nice body. Mine. I decided to keep it."

• • •

After finally sitting down and reading Cixous, I concluded that my secret assignation with Erica Jong had been serendipitous—for the two of them actually fit together nicely. Cixous is pushing women to find their own voices, to capture their own desires. "Decide for yourself on your position in the arena of contradictions where pleasure and reality embrace," she urges, adding, "When I write, it's everything that we don't know we can be that is written out of me, without exclusions, without stipulation, and everything we will be calls us to the unflagging, intoxicating, unappeasable search for love. In one another we will never be lacking." If Cixous created the manifesto for why women should write, should *fly*, then Jong chronicled the accompanying emotional journey in *The Fear of Flying*. Isadora may not know whether her desires are fully her own, or a reflection of male images of women's sexuality, but nonetheless she sets out to write, however falteringly, the script of her own desire, in her own words.

Dora

Desire. What *is* desire? When confronted with this question in class one day, Professor H. had walked up to the chalkboard and scratched out the following:

$$\text{Demand} - \text{Need} = \text{Desire}$$

We were back to Lacan, and, on the face of it, his equation had a soothing mathematical cleanliness that belies the fickle, mysterious nature of desire—and not just the peculiar brand of sexual desire. Desire, after all, spans the whole of human experience; it forms wheels and chains with other impulses, rising and falling in varying synchronicities. To further complicate the nature of the beast, our "organic" desires are layered with a host of "artificial" desires formed through cultural expectations, social pressures, advertising. Big and small desires pulse throughout our everyday life like so much background music. Sometimes we listen; sometimes we don't. Problems develop, however, when one desire conflicts with another. You want to go on vacation, but you also want to save money; you want to get a promotion at work, but you also want to spend more time with your children; you care about your spouse and don't want to hurt your family, but you have fallen desperately in love with your coworker. You get the drift. As our desires criss and cross, it gets more difficult to make out in the rumpus what we truly want rather than what we *should* want. But here's the kicker: The Lacanian precept insists that demand must always outstrip need; otherwise, a desire fulfilled ceases to be a desire at all.

Freud, of course, had his own ideas about female desire, incriminating sexual repression and dysfunction for causing a host of psychological disorders ranging from hysteria to the Oedipus complex to yet more penis envy. His classic study of female hysteria, *Dora*, which we also discussed in Fem Texts when I was an undergraduate, continues to show up on the syllabus, mainly to provide context for later feminist critiques—even Jong's *Fear of Flying*, with its heroine, Isadora, establishes itself as a rebuke to Freud. Although I admire many of Freud's writings, I am most definitely not a fan of *Dora*, neither then nor, as it turns out, now.

Dora chronicles the psychoanalysis of an eighteen-year-old woman named Ida Bauer, a.k.a. Dora, who entered Freud's care at the turn of the twentieth century. Since the age of eight, Dora had been experiencing various "nervous" episodes, including bouts of depression, migraine headaches, and chronic coughing fits, which, quite symbolically, would lead her to lose her voice for weeks on end. She had already endured countless therapies and medical exams when her father, Herr Bauer, insisted she undergo psychoanalysis with Freud.

As Herr Bauer explained to Freud, a schoolgirl fantasy was to blame for his daughter's latest fit. Dora had openly accused one of their closest family friends, Herr K., of propositioning her for sex while she was staying at his lake house. Herr K. had emphatically denied the charge, implying instead that Dora herself might be sexually deviant. Given his daughter's unstable mental history, Dora's father chose to believe his friend over his daughter and wanted to make the whole affair go away, but Dora was making this impossible. She ordered her father to break off all ties with the K family in light of Herr K.'s impropriety. When he refused, calling the episode a figment of her imagination, Dora became hysterical and threatened suicide, which in turn prompted her father to visit Freud's office.

"Please," Herr Bauer begged Freud, "try to bring her to reason."

Freud, once he agreed to treat Dora for her hysteria, came up with his own plans for this "girl of intelligent and engaging looks" as she began to answer his probing questions, stringing together a tale of operatic proportions. In the case history, Freud notes that Dora first became her father's caretaker at the age of six, when he fell ill with what she would later learn was syphilis, one of the venereal diseases running rampant through fin de siècle Vienna. As a result of his illness, father and daughter formed an unusually close relationship, while Dora's mother, whom Freud describes as cold and distant, suffered silently from "housewife psychosis"—Freud's version, it would seem, of Friedan's "problem that has no name"—a disorder in which a woman cleans house to such an obsessive degree that no one can relax for fear of dirtying something.

Dora eventually discovered that her father and Herr K.'s wife were having an affair, although she continued to be quite fond of the Ks and their children—until the incident at the lake, which, she confided to Freud, was not Herr K.'s first advance. When she was fourteen years old, Herr K. had grabbed her while they were alone in his office and kissed her. Dora had pushed him away in disgust and run, an action that Freud interprets as a repression of her true feelings. For Freud, *no* never actually means *no*, but merely obfuscates some subconscious desire. "I should without question consider a person hysterical," he writes, "in whom an occasion for sexual excitement

elicited feelings that were preponderantly or exclusively unpleasur-
able." As he dug further into Dora's history and her two recurring
dreams, which are the focus of his case study, he assembled the os-
tensible symbols from her dreams and her narrated story into what
he believed was a cohesive analysis of Dora's condition.

On one occasion, Dora told him that her father was impotent, and
Freud asked how, then, he could possibly be having an affair with
Frau K. Her answer was exactly as he hoped. Freud writes:

> She knew very well, she said, that there was more than one way
> of obtaining sexual gratification. . . . I questioned her further,
> whether she referred to the use of organs other than the genitals
> for the purpose of sexual intercourse, and she replied in the affir-
> mative. I could then go on to say that in that case she must be
> thinking of precisely those parts of the body which in her case
> were in a state of imitation—the throat and oral cavity. To be sure,
> she would not hear of going so far as this in recognizing her own
> thoughts. . . . But the conclusion was inevitable that with her spas-
> modic cough, which, as is usual, was referred for its exciting cause
> to a tickling in her throat, she pictured to herself a scene of sexual
> gratification per os between the two people whose love-affair oc-
> cupied her mind so incessantly. A very short time after she had
> tacitly accepted this explanation her cough vanished—which fitted
> in very well with my view.

Now, I'll willingly concede that the mind works in strange and
mysterious ways, but I nevertheless have a hard time attributing
Dora's cough to some covert imagining of her father getting a blow
job. As Freud would have it, *no one* was spared from poor Dora's tortured and subliminal affections—except perhaps her own mother:
Dora was obsessively in love with her father, Herr K., Frau K., and
even Freud himself; it was a veritable love hexagon. Dora, of course,
resisted Freud's clever analysis, as psychoanalyst and patient engaged

in a pas de deux. But such denials only reinforced his conviction that she was fundamentally repressed, her protests themselves becoming evidence of this.

No matter what she said or did, Freud describes this girl as a hotbed of subterranean passion, of water and fire, anger and vengeance, and ultimately she took her "revenge," as he puts it, by abruptly ending her treatment with him after just three months. In the postscript, Freud informs us that Dora got back at Herr K., too, by confronting him and forcing him to admit to his sexual advances. The news that his young patient was telling the truth all along is irrelevant to Freud. He never entertains the possibility that Dora could have genuinely been disgusted at being fondled by a family friend more than twice her age, nor does he acknowledge that having your father call you a crazy liar, even as you're telling the truth, could send you into despair. Also galling is Freud's conviction—for all his caveats that *Dora* is incomplete, is but a fragment of a case study—that he has successfully isolated the sources of Dora's hysteria, and that, as he writes to a friend, physician Wilhelm Fleiss, her case "has opened smoothly to my collection of picklocks."

But I'll give the doctor his due. Freud did make great strides in unraveling taboos and speaking about sex and genitalia in candid terms. He also encouraged people to think more openly about the varieties of sexual intercourse. In *Dora*, he cautions against judging other people's sexual habits. "Each one of us in his own sexual life transgresses to a slight extent—now in this direction, now in that— the narrow lines imposed upon him as the standard of normality. The perversions," he states, "are neither bestial nor degenerate in the emotional sense of the word." Yet despite these somewhat progressive views on sex, I cannot hold Freud up as a champion of women's sexuality, especially after reading Cixous and Lacan and their critiques of his work. Mainly, what I see is the damaging legacy of Freud's theories on the expression of a woman's voice and, by extension, of her desire; even today, any feminist discussion of female desire must do battle with muzzling the demons Freud let loose, which the class attempted to do with ferocity.

"I think Freud is trying to deny that Dora has any active sexuality at all," said Gillian, "beyond serving as the object of male desire. But then he also says that her hysteria stems from the fact that she didn't surrender to Herr K., but *wanted* to . . ."

"How is Freud not just, like, a total product of the patriarchy?" asked Sarah rhetorically. "Isn't it all just totally contextual anyway? For instance, the ancient Greeks believed in women's sexuality, but they went to the opposite extreme and saw it as ravenous. Women weren't even responsible for adultery because it was considered so outside of their control."

"So are women ravenous or passive?" Professor H. asked.

"Oh, we're just blobs," Sarah said darkly. "We just *absorb*."

The class emitted a few snickers and groans.

Professor H. smiled. "You're right, Sarah," she said. "Freud neglects to ask how a woman who is constructed as an object comes into possession of her own story. How does an object tell a story? And how does hysteria tell a story through its symptoms? A *good* psychoanalyst— these days, at least—will try to get you to tell your story *without* pushing you forward. That's why the struggle for story can take years. In other words, how can Dora tell her story when Freud already seems to believe that he knows what her story *is*? Remember that Dora was a real person—she was Ida—but Freud's *Dora* is a paradigmatic text based on a set of patriarchal assumptions about female desire that, even today, stands as culturally authoritative. So is this still how women are constructed—by an imposed set of assumptions?"

The class was silent, and Professor H. comfortably let us sit in silence before, satisfied the point had been made, she moved us in a slightly different direction. "Is Freud's desire for total knowledge, do you think, a penetrative power?"

More uncertain this time, Sarah raised her hand. "But what if Dora was trying to penetrate *Freud*? Although, really, this metaphor is making me nuts! I don't know—maybe *enfolding*?" Her mouth turned in a half-smile, half-grimace. "Or no—now we're back to the blob!" A couple of students groaned again. "Sorry," she said, with a glint of mischief in her eyes.

Professor H. considered Sarah's comment. "Maybe Dora is resisting being either penetrated *or* penetrator," she said. "After all, to be penetrated is to be made into the passive, the lackey, the other. So how can we identify new and different tools? How do women claim subjectivity to tell *their* stories?"

"But our language, and our vocabulary, is at its core a patriarchal creation," said Sarah, "so how are we ever going to get around that?"

"True, but there are ways, " Professor H. said. "For instance, Luce Irigaray—another contemporary European feminist—asks why we have to start with the phallus as Freud does. Maybe castration isn't the main break, but rather the cutting of the umbilical cord. What if it's the symbiotic state of the womb we want to get back to? What if we look at the labia as the *lips*, and we start with that, rather than the phallus?"

All through this conversation, I had been sneaking peeks at the lone male in our class, James. When I was an undergraduate, it was practically unheard of for men to sign up for Fem Texts, although some men wrote down "women's studies"—*wink, wink, nudge, nudge*—as their intended major in the Freshmen Facebook. Their reluctance was perhaps understandable, given that back then a lot of bile was flung at the white man for being a building block of the Patriarchy. Over the years, as the definition of patriarchy has become more nuanced, more men have signed up for women's studies classes—not a huge number, mind you, but professors reported that there were usually one or two men in each class. James' presence as our resident man was never unduly remarked upon. Not once had Professor H. called on him to speak from the male point of view, nor did he ever volunteer to give it.

As far as I could tell, James did not seem perturbed by all this recent talk of penises. A soft-spoken, wiry young man, he regularly contributed to class discussions, speaking earnestly and without any overt reference to his gender. Now he was listening carefully—head slightly to one side, his longish dark hair brushing against his shoulder, his expression impressively neutral, neither uncomfortable nor, apparently, titillated. He raised his hand, and Professor H. readily called on him.

"I like the idea of starting with the lips," he said. "In fact, I think it's in these, I don't know, *puns* that the gaps occur, the possibilities. The lips, for instance, are self-referential and reciprocal. So maybe by starting with the lips, we give primacy to the voice. Maybe it *is* a good way to break down some of these patriarchal constructs of language."

I didn't know what the hell he was saying, but it didn't really matter. His thoughtfulness was enough to remind me that feminism does not occur wholly in an all-female vacuum, but affects men, too, whether through their mothers, sisters, wives, or daughters, influencing their conception of women. Even as women have been chipping away at the patriarchal structure simply by succeeding in formerly male-dominated professions, many men, too, have been doing the same by learning to listen to women, to support their ambitions, to see them not as blobs, but as individuals. I thought then of my father, my husband, my male friends and colleagues—all of the many men who would view the Patriarchy as our common enemy—and was gratified to see that the old division of women versus men had been all but absent in my Fem Texts classes; after all, some of my favorite feminists are men.

In a Different Voice

When Sylvia was first born, John and I took great pains to be gender neutral, without drawing too much attention to these pains, and for a while it seemed to be working. Her favorite toys were a wooden toolbox and some baby approximation of whack-a-mole, and she had no qualms about tumbling in the dirt, building fortresses with Legos, or picking up dead bees on the playground—all those ridiculously stereotypical categories we have for "boy" things. Then, somewhere around age four, the Pink Princess Phase snuck upon us, and it was all pink and all princesses *all* the time. "Mommy, who's your favorite princess?" she would ask me with the utmost seriousness. After discovering that there was really no avoiding the question, I finally gave in. "Belle," I answered, "because she loves to read." Whenever possible I tried to inject my own helpfully subversive comments, but it was like doggy paddling against a tsunami—a powerful pink tidal wave of commercialism.

"I kind of *like* Maleficent," I said cheerily after watching *Sleeping Beauty* for about the hundredth time. "At least she has personality, you know? And that black cape and that headdress with the horns? Very cool."

Sitting on the other couch, John tried not to laugh too hard.

"Mommy," Sylvia said, sighing, as if dealing with a dimwitted child, "she's the *Mistress of All Evil*."

"Yeah, she's evil, Steph," John said, enjoying every minute of this exchange. "Get with the program."

"Hey, John," I shot back with fake sweetness. "Weren't you saying you wanted to play a game of Pretty, Pretty Princess after the movie?"

Sylvia clapped her hands in glee at the prospect of dressing her daddy up like a princess, then snuggled up next to me and rewound to her favorite scene: Prince Charming coming across the long-haired, funnel-waisted Aurora singing in the forest with all the cute, furry animals.

"Well, maybe Maleficent is just misunderstood," I mumbled, in vain. "She was the only fairy not invited to Sleeping Beauty's coronation—her feelings were hurt!" This is what I had been reduced to, defending the villain in a Disney movie and making my poor husband play princess games. But what else was a feminist mother to do?

• • •

Princess fever, it seemed, had infected almost every girl in Sylvia's preschool class. Whatever the parents' reaction, which ranged from befuddlement and concern to an enabling enthusiasm, the girls continued to band together in princess solidarity. Having grown up in the era of Marlo Thomas, I was loath to buy into the girlie culture and all it represents, but it became more and more difficult to hang on to my staunch belief that the sexes should be raised without regard to gender in the face of my daughter wobbling into the living room on plastic feathered heels, dressed in a floor-length poofy dress, a tiara atop her head—and a smile spreading from ear to ear. Even in the liberal bastion of Brooklyn, my five year old would come home from school and say things like, "Of course he doesn't like princesses—he's a *boy*—he just likes to play with trucks." I was stumped.

Then I picked up *In a Different Voice* again, which shed some light on understanding princesses as the currency of connection among preschool girls. In this 1982 best-seller, Harvard psychologist Carol Gilligan proposes that men and women typically exercise two modes of thought—women generally tend to view the world as a tightly bound network of relationships, while men view it more as a hierarchy. Although both, in her estimation, are equally valid perspectives, the male model of moral development served as the standard in scientific and educational research, and the female model was devalued and marginalized. Gilligan observed during her years of research that adolescent girls "struggle against losing voice and against creating an inner division or split, so that large parts of themselves are kept out of relationship," placing their psychological development at risk.

In a Different Voice was part of a trend during second-wave feminism that emphasized a politics of *difference* between women and men, as opposed to a politics of *recognition*, in which women were believed to be the same as, or as good as, men. Rather than focus on the similarities between the sexes, these second wavers honed in on the differences—such as the female tendency to cooperate—and demanded respect for those differences, not in spite of them. Unfortunately, the postpublication fallout from Gilligan's book demonstrates how this approach could backfire. Though Gilligan was very careful to point out that any difference in modes of thought between men and women is most likely caused by socialization rather than biology, the notion of difference soon became a wedge for concerted inequality. In 1999, when pressure mounted on the Virginia Military Institute to admit women, the school cited Gilligan's work repeatedly before the Supreme Court—arguing that it was inherently unworkable, even cruel, to place young women in a competitive and adversarial environment hostile to their very nature. Gilligan herself testified for the opposite side in support of integration. *Newsweek*, too, used Gilligan's book to support the claim that career women pay a "psychic price" for professional success. Retrograde pop-psychology books invoked Gilligan's work to bolster their claims that independence was unhealthy for women. And, in the years that followed, a virtual cottage industry sprouted in the ongoing attempt to foster some sort of understanding between these Men from Mars and Women from Venus.

Given its contentious legacy, I was pleased to find Gilligan's book was more literary and less political than I remembered and, after the arcane symbolism of Cixous and Freud, refreshingly empirical. She starts out by examining a study designed by Lawrence Kohlberg that has been used to measure moral development in adolescence by presenting a conflict between moral norms and exploring the logic of the subject's resolution of that conflict. Here is the test question: *A man named Heinz considers whether to steal a drug that he cannot afford to buy in order to save his wife's life. Should Heinz steal the drug?*

Two bright eleven-year-old students, Jake and Amy, are recruited to take the test. Jake answers confidently that, yes, of course, Heinz should steal the drug, because life is worth more than property. His answer, perfectly rational, shows that he can distinguish morality from the law, one of the benchmarks on the scale of moral development. Consequently, Jake scores high marks. Amy, on the other hand, is more evasive in her answer. "It depends," she says. Unlike Jake, Gilligan observes, Amy sees the dilemma less as a math problem involving humans than as a narrative of relationships that extends over time. Taking account of both the husband's concern for his wife and the wife's ongoing *need* for her husband—a need that could well be failed, were he to be sent to jail for any extralegal problem solving— Amy seeks to respond to the druggist in a way that would sustain, rather than sever, that connection. She wonders whether the husband could borrow the money, or perhaps strike a deal with the druggist to pay for the drugs at a later date.

As Gilligan puts it, the two children conceive of the question differently: Amy is not wondering whether Heinz *should* steal the drug, but should Heinz *steal* the drug. In fact, these two children see two entirely distinct moral problems—Jake identifies a conflict between life and property that can be resolved by logical deduction, while Amy sees "a fracture of human relationships that must be mended by its own thread."

If Amy's view made sense to me as an alternative way of viewing the issue, it clearly did not to the researchers running the study. As Amy continues to give the "wrong" answers, as evidenced by her interviewer's constant repeating of the question, and the circularity of the conversation, her confidence crumbles, her voice growing more diffident. In the end, she scores a full stage below Jake, according to Kohlberg's scale of moral development, the researchers noting that her responses reveal a feeling of "powerlessness in the world, an inability to think systematically about the concepts of morality or law, a reluctance to challenge authority or to examine the logic of received moral truths, a failure even to conceive of acting directly to save a life or to consider that such action, if taken, could possibly have an effect." Amy is, in essence, "cognitively immature." In person, however, she is none of these things. This is Gilligan's point. The "female" way of viewing the world, which she calls the "ethic of care," should be given as much credence as the "male" point of view, the "ethic of justice."

• • •

While I may have dismissed Gilligan's gender-based analysis as an undergrad, as a parent I was having second thoughts. I remembered back to Sylvia's first morning at preschool. Parents of new students were required to spend the day observing their child quietly from the corner of the classroom, in case there were any transitional issues. As I tried to fit my body into a pint-size wooden chair, Sylvia stood next to me, unsure of what to do. She looked so uncomfortable that my chest tightened up in sympathy. The other girls in the class were sizing her up. I knew it. Sylvia knew it. Waiting and watching, she stood absolutely still. The boys, meanwhile, were oblivious to Sylvia, too busy wrestling on the ground, laughing. Soon the teacher called snack time, and asked one of the older kindergarten girls to pick someone to help her set up. I sensed this was a major social event, and several of the other kindergarten girls tensed, hopeful, longing to be chosen.

Scanning the room, the girl's eyes rested on Sylvia. "Sylvia, do *you* want to help me?" she said.

"Okay," Sylvia said evenly, finally leaving my side.

No doubt a kind gesture, but also one surprisingly freighted with subtext, laying out the possibility both of acceptance and of rejection. This act of invitation seemed to me more measured and calculated than I would have expected among five and six year olds, and teetering on the chair in my daughter's brightly decorated classroom as I watched this exchange, I flashed-forward to junior high, then high school, and all the terrible social politics to come. A pit opened up in my stomach. I was a girl once.

That night, after Sylvia was fast asleep, I related the entire incident to John in detail. He sat on the couch next to me, listening patiently, and then admitted he just didn't get what I was so worked up about. During his own school years, he had never been made aware of the constantly shifting alliances of best friends, enemies, and "frenemies," while I was all too conscious of these machinations—often more so than I would have liked. I had seen how girls close ranks or whisper to each other as a way of undermining another girl who has fallen into disfavor. This tactic, what experts call "relational aggression," can be every bit as damaging, we are told, as, say, a punch in the nose. From an early age, girls are more likely to learn the importance of being judged by a jury of their peers, and, as Gilligan points out, eventually they mature into women who, naturally then, see the world as a complex network of relationships.

● ● ●

Whether women inherently tend toward a more humanistic view of relationships or are simply socialized in that direction, the result is often a growing inability—caught as we are in the fear of social exile— to enunciate our own desires. To demonstrate this difference be- tween the male and female entry into adulthood, Gilligan contrasts two literary coming-of-age stories. In James Joyce's *Portrait of the Artist as a Young Man*, the main character, Stephen, cuts off his relationships in search of personal freedom; for Mary McCarthy in *Memories of a Catholic Girlhood*, on the other hand, a "farewell to childhood" means relinquishing her autonomy in favor of *preserving* her relationships. Whereas Gilligan describes Stephen as suffering from a problem of human connection and Mary with a problem of truth, their respective deficits, in fact, mirror each other. Men suppose that by following the Socratic dictum "know thyself," they will also come to know others—including women; women, on the other hand, believe that if only they know *others*, they may also come to know themselves. Given these disparate relational approaches, "men and women tacitly collude in not voicing women's experiences," writes Gilligan, as they build their relationships around this silence.

Apparently, this collusion of silence continues. With women now outnumbering and outperforming men on most college campuses, I had assumed the women in Fem Texts would take issue with Gilligan's theories on gendered ways of communicating and how women's voices are hushed. On the contrary, many admitted that they still felt overshadowed by male students both inside and outside the classroom. Men talked more, I was told, louder, too, and with an air of authority that most women did not assert.

"I find I'm always apologizing, you know? Even if someone bumps into me or, like, hits me," said Cindy. "I don't know how to change this."

"*Hits* you?" Sarah interjected.

"Well, no, not *hits* me," said Cindy, flustered, "but, you know, knocks into me accidentally."

"You know, it's interesting," said Jen. "In other classes, women often start out by saying something like, 'This may be wrong, but . . .' Women are just *so* apologetic for expressing an opinion." She paused and glanced furtively at Professor H. "I'm sorry," she said quickly, "I don't know if this is even on topic."

"No, Jen, I think it *is*," said Professor H.

"Joke!" Jen called out—a Cheshire cat grin spreading over her face.

Everyone laughed. "See?!" said Professor H., laughing along with the rest of the class. "I'm so used to it, I couldn't even tell you were joking!"

All joking aside, the class agreed that there were some serious real-life consequences for women in the perceived conflict between their rights and their professed responsibilities, as Gilligan suggests. If the embittered, yet apparently tenacious, belief that a woman's greatest virtue—her very moral goodness—lies in her willingness to sacrifice herself for others, then how can she possibly approach adult decision making without "raising the specter of selfishness," as Gilligan calls it, and completely submerging her own desires?

To explore in more depth how women deal with life choices, Gilligan conducted a study tracking the decision making of twenty-nine pregnant women as they contemplated getting an abortion. The women came from varying ethnic and economic backgrounds, ranging in age from fifteen to thirty-three years old, and all of them had become pregnant unexpectedly due to faulty or absent contraception. Gilligan intentionally chose a situation involving a woman's reproductive choices because, as she explains, "It is precisely this dilemma—the conflict between compassion and autonomy, between virtue and power—which the feminine voice struggles to resolve in its effort to reclaim the self and to solve the moral problem in such a way that no one is hurt." The constant reappearance of the word *selfish* during the interviews, Gilligan reports, signals the tension a woman feels as she strives to include her own needs within the compass of care and concern.

This observation gave me an aha moment: How many times had I—like any number of adult women I knew—routinely characterized my desires as "selfish"? The recognition was stunning, really. *Selfish* was our go-to word, yet rarely, if ever, had I heard a man utter the same accusation of himself or his desires. I tried to picture John or one of my male friends saying that he felt "selfish" for working too much, or taking a night out with his friends—bad, maybe, or hangdog, even guilty, but not selfish. But ignoring one's own needs in the name of selflessness can have a toxic effect. Ironically, as Gilligan points out, a woman who expresses care for others but at the expense of her own desires invariably creates destructive distance within the very relationships she is trying to uphold, because she is effectively putting on a mask; likewise, men acting the part of lone ranger, when they exist within a system of relationships, are also living a lie. The ideal then is to integrate the two approaches of the ethic of justice and the ethic of care, in order to create more meaningful work and family relationships. Or, to put it in Disney terms, perhaps men need to channel Prince Charming more often and women their Maleficent.

The Morning After

Finally, I had arrived. We had left the second wave behind, with its politics of difference between the sexes, and were fast moving into the third wave—the very one I rode into adulthood. Unlike previous waves, third wavers argued that differences existed, but *among* women, and thus set out to examine problems of identity and how to form a politics within this fragmentation. And like previous waves, this one produced a formidable undertow. We were reading one of the products of this backlash, postfeminist Katie Roiphe, whose controversial 1993 book, *The Morning After: Sex, Fear, and Feminism*, came out the year I graduated from college. A Ph.D. student at Princeton when the book was published, Roiphe charged that a "rape crisis hysteria" had gripped college campuses across the country, mostly engineered by feminists who propped up women as weak and ineffectual beings, lacking in sexual agency. In particular, she accuses events like "Take Back the Night," an annual march and speak-out against sexual violence held on college campuses, of being little more than exercises in fabricated drama, emblems of a counterfeit rape culture. Her polemic caused intense indignation among many feminists of my generation. Years later, though as I listened to my classmates discuss the book, the reaction to Roiphe's manifesto bordered on uninterest. Not only had postfeminism's poster child moved, but so, it seemed, had many members of a new generation.

"I have to say I'm not really a fan of 'Take Back the Night,' either," said Valerie. "It seems pretty touchy-feely to me, all this rhetoric. I don't know—I guess some people really love it."

"I mean, I have no problem with wallowing in victimization," said Lisa, making clear her opinion on the event. "But I do know *guys* are pretty turned off by it."

"Not necessarily," countered Sarah. "Columbia Men Against Violence actually plays kind of a big part in 'Take Back the Night.'"

"Oh, *please!*" Heather cut in. "There are, like, five guys in Men Against Violence."

"I just don't like the fact that 'Take Back the Night' hasn't changed over the years," said Valerie. "It hasn't evolved."

"Well, I don't know if that's necessarily true," said Sarah. "The group has been discussing whether to include men in the march itself, and then there's Sexhibition"—(some later Googling revealed Sexhibition to be "an annual fun-filled fair held by the Take Back the Night organizers that celebrates consent-based sex with penis-shaped cookies, exotic dancers, and sex toys")—"I actually think they're pretty careful to send the message that we're antiviolence, you know, not antisexuality."

"Anyway, there are better organizations," said Jen. "Like 'Night Rides,' you know? You can call a security van to pick you up and drive you back to your dorm. But only women get transported, not men."

"I love Night Rides!" said Lisa, "I use them all the time, although I'm never calling because I feel unsafe. Usually just 'cause I'm lazy." She laughed. "And there's hardly ever anyone else on the van."

As I listened to the discussion, even I had to agree. Roiphe's flaying of feminism seemed so, well, *nineties*, in this age of "do me" feminism. But I was troubled that, save for Roiphe's book decrying the rape crisis, the subject of rape appeared to have fallen completely from the Fem Texts curriculum. Despite statistics showing that the incidence of rape has dropped around 60 percent since 1993, someone in this country is still sexually assaulted every two minutes, according to a 2007 survey by the U.S. Department of Justice, and college students are four times more likely to be assaulted. Part of me was glad to hear these women speak up in class about how safe they feel on campus, glad that antirape programs were seen more as a convenience than a necessity. On the other hand, I worried that the voices of this new generation may have made Roiphe's once contrarian postfeminist cry into a new norm.

"People have asked me if I have ever been date-raped," Roiphe writes in *The Morning After*. "And thinking back on complicated nights, on too many glasses of wine, on strange and familiar beds, I would have to say yes. With such a sweeping definition of rape, I wonder how many people there are, male or female, who haven't been date-raped at one point or another. People pressure and manipulate and cajole each other into all sorts of things all the time." For Roiphe, this is all part of the dangerous game of desire between men and women, and, back in the '90s at least, college administrators and campus feminists were rudely trying to intrude where they didn't belong.

• • •

When I was in college the statistic that one in four women would be raped in her lifetime hung over our heads, although later skeptics like Roiphe would argue the number was overblown. I have never been raped, but I have, in one of the most terrifying moments of my life, felt the fear: When I was fourteen years old, a car filled with drunk, rowdy middle-aged men followed my friend and me while we were walking around our neighborhood one summer night. We ignored them, as they shouted out obscenities from the window, their voices bruising the quiet night of our suburban town, smothering even the sound of the crickets. In an effort to get away from them, we walked toward someone's house, certain that these men would just keep on driving and disappear into the night. I waited for the screech of tires as their vehicles accelerated away. Instead, the engine died, and four doors slammed shut like gunshots. I'll never forget the sound.

"Run!" I yelled to my friend, and we did, arms and legs pumping in the darkness, the grass wet and slick beneath our feet from a rainstorm earlier that day. One of the men was soon right behind me; I could almost feel his breath on my neck. He stretched out his arm to swipe at my T-shirt, almost getting a hold of it. Of me.

"This is going to be the worst night of your life," he growled shakily over the labored breaths of his pursuit. I screamed, or at least I think I did, and pulled away in a rush of adrenaline. My friend was running just as fast, pursued by yet another man. They were everywhere. Then, spotting a house across the street with the lights on inside, we converged on it like moths. I pounded on the door, heaving. My lungs burned, and I could taste metal at the back of my throat. I looked back over my shoulder. There were three of them standing across the street. Waiting.

A woman came to the door in her bathrobe. It was pink terry cloth, the belt tied tight around her waist. She stood nervously behind the screen, the yellow light from the hallway brushing against one side of her face. She was blond, early thirties maybe.

"Please!" we pleaded, our voices rising. "Please, just let us in. Those men out there are *following* us." I waved across the street.

She peered out into the darkness, then looked back at us, suspicious. At last, she decided that our hysteria must be genuine. She unlatched the door and let us in. We fell inside, shivering with relief. "You girls shouldn't be walking outside so late," she said sternly. My father said the same thing when he came to pick us up a few minutes later, my phone call having roused him from bed. But his anger was just the thinnest veneer over his own fear. His knuckles were white on the steering wheel the whole way home. I craned my neck out the window as he drove, looking for the men, but they were nowhere to be seen.

Back home, I went into the fetal position under the bedcovers, and, even then, I couldn't still my fear. I shook for hours. I imagined what might have happened. I worried that they had hidden in the shadows, following us, and now knew where I lived. I got out of bed, checked all the locks on the doors, the windows. The night had taught me a lesson that I would not soon forget.

In college, I learned to analyze the act of rape, to understand it as a tool used by men throughout the ages to dominate women; rape wasn't about sex but about oppression and power, explained Susan Brownmiller in her pioneering 1975 book, *Against Our Will*. This book was required reading in my Fem Texts class back then, and my professor devoted several classes to discussing both rape and sexual harassment. Talk of rape was everywhere, most of it centered on acquaintance or date rape, not the more starkly defined stranger-in-the-bushes rape that I had almost fallen victim to. The William Kennedy Smith rape case was unfolding on TV, and clumped together with the Thomas hearings, and the sexual abuse allegations against Senator Bob Packwood, to say nothing of the systematic rape of women during the genocide in Bosnia, the female body was highlighted as especially embattled territory. Sexual relations on campuses across the country grew strained, as students and administrators clashed over when and how to prosecute possible rapists. Women scrawled the names of accused rapists' names on bathroom walls, a way to convict without facing the prying questions of an administrator in the university, let alone a judge and lawyers in the public forum of a courthouse.

It would appear we talk about rape differently today. Roiphe's contention that only a thin line separates bad sex and date rape has spawned, among other things, something called "gray rape," which *Washington Post* reporter Laura Sessions Stepp defines as "sex that falls somewhere between consent and denial and is even more confusing than date rape because often both parties are unsure of who wanted what." This definition in itself rings alarm bells—*unsure of who wanted what*? Many of these maybe-rape victims, operating in a culture where women are supposedly sexually liberated to pursue casual, alcohol-fueled hookups, have lost the language to explain what has happened to them. Rarely do they press charges against their assaulter. They doubt themselves. They doubt their own desires. They doubt their actions. One woman interviewed in the article describes how she said "No," how she said "Stop," how she *felt* afterward like she had been raped. Yet she doesn't call it rape because "she thinks of herself as a strong and independent woman, not a victim." This scenario seems to me a particularly disturbing legacy of postfeminism.

· · ·

Aside from these broader social concerns about rape, I also had another, more personal, reaction to Roiphe's book the second time around. Reading *The Morning After* again was like opening a time capsule, a chronicle of a specific period in time, one I lived. Here was Roiphe, daughter of renowned feminist novelist Anne Roiphe, who had gone to an elite all-girls school in Manhattan, then to Harvard, and then Princeton. She was, if anything, the ruby-red fruit of feminism's struggles. She should have been ready to take on the world, yet the woman who steps forward from these pages is awash, at times, in an almost paralyzing uncertainty. Roiphe longs for the landmarks that might give her comfort as she makes her way through the emotional turmoil of young adulthood. She waxes nostalgic for the hedonistic and carefree days of the 1960s and '70s, viewing them as a sexual golden age in which orgasms were plentiful and no one worried about AIDS or rape. She even speaks sentimentally of her mother's age, the '50s, which had imposed a set of distinct and recognizable markers of adulthood. At least the expectation of early marriage offered some form of security, "however illusory, however insubstantial," while for her, the future remained clouded by uncertainty.

Roiphe was obviously afflicted with a touch of generational myopia, a wistful nostalgia for the past, which, when looked at more closely, is simply a disguise for a fear of the future. I felt much the same way as Roiphe as I contemplated a blank future after college graduation, along with a worsening recession and a mountain of debt. The path my personal life would take cambered into the distance, with no discernible destination; I struggled, along with the rest of my generation, through this insecurity, this sense of crisis peculiar to our time. History had marched through our lives, too, as surely as it does with any other generation, leaving behind its own set of social and cultural trials that we alone had to navigate. We had grown up in the wake of the political upheaval of the 1960s and '70s, during an unprecedented age of social and sexual transformation that redefined our most intimate relations. Parents divorced and families split apart, leaving children to deal with the fallout. Mothers left the home and entered the workplace; deadbeat dads left the home, period. The accessibility of birth control removed one big risk from sex—pregnancy—while the spread of AIDS added another. Perhaps for my generation, then, the conundrums of love, sex, and relationships were our albatross. We were left dangling in this joyless gap between sweet romance and scripted sex. Instead of varsity pins, we got venereal diseases. Instead of key parties, we got date-rape pamphlets. Instead of clarity, we got *complicated*.

Roiphe's polemic closes by sounding a plaintive note that has nothing to do with rape and everything to do with her fear of ending up alone. "Ten years from now, all of my friends would be in couples," she writes, "filing two by two into the Noah's ark of adulthood, leaving me behind, looking up anxiously at the sky." She reminisces about her high school graduation; to protest the school administrators' investment in South Africa, the students wore black armbands over white graduation dresses. "I miss the clarity of high school sometimes," she admits. "The white dresses, the black armbands, the underground paper, Xeroxed and distributed, filled with new outrage each month."

I don't blame Roiphe for stewing over our raw deal, but nor do I blame feminism. Feminism stands for equality, for giving women both voice and choice. Education about rape on campus aims to instruct women and men on the importance of communicating their desires to each other. Pinning the paradoxes of youth, campus culture, and human nature on the failings of feminism is indeed misguided. "Desire, anxiety, feminism, and ambition clash, and what emerges is this strange new hybrid species: the radical cover-girl chic feminist," Roiphe writes, referring to her peers, the women who dance half-naked at fraternity parties yet also scream until they are hoarse at "Take Back the Night." The same could be said, however, for women who, reaping the benefits of feminism, also impeach it for giving them too many choices.

Gender Trouble

We were nearing the end of the semester, and the class had reached a comfortable pitch. The students chatted easily, their casual conversation pinging across the table in the minutes before class started and during the short break after the first hour of the seminar. During the semester, I had become particularly friendly with Priscilla, a graduate student from West Africa who was studying at Columbia for the year. From the very first day, we had both gravitated to the couch, sitting slightly outside the circle of conversation, although Priscilla spoke up often, her voice smooth and confident. She read the French feminists in their original tongue, picking up on the many nuances of language that are lost in translation. Always, she was impeccably groomed, elegant, smelling of musk and vanilla, her cotton shirts freshly ironed; next to her I often felt underdressed in my jeans and

T-shirt. Equally attentive to the class, she was always game to discuss the latest reading during our breaks, and so was I. For Priscilla, feminism was primarily about establishing equal economic and educational opportunities for women, not things like feminist psychoanalysis or, even more perplexing, radical lesbianism, the subject of one class toward the end of the semester. Speaking to her gave me some perspective on the occasional indulgences of Western feminism.

"It's very strange to me, this theory," Priscilla said, referring to French feminist Monique Wittig's proposition that the only way to escape the myth of "woman" is to escape the "binary" altogether and become a lesbian—and not just in the sexual sense; Wittig wants to take men out of the equation entirely. "I don't think we would discuss such a thing in my country."

"I know, it's a bit abstract, isn't it?" I murmured. "I don't exactly see how it's a practical solution." Too many women had beloved men in their lives, whether fathers, husbands, or sons, and portraying them as disposable would only ward these women from feminism's ranks. But aside from the fact that adopting a man-free life was simply not going to fly with many women, Wittig's suggestion inadvertently raises a larger point—one that we didn't address in class: Not all sacrifices women make are borne in oppression. Sometimes women act, not out of oppression, but out of love, responsibility, and a sense of community. And so do men.

Over the weekend, John, Sylvia, and I went out to dinner, and about halfway through the meal, Sylvia shoved her plate away. "My tummy hurts," she said. Only a few minutes before, she had been laughing as John made funny faces, and the change seemed too speedy to be true. Well acquainted with this "I'm sick" ploy as a way to try to get out of eating her vegetables, John played bad cop, informing Sylvia that if she didn't finish dinner, she wouldn't get dessert—a tactic that usually worked like a charm. But instead of protesting as expected, she bolted out of her seat and ran to the bathroom. I followed in quick pursuit to find her crying on the toilet.

John paid the check and bundled our girl up in his arms, carrying her the few blocks home, as I stroked her hair. "Mommy," she whimpered, her cheek resting on John's shoulder, "I feel like I'm gonna throw up."

Back at home, I passed the next few hours sitting by Sylvia's bed, smoothing her matted hair away from her face and wiping her feverish brow with a damp cloth. John sat on the other side of the bed, a large mixing bowl—now dubbed the puke bowl—ready on his lap. She couldn't keep anything down, except small sips of water. In between fits of coughing and scratching, she lay listless, her eyes half-closed and glassy from the sheer exhaustion of it all. Few things, I think, are more wrenching that a sick child. John and I wrapped our bodies protectively around her, and together, we watched over her all night, finally coaxing her to sleep; around dawn, we at last drifted off ourselves, his arm resting on mine. And we repeated this ritual, the three of us cuddled together in Sylvia's bed the next night, until the virus had run its course and Sylvia was again begging to go to the park and bargaining for an extra scoop of ice cream.

Sitting there in the corner, as the class debated the finer points of radical lesbianism, I sensed the big white elephant in the room: love. And not just women's love for their partners and children but also men's love for their families. I am a strong supporter of gay marriage and believe that no one should be denied the opportunity to express and celebrate love—but radical lesbianism as a political statement left me cold. If feminism was intended to enlarge the fabric of women's experiences, how could some of life's richest threads—love, romance, parenthood—be ignored?

• • •

I was feeling weary enough, and then I fell over the cliff, a steep descent into confusion otherwise known as Judith Butler's *Gender Trouble*. A poststructuralist philosopher, minted by Yale, Butler essentially turns theory on its head by taking feminism's reliance on "the Patriarchy"—namely, the Beauvoirian notion that a man's power as subject depends on viewing the woman as object—and then refining the concept even further by arguing that it is not "Man" per se who is oppressive but this "binary" way of thinking. As Butler sees it, this structured view of the world as composed of only men and only women reinforces sexism, because we must then perform stylized bodily acts that mimic gender. Like her predecessors, Butler agrees that gender is a social and psychological role, but she boldly asserts that sex, which feminists have typically accepted as an immutable biological category, is *also* socially constructed, especially when one considers that an estimated 1.7 out of 100 live births have no clear sexual designation, anatomically speaking. Our ideas of "man" and "woman" are, as Butler puts it, copies that have no original.

So let's scratch these categories of man and woman, Butler suggests, and instead view sex as a spectrum. Terms like *intersex* and *transgendered* were not yet in vogue when I was an undergraduate, and I had to figure out their definitions initially. *Intersex*, as Butler explains, refers to any individual "who deviates from the Platonic ideal of physical dimorphism at the chromosomal, genital, gonadal, or hormonal levels." Taking the political out of the science, Butler points to physiological instances that confuse the assignment of gender. Men, for example, with gynecomastia grow breasts, while women with hypertrichosis grow beards. And ironically, as described by *New York Times* science writer Natalie Angier in her book *Woman: An Intimate Geography*, "women" suffering from androgen-insensitivity syndrome resemble the ideal woman—tall, buxom, docile—yet are chromosomally male and without a uterus.

Then there's the element of choice. With the aid of the right surgery and drugs, even someone born squarely into a certain sex can transform into the other; as one student had already proved, you could enter Barnard as a woman and graduate a man. Given these examples of "gender trouble," Butler asserts the world cannot be neatly divided into men and women, and therefore the whole bedrock of sexism disintegrates. The argument sounds persuasive enough when batted around the classroom. Problem is, postmodern theory is just that, theory. And postmodernism, with its central precept that everything be questioned, does not make for easy comprehension or application.

In college, this was the sort of intellectual exercise I would have loved, but now—as I tried to fit Butler's theories into the four corners of my daily life—I was having a hard time getting on board, and soon I was feeling downright grim about the prospects of feminist theory to improve women's lives in any concrete way. Most of the class seemed to feel the same way.

"I'm not buying Butler," Courtney said. "So it's just a random accident that 51 percent of the population can reproduce?" She sat back in her chair, arms crossed. Since the beginning of the semester, Courtney had assumed the position of class gadfly. A brunette with a thick don't-mess-with-me Long Island accent, she stared at her classmates through horn-rimmed glasses, her gaze inviting someone to disagree with her. A number of students in the class, like Courtney, were majoring in economics, not women's studies, which I found heartening. When I took Fem Texts, the class was mainly filled with women's studies and sociology or political science majors, but now the students ran the gamut.

Yet if feminist values had crossed over into the mainstream, appealing to students with broader academic interests, then feminist theory itself seemed to have taken a contradictory turn to become more esoteric. The psychoanalytic and linguistic theories of earlier classes were baffling enough, but they were nothing compared to this.

Butler's work, an academic text that sold more than 100,000 copies worldwide, signaled a popular shift in feminist theory. In the late 1980s, postmodernism had emerged as a challenge to Enlightenment ideas and the belief that there are any universal truths.

Within the postmodern movement grew poststructuralism, a related school of thought that looks specifically at systems as totalities. And although the two terms are connected and overlap, postmodernism is considered the roomier concept. Eventually, postmodernism and poststructuralism gave rise to queer theory, which, despite the use of the word *queer*, has less to do with sexual identity than with "problematizing" prevailing norms. As a class, we spent some time just trying to sort through the jargon.

"Being queer is a position vis-à-vis the normal," said Sarah. "You know—the legitimate, the dominant."

"But what's so wrong with normal?" asked Greta. "I mean, I'm queer in the sexual sense, but I want to get married and have kids and stay at home. I *want* all that."

"I *don't* want that," said Blaine. "I think marriage is on its way out, actually."

"But the statistics don't support that at all," said Lisa. "More people are getting married than ever, you know? And having, like, these *crazy*, over-the-top weddings."

"But going back to what you said, Greta—if queer's going to encompass that traditional lifestyle, too, then, hey, anyone could be queer," said Heather. "Isn't that just degaying gayness?"

Exasperation with Butler and the lingo of theory had set in, and Emily, the resident philosophy major, leaped to Butler's defense, right in her element, her body full of animation. "First of all," she said, "not all women can reproduce, so where do they fall in the binary structure? I don't know—the fact that we tend to view biology as somehow essential is just flawed. Biology is a discourse in and of itself. In fact, the scientific Enlightenment changed society's view of biology to begin with. I mean, up to that point, people believed that men and women shared the same genitalia, just that one was external and the other was internal. So Judith Butler's saying that the natural sex on which we build gender is already gendered, and the existence of intersexed and transgendered peoples only further problematizes the binary."

"But I don't understand," said Cindy. "If you're a man dressing as a woman, you're still a man . . . aren't you?"

"Postmodernists would say to your face that you're wrong," answered Professor H. lightly. "Think about it this way: What is a tomato? It still boggles my mind that it's a fruit. I think, 'No, no—it's a *vegetable* I'm putting on my salad!'"

Next to me, Priscilla raised her hand. "In my country, it is a bit different," she said. "There are some women who have beards and hair on the chest and masculine voices, but somehow it is accepted, and they get married and have children. No one pays any attention."

Courtney was vigorously shaking her head. "I still don't buy it," she muttered. I could tell from her scowl that she was not expecting, when she signed up for Fem Texts, to debate whether a person with breasts, vagina, and a beard was, in fact, a woman or something akin to a tomato.

While contemplating these questions had the appeal of a brain-teaser, I was similarly exasperated. So *what*? I thought.

Professor H. valiantly took on the task before her, trying to show us the possibilities of postmodern theory and its embrace of the multiplicity of identity. For Butler and others of her ilk, there *is* no "is"—there is no stable self. Our identities are always being constructed as we take part in presentation that necessarily contains an element of voluntarism, and this voluntarism is where the individual can assert agency. Or, as Professor H. put it, "Every time we walk outside the door, we are 'performing' a gender."

"Yeah, now you can be girly with *irony*," quipped Lisa.

"Exactly," said Professor H., clearly amused. "Although that's also one of the big criticisms of postmodernism: Irony allows you to vent without in any way effecting change. When *Gender Trouble* came out, it was very destabilizing. How can we have a movement without categories? If we go with Butler's argument that we're just a range of bodies, we take away the category of man, too, and all we have left is our common humanness."

"I gotta say, I'm having trouble seeing this as the future of feminism," said Heather. "So we have men paying—what?—two hundred dollars to dress up as women, and then we teach them how to act like stereotypical women. I wish it were twenty years later already— you know?—and we had moved past all this PoMo crap. I mean, it's just not *relevant* to my life."

"I know, it's frustrating, particularly when one is trying to put together a movement in this postmodern world," said Professor H. "A lot of people say that postmodernism has hobbled politics, making political activism seem almost old-fashioned and outdated. But on the flip side, the theory has introduced more tolerance and more capacious definitions, with more maneuverability within these definitions."

Emily raised her hand, and Professor H. gave her a nod to speak. "Look, I'm a total fan of theory and think it can change the world and everything," she said testily, still trying to salvage Butler's reputation as best she could. "I'm down with that. But I guess we happen to live in a gendered world, and to some extent we *need* the category of woman, so I think the goal, at least for now, should be to expand the available performances of 'woman.' Maybe we just need to perform this role in new and different ways."

I liked this bridge Emily had built between theory and real life, and so did Professor H. "Yes," she said, "and that's why some feminists have adopted 'strategic essentialism,'" she explained, referring to the work of literary theorist Gayatri Chakravorty Spivak. "It's important to understand the distinction. Strategy is not meant to be a theory, but rather something used to address a situation. The categories of 'man' and 'woman' are powerful—absolutely—and we can't simply do away with them." She nodded at Courtney here. "We just have to critique the things that are most important and useful and look at them from different perspectives."

The final hour was almost over, and the students were fidgety, keen to bolt the classroom and leave behind postmodernism; or I might have been projecting, because that's how I was feeling. I had already started packing my books in my bag and moving to the edge of my seat, so that when Professor H. officially dismissed us, I was already halfway to the door.

• • •

That weekend John and I were driving south on the New Jersey Turnpike, heading toward I-95, taking us back to Maryland to help my father move out of the house I grew up in. Sylvia had fallen asleep in her car seat, her chin resting awkwardly on her chest so that whenever John stepped on the brakes or accelerated, her head snapped forward and then back. Each time this happened I cringed, swiveling my body around, trying to arrange Sylvia's head into a more comfortable position against the cushion. The dog was staring intently at the passing cars, whimpering. I opened the back window, and her snout lifted into the humid air, nostrils flaring as she investigated the breeze. Night fell. The trees joined into one long, unbroken silhouette. Sylvia let out something between a snore and a sigh. We drove on, zooming through the darkness, our way lit by a dizzying array of headlights and taillights approaching and receding.

It was almost midnight when we reached my father's house. We pulled up in front, tires crunching to a stop on the deteriorating pavement, and John cut the engine.

"Oh, my God," I said.

The entire half acre of my father's well-lit front yard was covered with boxes, random bottles of cleaning fluid, and various pieces of heavy machinery, including a tractor with backhoe—not a blade of grass was visible. Dominating the driveway was a metal storage pod with the words *Pack Rat* written across the side. I had been expecting things to be bad. They were worse.

Some doctors have a penchant for fine brandy and golf; my father's therapy was of the retail variety and involved buying power tools and motorized equipment: the bigger, the better. When my parents divorced, he turned our basement into a workshop crammed with metal lathes, circular saws, drill presses—all of which now had to be transported to new digs. He took pleasure in building and fixing, not only people but also machines. For most of my childhood, a rusting avocado-green BMW sat propped up on blocks in the front yard, and every weekend my father would tinker with the engine, taking parts out, putting parts back in, as I sat cross-legged on the grass next to him, handing him wrenches out of his toolbox. We affectionately called it the "penicillin factory" in honor of the mold growing in the backseat and talked excitedly about the day when the BMW would run again. The neighbors, needless to say, did not share our enthusiasm and filed a public-nuisance complaint with the police, who came over to our house one evening during dinner to inform us the offensive heap must be removed.

The BMW may long since have been hauled to the junkyard, but my father refused to surrender. The last time John and I came to visit, he escorted John out to the backyard to show off his latest purchase: a pneumatic log splitter. The two of them then proceeded to spend the afternoon merrily splitting logs, protected from a hail of wood chips by plastic goggles. Sylvia and I occasionally observed them from the upstairs living room window, forced to raise our voices in order to hear each other above the racket.

"Boys with toys," I yelled, shaking my head. I couldn't resist.

After thirty years, my father had put his house on the market and taken a new job in Florida, trading in the Washington, D.C., winters for perennial warmth. I suspect his suburban neighbors were not too sorry to see him—and his diesel pickup—go. That is, if he could manage to clear out the house in time.

John's eyes were wide. "Isn't he closing on Monday?" he asked.

I nodded. "Yeah, not sure that's gonna happen."

Just then, a figure emerged from behind the house, bearing yet another box. A man walked stiffly into the light of the streetlamp, wearing a white T-shirt and shorts, a brace around his back, bandages wrapped around each knee.

I got out of the car, gently closing the door so as not to wake Sylvia, and walked up to my sixty-one-year-old father. John followed. "Dad, I can't *believe* this," I said, trying to help him with the box. "You're moving everything by yourself?"

He put down the box, wiping an arm across his perspiring forehead. He nodded, surveying the scene. "Maybe it wasn't the best idea."

It turned out he had been moving since six that morning, and once we got inside the house, Sylvia slung over John's shoulder, I could see why. The inside of the house was even more chaotic than the yard. And so we spent the next forty-eight hours trying to scrape the house of its decades' worth of accumulation. As the hours raced by, there was no room for sentiment. All the furniture, books, and various knickknacks were unceremoniously carted to the Salvation Army or the dump. John helped my father disassemble the waterbed, in the process dropping the heavy-as-lead frame on his big toe, which immediately swelled bright red before turning to an ugly, bruised black. We rushed to the kitchen, the bed forgotten, and I put together an ice pack as my father checked to see whether John's toe was broken, pressing on the toe while John's lips curled in pain. Meanwhile, Sylvia hovered around us, asking a million questions, and I did my best to shoo her away. She rushed down the hallway to see for herself the bed frame that crushed her father's big toe.

A minute or two later from the bedroom, she cried out, "Mommy!"

"What is it sweetheart?"

"Something smells funny."

Declaring John's toe officially intact, my father headed back to the bedroom; I trailed behind him. The smell of burning synthetic stung the air, and we quickly figured out the source: the water-bed heater, still hot, had seared an ugly black scar on the blue carpeting.

We all stood there, looking at the gaping hole. A laugh bubbled up in my throat at the absurdity of this latest disaster, but I fought it back down.

"*Shit*," my father, who never swears, spat out under his breath. Then he got to work peeling the heater from the melted fibers of rug.

By ten o'clock that night, John and I could barely move, so sore were we from the sheer physical labor of moving. We crept into bed with Sylvia, sharing the queen-size Ikea bed that occupied what was once my old bedroom, long since emptied of my own belongings. Lying there with my family on the bed, the room was almost familiar, but not quite, like a word tripping on the tip of one's tongue. Outside, a storm front had moved in, letting loose a heavy artillery of rain against the roof and windows.

"What a *day*," John whispered.

"I know," I whispered back. "How's your toe?"

"Better," he said. Sylvia was splayed out between us, and I absently brushed away a hair that had fallen across her cheek. I was about to say more, but already I heard rumbling snores coming from John's side, and before I knew it, I was asleep, too.

The next day brought a similar marathon of activity, until, miraculously, everything had been stripped clean, the metal pod sealed, and my father, though no longer able to stand, lifted his arm to wave from the kitchen window as we drove away from the house one last time.

"It must be weird for you, packing up your old house," John said later, after the trees and buildings had been replaced by seemingly endless highway.

I murmured my assent, suddenly overwhelmed by the passage of time. I thought back to another time I had traveled down this very same highway going from Annapolis to New York City, before we moved. John and I had barely been speaking then, the air crackling between us with all that was unspoken. Feeling terribly alone, I had stared out the car window as we cruised through the industrial wasteland of New Jersey, until at last we hit Holland Tunnel traffic, which brought us to a dead stop. I wondered whether we would make it to the other side. I turned my head now to look at John, his profile and his hands on the steering wheel illuminated by the dashboard light, and thought of how much I had changed since then—how much we *both* had changed.

The storyteller in me wishes I could point to one watershed event, but the truth is that we had changed slowly, incrementally, coming closer together through the thousands of tiny moments that make up a day, a life. This didn't have to happen. I knew from experience, both my own and others, that these moments could have just as well pulled us apart, if even one of us had chosen otherwise. We had chosen each other. As I studied John's face in the glow of the dashboard, his features intermittently lit up by the bright lights of other drivers, what I knew of him, the flashes of kindness and love that had been revealed to me over the years, hung like stars in my imagination. We may have been many things to each other, woman and man, wife and husband, mother and father, but underneath it all we were, in the end, just us, two individuals, Stephanie and John—and for a moment I wondered if postmodern theory, with its claim that that there is no sex and no gender, only figments of identity along a spectrum, was trying to make this basic point.

Riverbend Girl Blog

For our last class, Professor H. chose to lead us in an unexpected direction. Rather than a traditional text, she had us read *Baghdad Burning: Girl Blog from Iraq*, a published compilation of blog entries from a young Iraqi woman going by the pseudonym Riverbend, who was living in and reporting from Baghdad during the U.S. occupation following 9/11.

"So this is the beginning for me, I guess," Riverbend writes in her first online entry. "I never thought I'd start my own weblog. . . . All I could think, every time I wanted to start one was 'but who will read it?' I guess I've got nothing to lose. . . . A little bit about myself: I'm female, Iraqi, and 24. I survived the war. That's all you need to know. It's all that matters these days anyway."

From this modest beginning, one woman—armed with a computer—managed to open up her thoughts and experiences to an audience of thousands around the world, in effect changing the way many people viewed Iraq, Iraqi women, and the war. Riverbend gives an inside look at what it means to be a young woman in a country torn apart both by conflict and by the religious fundamentalists who have gained a foothold in the ensuing chaos. In one entry, she writes, "Men in black turbans (M.I.B.T.s as opposed to M.I.B.s) and dubious shady figures dressed in black, head to foot, stand around the gates of the bureau in clusters, scanning the girls and teachers entering the secondary school. The dark, frowning figures stand ogling, leering and sometimes jeering at the ones not wearing a hijab or whose skirts aren't long enough. In some areas, girls risk being attacked with acid if their clothes aren't 'proper.'"

By turns acerbic and hopeful, *Baghdad Burning* was the first text—if one could call it such—that didn't address feminist ideals head-on, but rather discreetly ushered them in through the context of daily life. Although Riverbend was clearly a woman—the subtitle was after all a "girl blog"—her entries covered a broad range of topics. She regularly offered a searing critique of the politicians on TV talking about Iraq, contrasting their words with her reality. She described how women were being oppressed under Iraq's new regime and how much she missed the days when she could drive, work for equal pay, dress the way she wanted to dress, and practice Islam according to her own values and beliefs. But she also wrote about the rain, the mossy smell of it, its cool relief, of escaping to the roof with her younger brother when the sweltering heat inside the house grew unbearable, and of the long spells without the crackle of electricity, the evening hours that stretched out endlessly in this darkness.

Although Riverbend doesn't describe herself as a feminist, the class examined her words through a feminist lens. Was she ultimately telling a feminist story? Or was it simply the story of one individual who happened to be a woman? Could anyone's story be labeled as "feminist"? And if so, what was the purpose of marshaling one's story into the service of a theory, a philosophy, a movement?

"One thing we should have learned by now is that feminism is not an either/or," Professor H. reminded the class. Indeed, above all, this I had learned. There are no neat conclusions, no A + B = C, no foolproof prescriptions. During my couch-bound adventures, I had read and pondered, listened and discussed, gathering the many small moments of clarity, understanding, and truth that had transpired along the way. More than two years ago, I had walked into a bookstore looking for answers on how to reconcile the identities of woman, wife, and mother, afraid that I was losing myself in the midst of negotiating these new roles. I could still see myself, sitting there cross-legged on the floor, a character partially shaped by the endless barrage of cultural images and partially made of my own creation, but entirely constrained. Lost though I may have been, revisiting the great works of feminism had opened up a path of discovery and rediscovery.

Never would I have expected to identify with the first-wave feminists, like Mary Wollstonecraft and Charlotte Perkins Gilman, or come to odds with my former heroines, like Beauvoir, or make peace with postfeminists like Roiphe. At times I felt exhilarated, inspired by these women who had crossed such heavily guarded cultural boundaries, surmounting obstacles on the faith of their convictions alone; other times, I felt aggravated, confused, and, yes, I'll admit, occasionally a little bored. Sometimes I grappled with the divisiveness of second-wave feminism and the ambiguity of third-wave feminism, while the postmodern theory I would have analyzed with delight as a college coed was cause for vexation when viewed in the framework of my daily life. Yet even these theoretically dense texts provided important opportunities to question and challenge my own beliefs, my own reactions.

• • •

Although at first I thought Riverbend's *Baghdad Burning* might be a strange place to end this journey—it's not even clearly a text, let alone clearly feminist!—I have come to believe it may be the perfect wrap-up to my Fem Texts adventure. With courageous determination, Riverbend found her voice and projected it into the public sphere to report on the inequities she was witnessing in her country. Professor H. was obviously excited by the possibilities of the Internet. In the virtual world, Riverbend could respond directly to readers who spanned the globe and link to other blogs and Web sites; she was authoring a sprawling work in progress, becoming part of a new generation of women who are successfully using the Internet to amplify their voices, encouraging a greater awareness of social issues, and connecting online communities geared toward advocacy. All the Fem Text canonical authors would have applauded her.

On this hopeful note of progress and change, Professor H. concluded class. But she was not ready to let us go, not quite yet. In the few remaining seconds, she gave us one final piece of advice to take with us out the door, a call to action as we transitioned from the classroom into the world. "Identity is constituted from experience, from being the subject of knowledge. And remember this," she said. "*Being* is a process, a story—and, if you will, a dialogue. Always try to tell the unexpected story."

I would remember Professor H.'s invocation, long after I had left the sanctuary of Fem Texts and returned fully to my life outside the classroom. History leaves a unique pattern of kisses and bruises on each of us, but many of the fundamental issues raised by being a woman have remained the same. Regardless of the gaps in years, place, and circumstance, women across the ages have all had to negotiate the borders of their identities; in this, we find a common ground. Certainly, our responses may differ. Burning a bra is a far cry from wearing a push-up. Both, however, can be considered expressions of female empowerment, as instructive in their similarities as in their differences. The intrinsic worth in reading and rereading feminist writings is that, in doing so, we are given the precious chance to compare and contrast other women's lives with our own, to liberate our imaginations from the predictable, the conventional, and thus gain greater insight into the various scripts assigned to us by our particular generation. Feminism gives us room to tell the unexpected story, and this, perhaps, is its greatest gift.

Living Forwards

....

Not too long after Fem Texts ended, I found myself back on campus for an alumni event. I was walking along on College Walk to meet up with John and Sylvia when Rowan, one of the students from T.'s class, fell into step next to me. She had a colorful Indian scarf wrapped around her neck, and its metallic threads glinted in the sunlight. Her hair had grown out since I had last seen her more than a year ago, forming a sleek brown cap on her head.

"Hey!" she said. "How *are* you?"

We caught up as we strolled together through campus. Rowan told me she was graduating, then taking a year off to work and travel before applying to graduate school, maybe in women's studies, maybe in English. She was not sure yet. Listening to her speak about the future, I was reminded of myself at her age.

"I can't believe college is almost over. It went by so fast." She smiled and groped for a cigarette out of her weathered leather tote bag. Then she gave me a sidelong glance. "I just wanted to say that I think it's really cool that you did this, coming back to school to read these books. I mean, I loved the readings and the discussion, but I didn't really get to enjoy them because I had so much other work to do."

We stopped below the steps of Low Library so Rowan could light her cigarette, by chance in front of the university's *Alma Mater* statue, her marble hand holding the scepter of wisdom and both arms raised skyward in a perpetual gesture of welcome. Directly across from us sat Butler Library, with the names of some of history's great thinkers—all men by the way—engraved into its vast facade: Homer, Herodotus, Sophocles, Plato, Aristotle, Demosthenes, Cicero, Vergil, Horace, Tacitus, Augustine, Dante, Cervantes, Shakespeare, Milton, Voltaire, Goethe. Standing there with Rowan, between the *Alma Mater*—Latin for "nourishing mother"—and Butler Library's homage to the Western canon, a flow of students, of men and women, streaming up and down College Walk, I suddenly pictured all of us, dead and alive, as allies taking part in a grand dialogue. Farther away, by the iron gates, I spotted John and Sylvia waiting for me, and I waved.

"Anyway," Rowan continued, "I hope I can do the same thing when I'm older and have kids."

A surge of affection came over me then for this bright, earnest young woman—for all the students I had met over the course of these two years. "You *should*," I said. "Promise me you will. Someday I'll probably read them again, too."

We smiled and said our good-byes. Watching her go, I felt a pang of sadness that my journey had come to an end, although, really, it had just begun.

• • •

Danish philosopher Søren Kierkegaard once said, "Life can only be understood backwards; but it must be lived forwards." The mind can trick the fates, however, through recollection. As my feet moved closer to the iron gates surrounding campus, to John and Sylvia waiting for me on the bench, memory took me back one last time to an image framed almost as clearly as my graduation photograph itself.

It is the day I graduated from college. And after three hours of creaky metal chairs, the four glasses of champagne, and countless congratulatory hugs, I am back in my dorm room. The windows are open, and the soft, cool breeze of spring floats in and out, like a whispered conversation. I've already returned my rented graduation gown, and my possessions are packed away into cardboard boxes neatly labeled with a black Sharpie. Only the posters remain, but I'm not yet ready to take them down; there's something too stark and final about bare walls in an empty room. Instead, I perch on the windowsill, dragging heavily on a cigarette and watching the smoke disappear into the sky as I slowly exhale, waiting until only the ghost of scent remains before I take another puff. I enjoy the feel of the cigarette between my fingers, the impression of toughness it imparts when I'm in a crowd, but alone, in my room, the cigarette is just an excuse to make myself stop for a moment and breathe. Outside, the air smells of ash and the damp of rain.

From where I'm sitting, I can look down on leafy treetops, the whoosh of traffic on Broadway, the sparkle of the Hudson River, a whole magnificent spread of New York City in miniature, and I experience the particular vertigo that occurs when one is passing through a life event so significant that it's impossible to absorb entirely right then and there; one has no choice but to fall into the feeling. Looking down, the wild chaos of the city seems suitably tamed, split into squares and grids—manageable, conquerable even.

Stubbing out my cigarette into a Diet Coke can, I take a deep breath; the future awaits me. Anxieties branch out in my mind, of course, but they are hung with hopes and dreams. Ready to go now, I slide off the windowsill and begin peeling the posters from my walls, trying not to rip them, although, of course, I do. I mean to take one last look at the view before I leave, but before I know it, my father is calling from the elevator, telling me to hurry up because he's double-parked. So, without a backward glance, I hurry from the room, my posters rolled up and awkwardly tucked under my arm, the door clicking shut behind me.

Outside, at the iron gates, on the threshold between city and campus, my older self paused to look back. I used to believe I left a version of myself behind that day, up there in that dorm room on the sixteenth floor. Whenever I thought of her, I would feel a loss, an emotional lightning bolt flashing in my mind's eye, and I would lament her passing. No longer.

Sylvia was running toward me, and as she reached me, I bent down to scoop her up. John caught up a moment later and encircled one arm around my waist, the other around Sylvia.

That girl I once was and the woman I am today, I see now, are simply points on the same line; she is me, and I am her, and together, with the map laid out by other women, other lives, we will continue to trace our route, both forward and backward, to where we are now.

Here, in this place.

AUTHOR'S NOTE

Roland Barthes once derided biography as "the counterfeit integration of the subject," and indeed, while all the quotes you have read were taken directly from the professors and students in class, I have changed their names and obscured their identities, as well as created composite characters in some instances, in order to maintain their anonymity. Although I had originally planned to take Fem Texts over the course of one year, with the same professor, circumstances beyond my control intervened that prevented my doing so. Instead, I ended up taking the course over two years, on both the Columbia and Barnard campuses, with four different professors and, for the most part, four different groups of students. As a result, I have taken the occasional narrative liberty to avoid confusion, while at the same time being careful to preserve the verity of what happened. Contrary to Barthes's notion, I believe these intentional tweaks actually get us closer to the essence of the story rather than further away.

I must also point out that my experience remains entirely circumscribed by the classes I happened to attend at Barnard and Columbia, which, as I have said, differed greatly from semester to semester. By no means am I making any statements about academic feminism in general, nor about Barnard and Columbia in particular.

And while I'm at it, another brief caveat: Let me be clear that I approached these books as neither critic nor scholar but rather, as Virginia Woolf put it, "the common reader," who "above all . . . is guided by an instinct to create for [herself], out of whatever odds and ends [she] can come by, some kind of whole—a portrait of a [woman], a sketch of an age, a theory of the art of writing." My thoughts and opinions are just that, and I'll wager that many a professor or doctoral student would gleefully tear my interpretations apart—and probably rightfully so. Although my purposes in returning to Barnard were literary as well as philosophical—to the extent that philosophy deals with how we choose to live our lives—they will, I am guessing, also be perceived as political, in that any discussion of women's roles, and the choices they make, is inherently political. Be that as it may, I hope no one will read this book as something more than it is—a highly personal investigation.

As someone who, at the root of things, identifies herself as a feminist, I turned to these books as a way of grasping the difficulties that I was facing at a specific time and place in my life when, as a woman, I felt drawn and quartered by love and guilt, confusion and frustration. The slant of my circumstances therefore determined the titles I selected to write about. Regretfully, given the sheer number of books I read during those two years, I had to omit quite a few wonderful texts in this book—not because I thought they were any less valuable, or lacked literary merit, but because they would have led me away from my central focus and into more contentious or theoretical realms.

Since this is, at its heart, a book about reading, my greatest hope is that others will be inspired to read—or reread—some or all of the books that have been mentioned on these pages and any I may have left out. In that spirit, I have included the combined syllabi from my four semesters of Fem Texts on page 265.

ACKNOWLEDGMENTS

I had the great fortune to have not one but two dear friends who were early champions of this book: Nina Collins, who pushed me with her unflagging enthusiasm and encouragement, as well as her sharp insights into my story (as someone who knows me so well), and Rob McQuilkin, who not only lent his incredible editorial eye to make this a better read, but also kept me going with his wit, charm, and fierce dedication to the project. Thanks to both of you for believing in this book and, more important, for your friendship over the years.

This book found a wonderful home in my publisher, and I have been grateful for all the support I have received from everyone at PublicAffairs. Special thanks to my editor, Clive Priddle, for his brilliant suggestions and clever titles; to Niki Papadopoulos, for her thoughtful and intelligent comments; and to my copy editor, Annette Wenda, for her attention to detail. All of their input made this book infinitely richer. Also to Susan Weinberg, Tessa Shanks, Kay Mariea, Melissa Raymond, and Lindsay Fradkoff.

To my parents, for their love and for being all-around good sports at having a daughter who occasionally trots them out in her writing, and to my sister, Caroline, for the countless hours of conversation on the couch, not to mention the chocolate and baked goods.

To the many friends who kept me on track and made me laugh (even when I felt like crying) during the many years it took to write this book, especially Jenny Lee, Tasha Blaine, Kristen Buckley, Nicole Hala, Barbara Messing, Hal Niedzviecki, Hugo Sandstrom, Jason

Anthony, Jill Grinberg, Susan Gregory Thomas, Lorenzo Dominguez, and last, but most definitely not least, Arnesto Katz.

Special thanks, too, to the Riordans: Lynn, John, and James.

Thank you to Barnard College and all the professors who so generously let me into their classrooms, as well as to the students who welcomed my presence with grace. Indeed, revisiting the campus only confirmed what I already knew: Barnard is a special place. Deciding to transfer there as a junior was probably one of the best decisions I ever made, and I have never looked back.

To John, for his unwavering love, his ineffable patience, his marvelous sense of humor, and for being with me on every step of this journey.

Finally, to Sylvia, my North Star, for being who you are, sweetheart.

READING LISTS

My Reading List

Elaine Pagels, *Adam, Eve, and the Serpent*

Joyce E. Salisbury, *Perpetua's Passion: The Death and Memory of a Young Roman Women*

Mary Wollstonecraft, *A Vindication of the Rights of Woman*

Lyndall Gordon, *Vindication: A Life of Mary Wollstonecraft*

Charlotte Perkins Gilman, *The Yellow Wallpaper*

Charlotte Perkins Gilman, *The Living of Charlotte Perkins Gilman*

Kate Chopin, *The Awakening*

John Stuart Mill, "The Subjection of Women"

Virginia Woolf, *A Room of One's Own*

Simone de Beauvoir, *The Second Sex*

Hazel Rowley, *Tête-à-Tête*

Betty Friedan, *The Feminine Mystique*

Pat Mainardi, "The Politics of Housework"

Shulamith Firestone, *The Dialectic of Sex*

Ruth Rosen, *The World Split Open*

Kate Millett, *Sexual Politics*

Catherine MacKinnon, *Only Words*

Ariel Levy, *Female Chauvinist Pigs*

Erica Jong, *The Fear of Flying*

Jacques Lacan, "The Meaning of the Phallus"

Helene Cixous, "The Laugh of the Medusa"

Sigmund Freud, *Dora: An Analysis of a Case of Hysteria*

Carol Gilligan, *In a Different Voice*
Katie Roiphe, *The Morning After: Sex, Fear, and Feminism*
Judith Butler, *Gender Trouble*
Riverbend, *Baghdad Burning*

Feminist Texts I
Texts

Ida B. Wells Barnett, *Crusade for Justice*
Sor Juana de la Cruz, *Poems, Protest, and a Dream: Selected Writings*
Sigmund Freud, *Dora: An Analysis of a Case of Hysteria*
Glueckel of Hameln, *Memoirs of Glueckel of Hameln*
Radclyffe Hall, *The Well of Loneliness*
Hildegard of Bingen, *Scivias*
Rokiya Hussayn, *Sultana's Dream and Padmarag*
Harriet Jacobs, *Incidents in the Life of a Slave Girl*
Nella Larsen, *Quicksand* and *Passing*
Roland Marchand, *Advertising the American Dream: Making Way for Modernity 1920–1940*
Murasaki Shikibu, *Diary of Lady Murasaki*
Elaine Pagels, *Adam, Eve, and the Serpent*
Christine de Pizan, *Book of the City of Ladies*
Huda Shaarawi, *Harem Years*
Thorstein Veblen, *The Theory of the Leisure Class*
Mary Wollstonecraft, *A Vindication of the Rights of Woman*
Virginia Woolf, *A Room of One's Own*
Anzia Yezierska, *Bread Givers*

Selected Essays

Susan B. Anthony, "Woman Wants Bread, Not the Ballot!"
Charlotte Perkins Gilman, "Women and Economics"
Angelina Grimke, "Appeal to the Christian Woman of the South"
Sarah M. Grimke, "Letters on the Equality of the Sexes and the Condition of Woman"
John Stuart Mill, "The Subjection of Women"

Rosemary Radford Ruether, "Woman, Body, Nature: Sexism and the Theology of Creation"
Elizabeth Cady Stanton, "Address to the New York State Legislature" and "Womanliness"
Sojourner Truth, "Ain't I a Woman?"
Frances Wright, "Education" and "Of Free Enquiry"

Feminist Texts II

Texts

Simone de Beauvoir, *The Second Sex*
Judith Butler, *Gender Trouble*
Nancy Chodorow, *The Reproduction of Mothering*
R. W. Connell, *Masculinities*
Mary Daly, *Gyn/Ecology*
Angela Davis, *Women, Race, and Class*
Barbara Ehrenreich and Arlie Russell Hochschild, *Global Woman: Nannies, Maids, and Sex Workers in the New Economy*
Shulamith Firestone, *The Dialectic of Sex*
Betty Friedan, *The Feminine Mystique*
Leslie Heywood and Jennifer Drake, eds., *Third Wave Agenda*
bell hooks, *Ain't I a Woman?*
Laura Kipnis, *Bound and Gagged: Pornography and the Politics of Fantasy in America*
Catherine MacKinnon, *Only Words*
Kate Millett, *Sexual Politics*
Cherríe Moraga and Gloria Anzaldúa, eds., *This Bridge Called My Back: Writings by Radical Women of Color*
Robin Morgan, ed., *Sisterhood Is Powerful: An Anthology of Writings from the Women's Liberation Movement*
Uma Narayan, *Dislocating Cultures: Identities, Traditions, and Third World Feminism*
Joan Nestle, *A Restricted Country*
Susan Moller Okin et al., *Is Multiculturalism Bad for Women?*
Riverbend, *Baghdad Burning*
Katie Roiphe, *The Morning After: Sex, Fear, and Feminism*
Ruth Rosen, *The World Split Open*

Ann Snitow, Christine Stansell, and Sharon Thompson, eds., *Powers of Desire: The Politics of Sexuality*
Imelda Whelchan, *Modern Feminist Thought: From the Second Wave to "Post Feminism"*

Selected Essays
Helene Cixous, "The Laugh of the Medusa"
Sigmund Freud, "Femininity"
Luce Irigaray, "This Sex Which Is Not One" and "And the One Doesn't Speak Without the Other"
Jacques Lacan, "The Meaning of the Phallus"
Audre Lorde, "The Uses of Anger: Women Responding to Racism" and "The Master's Tools Will Never Dismantle the Master's House"
Pat Mainardi, "The Politics of Housework"
Adrienne Rich, "Notes Toward a Politics of Location" and "Compulsory Heterosexuality and Lesbian Existence"
Gayle Rubin, "Thinking Sex: Notes for a Radical Theory of the Politics of Sexuality"
Carroll Smith-Rosenberg, "The Female World of Love and Ritual"
Alice Walker, "In Search of Our Mother's Garden" and "One Child of One's Own"
Monique Wittig, "One Is Not Born a Woman"

READING GROUP GUIDE
FOR READING WOMEN

Discussion Questions

1. What did you think of the author's decision to return to Barnard and take Feminist Texts? If you could go back to college and retake one course, which one would it be?

2. Have you read any of the books from the Fem Texts syllabus? Which have affected your life?

3. Staal writes a lot about the work/mother dichotomy and how difficult it is for women everywhere to inhabit these roles fully simultaneously. If you are a parent, how have you handled this situation?

4. At a panel the author attends, one of the panelists says "Well, I don't know if we should tell our daughters that they have *limitless* possibilities." Do you think it's disingenuous to tell our daughters that they can "have it all?"

5. The class encounters different types of feminists throughout the course of their readings—from the radical feminists like Shulamith Firestone to the "post-feminists" like Katie Roiphe. How do you define a feminist? Do you consider yourself a feminist?

If you do consider yourself a feminist, can you attribute it to a particular event or experience in your life?

6. The last text Staal reads for her class is a blog called *Baghdad Burning*. What noncanonical texts—whether it be fiction, nonfiction, poetry, blog, book, magazine, or other types of writing—have contributed most to your understanding of feminism?

7. Staal observes many differences between opinions she espoused while in college and those of her Gen Y classmates. How do you think the younger generation, raised in the social network/Facebook era, will respond differently to the challenges of reconciling adulthood or motherhood with feminism? Will it be any easier for them than it was for the author's generation?

8. Staal is upset by the *New York Times* article about Ivy League women opting out of the workforce "not so much because these young women wanted to be stay-at-home mothers, but for their seeming readiness, at nineteen years old, to resort to traditional gender roles without a peep." What do you think of that article? Of Staal's opinion?

9. Of all of the books the author writes about, which one intrigued you the most? Which author was the most interesting to you?

10. What would you say are the most pressing issues that feminists should be concerned about today?

Stephanie Staal on Reading Beyond Reading Women

Five Novels I Love That Further Explore the Themes of Reading Women

• THE PASSION *(1997)* BY *JEANETTE WINTERSON*

A friend passed along this book to me the summer after I graduated from college. "You will love it," he said. And I did—and still do, every time I reread it. A magical fairy tale of love and war set during the Napoleonic Wars, the story is told in the alternating voices of Napoleon's cook Henri, who eventually makes his escape from military life, and Villanelle, the gender-bending, gambling daughter of a Venetian gondolier who falls in love with a married woman and loses her heart to her—literally. For a fairly slim book, Winterson delves deep into issues of sex, violence, identity, and of course, passion. Gorgeously written, evocative and provocative, this book always tops my list of must-read recommendations.

• THEIR EYES WERE WATCHING GOD *(1937) BY ZORA NEALE HURSTON*
I was first introduced to Zora Neale Hurston, one of the major figures
of the Harlem Renaissance, when I transferred to Barnard. A Barnard
alumna, Hurston also majored in anthropology, studying with Franz
Boas, Ruth Benedict, and fellow student Margaret Mead during the
1920s. After reading her groundbreaking nonfiction and ethnographic
works—*Mules and Men* and *Tell My Horse*—I eagerly picked up this
novel, which follows the life and loves of an African-American woman
named Janie Crawford. I love this book, not only because it offers a
poetic glimpse into a black woman's experience during a particular
time and place (the narrative is written partly in dialect), but also
because Hurston so masterfully reveals the universal tangle of emotions we experience in human relationships.

• WIDE SARGASSO SEA *(1966) BY JEAN RHYS*
I was drawn to this novel as soon as I heard the premise. Rhys, inspired by the "madwoman in the attic" in Charlotte Bronte's *Jane
Eyre*, sets out to imagine this woman, giving her voice and thought
and desire of her own. The lunatic wife, Bertha, in *Jane Eyre* is, in
Rhys's version, Antoinette Cosway, a white Creole heiress raised
in Jamaica and forced by circumstance to enter an arranged marriage
to an Englishman. The union is an unhappy one, with both husband
and wife caught up in a fever of distrust and discontent. They leave
the tropics for England, where Antoinette, already mentally unstable,
descends into madness. Rhys writes in lush prose, shifting between
Antoinette's and her husband's point of view, illustrating the power
of a narrator to control reality. I found myself still haunted by this
book long after I had finished the last page.

• THE BELL JAR *(1963) BY SYLVIA PLATH*
A semi-autobiographical novel about a young college woman, Esther,
who, following a prestigious summer internship at a woman's magazine in New York City, returns home and becomes increasingly

depressed, then suicidal, eventually ending up in a mental hospital. I can picture myself in my peach-walled childhood bedroom, reading Plath's novel the summer after my junior year in college, and coming across one passage in particular in which Esther describes the choices before her as plump figs on a tree. And as she is standing there, trying to make up her mind about which one to choose, she watches them shrivel and fall off the branch one by one. Being around the same age as Esther, and feeling a similar anxiety about the future, I could totally relate. I think I carried that book around with me all summer.

• COMMENCEMENT *(2009)* BY J. COURTNEY SULLIVAN
I'm more than a few years older than the four women in *Commencement*, but I nevertheless found myself really connecting with the story. By following the lives of these different women, the novel takes a look at why we make the choices we do and how the consequences of those choices come to shape us. Meeting for the first time at Smith College in the late '90s, these four college friends form a tight bond, one that is later tested as they face various crossroads in their relationships and careers during their 20s—dead-end jobs, parental disapproval, dealing with romantic partners, weddings, babies, etc. Reading this book transported me straight back to that period in my life, reminding me of the importance of female friendship, camaraderie, and support.

Five Provocative Books About Marriage/Motherhood
• PARALLEL LIVES *(1983)* BY PHYLLIS ROSE
In this utterly fascinating book, Rose takes a microscopic look at five unconventional Victorian marriages to illuminate more universal themes, like the shifting balance of power within a relationship and the constraints of social mores. Each union contains a famous writer—Thomas Carlyle, John Stuart Mill, Charles Dickens, John Ruskin, and George Eliot (Marian Evans)—and Rose, taking on a feminist lens, portrays the relationships in voyeuristic detail. By

shedding light on how these marriages unfolded in the past, Rose also gives insight into how marriages operate today. George Eliot and George Henry Lewes provide one of the most intriguing case studies; already married, Lewes could never formalize his arrangement with Eliot, and yet they were, perhaps, the happiest of all. This book is an engrossing read that will make you think carefully about your expectations in marriage.

• FRUITFUL *(1996)* BY ANNE ROIPHE

As the second wave of feminism was crashing around her, Roiphe (mother of Katie Roiphe) found herself divorced, a single mother, and an aspiring novelist. She eventually remarries—a man also divorced with children from a previous marriage—and has more children, facing new and complicated challenges of being part of a blended family. In this highly personal account, she speaks of her struggle to reconcile her feminism with motherhood, steering a wavering course between the extremes of '70s feminism and the religious right's trumpeting of "family values." Roiphe, who was born in the '30s, addresses many issues that speak to a different era; nevertheless, I found her lyrical and honest examination of some of the tensions between motherhood and the feminist movement still resonated with me.

• COMPOSING A LIFE *(1989)* BY MARY CATHERINE BATESON

Bateson, a cultural anthropologist and daughter of anthropologist Margaret Mead, chronicles the complex lives of five women (including herself) as they engage in what she calls the creative act of "composing a life." I read this in my 20s—and again in my 30s—intrigued by this idea of life as an ongoing improvisation, with the conflicts, interruptions, and divided energies forming part of the symphonic range of experience. Bateson urges us to look at problems, not as roadblocks on the path to achievement of a single goal, but as creative opportunities that allow for reinvention and fluidity. I found this book especially illuminating after I became a mother and grappled with the discontinuities in my own life. Also of personal interest was how growing up with a world-famous mother affected Bateson's expectations and sense of self.

• AGAINST LOVE BY LAURA KIPNIS

Sharp, witty, and at times so undeniably on target, it hurts. I practically inhaled this book when I got my hands on it. A self-proclaimed polemic, *Against Love* takes the act of adultery as its main line of attack, drawing on everything from scandals to pop psychology books to Marxism as back up. In one brilliant passage, Kipnis enumerates all the things you can't do when you're part of a couple—this alone goes on for almost six pages. Kipnis warns in the early pages that polemics are not balanced. "They overstate the case. They toss out provocations and occasionally mockery, usually because they're arguing against something so unquestionable and deeply entrenched, it's the only way to make a dent in the usual story." Here, she succeeds in doing just that. You might never look at love the same way again. At the very least, you will have fun ripping through this clever book.

• OPTING IN *(2008)* BY AMY RICHARDS

I was thrilled when this book came out just as I was in the midst of thinking and writing about feminism and motherhood. Richards is a prominent feminist activist, writer, and organizer who had previously co-authored a guide to third-wave feminism titled *Manifesta* (and, coincidentally, another Barnard alumna!). In response to the 2004 *New York Times* Magazine cover article heralding an "opt out" revolution of well-educated women abandoning their careers in favor of motherhood, Richards tells a different story. Through interviews, historical analysis, and her own experience, she not only looks at the positive opportunities forged by feminism for women in negotiating their careers and family life, but also how becoming a parent goes beyond the workplace to affect our relationships with our partners, friends, and families. An inspiring read that encourages women to cut through the cultural noise about motherhood and make the choices that are truly the best for them.

STEPHANIE STAAL has written for several publications, including *Cosmopolitan, Glamour, Marie Claire*, and the *Washington Post*. She is the author of *The Love They Lost*, a journalistic memoir about the long-term effects of parental divorce. A graduate of Barnard College and Columbia University's Graduate School of Journalism, she lives with her husband and daughter in Brooklyn, New York.

PublicAffairs is a publishing house founded in 1997. It is a tribute to the standards, values, and flair of three persons who have served as mentors to countless reporters, writers, editors, and book people of all kinds, including me.

I. F. STONE, proprietor of *I. F. Stone's Weekly*, combined a commitment to the First Amendment with entrepreneurial zeal and reporting skill and became one of the great independent journalists in American history. At the age of eighty, Izzy published *The Trial of Socrates*, which was a national bestseller. He wrote the book after he taught himself ancient Greek.

BENJAMIN C. BRADLEE was for nearly thirty years the charismatic editorial leader of *The Washington Post*. It was Ben who gave the *Post* the range and courage to pursue such historic issues as Watergate. He supported his reporters with a tenacity that made them fearless and it is no accident that so many became authors of influential, best-selling books.

ROBERT L. BERNSTEIN, the chief executive of Random House for more than a quarter century, guided one of the nation's premier publishing houses. Bob was personally responsible for many books of political dissent and argument that challenged tyranny around the globe. He is also the founder and longtime chair of Human Rights Watch, one of the most respected human rights organizations in the world.

·   ·   ·

For fifty years, the banner of Public Affairs Press was carried by its owner Morris B. Schnapper, who published Gandhi, Nasser, Toynbee, Truman, and about 1,500 other authors. In 1983, Schnapper was described by *The Washington Post* as "a redoubtable gadfly." His legacy will endure in the books to come.

Peter Osnos, *Founder and Editor-at-Large*